FANTASIES OF SALVATION

FANTASIES OF SALVATION

DEMOCRACY, NATIONALISM, AND MYTH
IN POST-COMMUNIST EUROPE

Vladimir Tismaneanu

PRINCETON UNIVERSITY PRESS   PRINCETON, NEW JERSEY

Library of Congress Cataloging-in-Publication Data

Tismaneanu, Vladimir.
Fantasies of salvation : democracy, nationalism, and myth in post-communist Europe /
Vladimir Tismaneanu.
p.   cm.
Includes bibliographical references and index.
ISBN 0-691-04826-6 (cl : alk. paper)
1. Ideology—Europe, Eastern. 2. Ideology—Former Soviet republics.
3. Post-communism—Europe, Eastern. 4. Post-communism—
Former Soviet republics. 5. Europe, Eastern—Politics and
government—1989– 6. Former Soviet republics—Politics and
government.   I. Title.

JA84.E92T57   1998   97-25602
320.5′094′091717— dc21   CIP

This book has been composed in Berkeley Book Modified

Princeton University Press books are printed
on acid-free paper and meet the guidelines
for permanence and durability of the Committee
on Production Guidelines for Book Longevity
of the Council on Library Resources

http://pup.princeton.edu

Printed in the United States of America

10 9 8 7 6 5 4 3 2 1

TO MY WIFE

Mary Sladek

MORE THAN EVER, MY LOVE AND GRATITUDE

Contents

Preface

Why Eastern Europe and Why Care?

SINCE George Washington's presidency, most citizens of the United States have disliked getting involved in European strife and bickering. But, two world wars, a cold war, and the demise of communism forced many people to admit that an ocean simply is not big enough to separate the United States from Europe's dilemmas, hopes, and torments. From both the virtues and vices of Europe (and of East-Central Europe in particular) Americans can learn a lot about their own present and future: the perils of ideological hubris, the risks of excessive rationalism and irrationality both, and the dangers associated with the hegemony of political myth in public affairs. We can also temper a certain missionary, almost providential zeal that elites or guerrillas and their followers in the Americas often indulge in.

In my view, the divide between Eastern and Western Europe is an artificial one, bound to vanish with the old millennium. If it persists, the fate of the continent (and therefore the world) will be less felicitous than envisioned by Jean Monnet and other architects of the European integration. For example, we should not forget that Bosnia is as much part of Europe as France or Poland. When Sarajevo was bombed and ethnic cleansing was applied by Radovan Karadžić and his neo-Chetnik thugs, it was the whole of Europe that bled. In the light (or should I say in the darkness?) of what has happened since 1989 in the former Yugoslavia, we should refrain from any self-congratulatory and self-glorifying discourses about Europe as "the continent of humanism."

So am I not contradicting myself by making a point that the Eastern part of the continent has a special lesson to offer? Not at all. First, East-Central Europe is not a homogeneous space. There are traditions of tolerance and dialogue there, as well as memories of exclusiveness, tribalism, and atrocious persecutions. East-Central Europe was, during the period between the first two world wars, as much a territory of cultural experimentation as one of vicious harassment of ethnic minorities. Americans, Europeans, Chinese, Africans—anyone interested in humanity's future—can look back to those times and realize how precarious the boundaries of civilization are, and how easily people oriented toward advancing technology and culture can fall into the temptation of barbarism. Eastern Europe (Russia and other once-Soviet republics included) is thus an accumulation of noble hopes, emancipating dreams of national dignity and, in the same vein, a region marred by many unfulfilled vindictive fantasies and excruciating neuroses. None of its economic or social problems was solved by the four (or seven) decades of communism; instead, they were exacerbated and distorted. At the same time, despair does not rule; Eastern Europe's experience also shows that from the deepest strata of human despondency the ideas of honor and solidarity can be born. It is an experience which demonstrates that human spirit endures even under the worst forms of duress. This is the Eastern Europe of dissidents, of people like Poland's Adam Michnik and Jacek Kuron, the Czech Republic's Václav Havel, Hungary's Arpad Göncz and Miklos Haraszti, Russia's Andrei Sakharov and Sergey Kovalyov, Romania's Mircea Dinescu, and Bulgaria's Zhelyu Zhelev.

In the 1990s, it became fashionable to dismiss the critical intelligentsia (the former dissidents like those mentioned above) for "having lost the political battle." But their ideas still burn as a reminder that individuals need something more than bread and water: human beings need to make sense of their very existence, to find a cause worth living for, to construct a set of values that allow one to make distinctions between good and evil. The most important thing the East European experience provides is knowledge that the region's citizens saw and endured radical evil in pure form. They know much too well the threats involved in any project of compulsory happiness, in the utopias of classless or ethnically "clean" societies. It was also in Eastern Europe that the hope for anti-politics, for an anti-Machiavellian order of public things took shape. During the post-1989 decade of transition, while the old paradigms collapsed and new ones gestated, an East European caveat emerged: beware self-appointed prophets, distrust mankind's charismatic benefactors, and respect those rather modest but immensely significant propositions normally associated with the notion of human rights. This is the East European legacy and promise that my readers may find familiar as well as both instructive and inspiring: the search for the deeper meaning of social life, the discontent with the frozen figure of an omnipotent bureaucracy, and the refusal to submit to the diktat of the pseudo-inexorable "laws of history."

This book is the result of years of research on the fate of values, memory, and ideas in communist and post-communist societies. I started in 1992, when the Department of Government and Politics at the University of Maryland (College Park) provided me with a summer grant to initiate research on the new ideologies in post-communist East-Central Europe. In the summer of 1993, I benefited from a research scholarship at the Woodrow Wilson International Center for Scholars (the East European Program), where I put together the main hypotheses for this book. I want to extend special thanks to the Joint Committee on Eastern Europe of the American Council of Learned Societies, which generously gave me a fellowship in the fall of 1995 to pursue research on post-communist political mythologies. Many of the ideas in this book have been discussed and developed during the graduate seminars on post-communism at the University of Maryland at College Park. Special thanks are due to my graduate students Beata Czajkowska (Rybczynski), Michael Turner, Trevor Wysong, and Jennifer Yoder, who have consistently helped me with suggestions and often barely accessible information. Stacy VanDeveer was an extraordinary research and editorial assistant. Trevor Wysong kindly volunteered to compile the book's index.

Earlier, much shorter versions of several chapters came out in *Common Knowledge, East European Politics and Societies,* and *Partisan Review,* and the author wishes to express his thanks for their editors' useful suggestions. Parts of the manuscript were read by friends whose critical ideas have helped clarify some of the less persuasive points in my argument. Let me also thank for their patience and important suggestions: Jan T. Gross (New York University), Gail Kligman (UCLA), Maya Latynski (Georgetown University), Nicholas J. Miller (Boise State University)—whom I met because of his participation in my National Endowment for the Humanities (NEH)-funded Summer Seminar for College Teachers on Democracy in Eastern Europe in 1994—Martin Palous (Charles University, Prague), Ilya Prizel (Johns Hopkins-SAIS), Ana Seleny (Princeton University), and G. M. Tamás (University of Budapest). Special thanks are due to Dan Chirot (University of Washington) and Ken Jowitt (University of California, Berkeley), whose critical reviews of the book manuscript have strongly influenced my own approach to the moral and intellectual dilemmas of the transition from state socialism. Needless to say, none of the above colleagues or funders bears any responsibility for my views. Their role was to participate in a dialogue, an engagement in common reflection, and for this I owe them a lot. But more than anybody else, my wife, Mary Sladek, has shown unswerving commitment to this book in terms of editorial support, intellectual stimulation, and moral encouragement. For these reasons, the book is dedicated to her

Finally, a word about my great joy of having this book published with Princeton University Press. Malcolm Litchfield showed great interest in the manuscript even when it was in a quite embryonic and excruciatingly unshaped stage. His encouragement and enthusiasm for this book have been tremendously important to me. Margaret Case deserves my warmest thanks for her perceptive and truly thoughtful editing of the manuscript. Working with her was a most rewarding experience for me.

FANTASIES OF SALVATION

Introduction ─────────────────────────────

After Marx: The Return of Political Myth

> There is something new in the world: not the end of
> history, or the clash of civilizations, or the inexo-
> rable terminal decline into criminal anarchy.
> Rather, we are at a point and in a time when well-
> delineated, predictable, familiar practices, institu-
> tions and ways of life give way to ill-defined, dif-
> fuse, anxiety-producing and violent realities. The
> kind of time Augustine may have had in mind when
> he said, "it was not absolute nothingness. It was a
> kind of formlessness without any definition."
>
> *(Ken Jowitt, "Our Republic of Fear")*

> I wonder if it is possible to give an intelligible ex-
> planation of the passage from principles to action
> without employing myth.
>
> *(Georges Sorel,* Introduction à l'économie
> moderne)

THE REVOLUTIONS of 1989 in Eastern Europe have shattered the world political
arrangements, confronting the individual, East and West, with new, unexpected dilemmas. Initially celebrated as the triumph of democratic individualism over the Leninist autocracies, these changes have led to the resurgence
of neoromantic, populist, anti-modern forces in the region. For all practical
purposes Leninism is extinct as a teleological project, but its leftovers continue
to affect the post-Leninist political cultures. Many of those who in the past
espoused the homogenizing logic of communist ideology are ready these
days to adhere to no less collectivist visions of society, viscerally inimical to
the very idea of individual rights, diversity, and difference. In all these societies, movements and parties have emerged that romanticize the past, idealize
authoritarian traditions, deprecate parliamentarism, and scorn the former
dissidents and their concept of freedom. In countries like Hungary and
Poland, astounding transmogrifications have allowed former communist apparatchiks to mutate into champions of privatization and free market competition. In the former Soviet Union and the Balkans, the ex-communists have
created gigantic networks of influence, preserved or restored many of the old

patterns of hypercentralized state controls over the economy and the media, and embraced nationalism as a convenient ideological substitute for the defunct Leninism.

A struggle between the friends and the foes of an open society is being waged in all these countries and, as the political turbulence in Russia has shown, its final outcome is not certain. Economic hardship, growing unemployment, and the disbanding of the socialist state's welfare system have generated discontent, anger, and rampant disaffection with the new order. This book focuses on the main threats to liberal democracy in East-Central Europe and the former Soviet Union. Refusing both the pessimistic scenario of democratic breakdown and the overly optimistic proclamation of a definitive liberal victory, my approach calls for moderate skepticism. Some countries have better prospects than others in their efforts to democratize and create successful market economies. These opportunities are directly related to the learning of deliberative procedures, the development of pluralist institutions, and the maturing of a political class committed to the values of an open society. In some countries liberal views and practices will prevail, in others civil society and pluralism will remain weak, problematic, and beleaguered. The time zones of Europe, with their uneven relationship to modernity, including democratic individualism, will continue to divide the continent's political and spiritual map.[1]

This book is an intellectual history and a critique of two major constellations of writings and ideas that have shaped the contemporary political climate in the former communist countries of East and Central Europe, including Russia and other republics of the former Soviet Union. One of these constellations consists of the liberal dissident thinking that contributed so significantly to the astounding collapse, and greatly influenced Western (including American) thinking about the importance of "civil society" by demonstrating the strength of classical Enlightenment ideas. The second strand of political ideas has emerged, or rather strongly reemerged, after the fall of communism. It loathes the Enlightenment and rejects Reason as a universal value. It opposes individual rights, liberal Western democracy, and the building of an independent civil society. It is collectivistic, chauvinistic, and in many instances quite explicitly racist with respect to Jews, Gypsies, and other minorities who live within the borders of the post-communist states.[2]

My main thesis in this book is that intellectuals played a key role in bringing about the demise of communism, and intellectuals remain a vitally important force in shaping the future. Therefore, the arguments raging between these two main strands of thought, between the once widely acclaimed but now increasingly marginalized "Westernizing" liberals and the resurgent xenophobic, nativist right, constitute a key battleground for the future of the entire region. Given the strength of the anti-Enlightenment, ethnocentric forces in the pre-communist period, and the ways in which they were coopted and even officially encouraged in many of these countries during the late communist stage, it is reasonable to fear that their latter-day revival is a grim omen for the future. The anti-capitalist and anti-democratic sentiments, including paternalistic, corporatist, and populist nostalgias, could coalesce in new authoritarian experiments.[3] In this book, I look at the key political intellectuals and figures in these various countries, trying to explain their weaknesses and strengths and to identify, primarily in the case of those on the far right, the sources of their thinking and the reasons for their degree of success.

To be sure, things differ from one country to another. In the Balkans, we have witnessed the devastating effects of vicious nationalist demagogy, especially in the former Yugoslavia. Forces directly linked to the old regime are in power in Serbia, whereas authoritarian tendencies have plagued the democratic transitions in Albania, Croatia, and Romania. In Central Europe, Slovakia is ruled by a parochial government, which sees any form of criticism as a direct attack on the country's national security.[4] An alliance of neo-Bolshevik and nationalist fundamentalists has emerged as a major political force in Russia. The situation is less dismal in Poland, Hungary, and the Czech Republic, but even there one can see the rise of anti-democratic and anti-Western forces. The vehement anti-communist rhetoric of the Solidarity union has incorporated, especially after 1993, traditional themes of the extreme right, including anti-parliamentarism and anti-Semitism.

The topics addressed by this book bear directly on the ideological polemics now convulsing the post-communist world around the question, which are the main dangers for the new democracies? In my view, which I share with many former dissidents, there is less risk that "communism" in the sense of Marxist-Leninist socialism will be restored, than that corporatist, populist, pseudo-democratic authoritarianism will prevail. The avalanche of studies and reports about the emergence of markets and Western-style institutions have tended to dismiss the role of political traditions, memories, and deeply entrenched attitudes—in one word, the role of political culture. In this book I point out that it is not just an economic model that is at stake in the former communist world. In fact, the main issue is the nature of the emerging political communities: will they be inclusive or exclusive, tolerant or intolerant, society- or community-oriented? How should these nations come to terms with their own history of suffering and backwardness? Can nationalism be "tamed" and transformed into a positive energy, conducive to civic dialogue and cooperation, or is it bound to further aggressive goals of ethnic self-aggrandizement?

If these societies are to reinvent politics in a humane, enlightened way, such fundamental values as truth, trust, and tolerance need to be defended in the political arena. This is the reason Václav Havel decided to remain politically active, and urged like-minded intellectuals to do the same. Deserting the political battle now, withdrawing into an imaginary ivory tower, would simply signify a capitulation to populist demagogy. It would mean, indeed, a betrayal of the most noble promises of the dissident struggle against lies, cynicism, and hypocrisy. At this juncture in the history of Eastern Europe, when political movements have reemerged that unabashedly revive the fascist mystique of blood, ancestry, and "organic" community, intellectuals are important as promoters of the values of Enlightenment, individual rights, and civic humanism. More than ever, knowledge and action are inextricably linked, and a failure of nerve among the critical intelligentsia would have abysmal consequences. For, one should emphasize, if they do not fight for the autonomy of the individual now, if they give in to feelings of nausea and helplessness, tomorrow may be too late.

The Post-Communist Condition

The post-communist landscape is propitious soil for collective passions, fears, illusions, and disappointments. The old ideological certainties are dead. Instead, new mythologies have arisen to provide quick and satisfactory answers to excruciating dilemmas. Political myths are responses to the sentiments of discontinuity, fragmentation, and the overall confusion of the post-communist stage. Analyzing the social functions of myth in man's social life, philosopher Ernst Cassirer perceptively wrote: "Fear is a universal biological instinct. It can never be completely overcome or suppressed, but it can change its form. Myth is filled with the most violent emotions and the most frightful visions. But in myth man begins to learn a new and strange art: the art of expressing, and that means of organizing, his most rooted instincts, his hopes and fears."[5]

I contend that the resurgence of long-suppressed passions, sentiments, and resentments can be rationally explained and analyzed. The issue is neither to indict nor to deplore but to offer a comprehensive approach that explores the deep causes of the ongoing ethnic and political tensions throughout the whole region as well as the appeals of populist rhetoric. The origins of this mythological revival can be detected in the deeply entrenched feelings of national humiliation experienced by all nations in the region as a result of their subordination to the "Moscow center."[6] All were deprived of their memory during the decades of coercive Leninist indoctrination. The fallacy of socialist internationalism was imposed in different degrees on all of the communist world's subjects as the only correct approach to interstate and interethnic relations. In reality, however, this was an empty slogan that could not inspire more than ironies and suspicion.

The decline of Leninist internationalism coincided with the rise of the national-communist state during the terminal stage of state socialism in East and Central Europe. In order to stay in power, the bureaucratic elites increasingly abandoned Marxism-Leninism and espoused the more appealing symbols of national interest. To deter independent groups and movements from challenging their authority, the established political class resorted to traditional forms of nationalist manipulation and mobilization. In the case of Serbia and Romania, this strategy continued even after the official end of communism: the ruling elites have exploited the demagogy of "the fatherland is in danger" and accepted any ideological transmogrification, including the adoption of long-denied religious values, *only* to conserve their power.[7] In many of these countries, after the downfall of the corrupt and incompetent Leninist regimes, the new elites—often recruited from among the second or third echelons of the previous ones—embraced nationalism as a source of ideological legitimation.

Post-communist nationalism is thus a political and ideological phenomenon with a dual nature: as an expression of an historical cleavage, it rejects the spurious internationalism of communist propaganda and emphasizes long-repressed national values; on the other hand, it is a nationalism rooted in and marked by Leninist-authoritarian mentalities and habits, directed against any principle of difference and primarily against those groups and forces that champion pro-Western, pluralist orientations. The first direction is related to the global tendency toward rediscovery of ancestry, roots, and autochthonous values. The second perpetuates and enhances collectivistic communist and pre-communist traditions by denying the individual the right to dissent, sanctifying the national community and its allegedly providential leader, and scapegoating or demonizing minorities for imaginary plots and betrayals. Indeed, taking the case of Serbia's strongman Slobodan Milošević, we are dealing with an astute demagogue who cynically exploited Great Serbian nationalism to further his own hegemonic-dictatorial purposes.[8]

Post-communist mythologies of salvation are ideological surrogates, competing with other intellectual and political trends. Their principal function is to unify the public discourse and provide the citizen with an easily recognizable source of identity as a part of a vaguely defined ethnic (or political) community. These mythologies minimize individual rights and emphasize, instead, the need to maintain an organic supraindividual ethos. Catering to mass frustrations, they speak in terms of collective guilt and collective punishment. Favoring a politics of anger and resentment, proponents of these mythologies often capitalize on legitimate aspirations and grievances. After all, there is a lot of despair in these countries, and the political myths provide fast, clear-cut explanations for the causes of the ongoing troubles.

The new mythologies tend to indulge in self-pity: "We Croats (or Lithuanians, Russians, Slovaks, Serbs, Ukrainians, and so on) have been the ultimate victims of communism (or of Western betrayal)." According to this vision, no other nation has suffered as much as the one of the speaker (or writer, or historian), who simply cannot understand why the outer world is so insensitive to his or her nation's unique plight. A political myth is needed around which the afflicted society or groups that have been displaced or uprooted by the stormy changes can identify themselves, can gather and attempt to restore their collective life. This longing for lost certitudes explains the growing nostalgia for the pre-communist national and cultural values, the resurrection of the messianic myth of the Nation (the People as One), and the burning belief in its regenerative power.[9]

Post-communist radical mythologies merge the Jacobin-Leninist logic of "vigilance and intransigence" with themes championed by the xenophobic extreme right of the interwar period. For practical political purposes, the "Other" is constructed as a demonical figure (the "Eternal Jew," the "bloodthirsty Hungarian," "the overbearing Czech," the "cheating, promiscuous Gypsy"), because as Eric Hobsbawm states: 'there is no more effective way of bonding together the disparate sections of restless people than to unite them against outsiders."[10]

In this book, I insist on the key distinction between anti-liberal, integral nationalism, which asserts the primacy of ethnic values over any others, and liberal or civic, nationalism, which admits the compatibility of civic and ethnic identities in a political order based on mutual trust and tolerance. The revolutions of 1989–1991 had a dual nature: they were simultaneously revolutions of political and national liberation. Hence it is not surprising that the first post-communist stage was predominantly civic, whereas the second has tended to be more ethnically colored. The two stages cannot be completely separated, as civic and ethnic elements may overlap in both official discourse and private political statements.

This book attempts to clarify many of the current confusions regarding the cultural and political debates about the future of post-communist societies. It shows how a climate of angst and despair, insecurity and disarray is conducive to the flourishing of mythologies promising immediate solutions and the elimination of troublemakers. It analyzes a number of paradigmatic political actors directly involved in the making (or unmaking) of prevailing post-communist myths: Lech Walesa, Adam Michnik, Václav Havel, Václav Klaus, István Csurka, Gennady Zyuganov, Vladimir Zhirinovsky, and soon. The book also examines the new coalitions of Stalinists, religious and nationalist zealots in Russia and the Balkans, strange alliances whose basis is the shared hostility to modernity, popular sovereignty, civic rights, and tolerance for diversity.

Although there are many books dealing with post-communist Eastern Europe, this may be the first one to explore systematically the successor mythologies to the extinct Leninist creed. It shows the power of collective beliefs and analyzes the risks of having these myths act as galvanizing forces for unrest, turmoil, and even regional war. It is a book that deliberately places itself between comparative politics and political theory: my goal is to understand mentalities and behavioral patterns that explain many of the current evolutions or devolutions in the post-communist world. And mental patterns (or, in Alexis de Tocqueville's and Emile Durkheim's terms "the habits of the heart") are stubborn, self-enclosed, and self-generating, particularly if giving them up appears as an externally imposed duty.[11]

The Longing for Political Myth

Political myths are not systems of thought but rather sets of beliefs whose foundations transcend logic; no empirical evidence can shatter their pseudo-cognitive immunity. French anthropologist Gilbert Durand spoke of "mythological constellations" to describe the ensemble of mythical constructs belonging to a common theme and structured around a central vision.[12] There exists an inner grammar of mythological discourse, a hidden syntax, to use Claude Lévi-Strauss's terminology. Political myth is intrinsically elusive, and some of its transrational aspects defy rigorous analysis. And still, precisely because of its elusiveness, political myth appears as a coherent and complete belief system: "it does not invoke any other legitimacy but its own affirmation, no other logic but its own development. And experience has without doubt shown that each of these mythological 'constellations' can emerge at the most opposite points of the political horizon, can be classified as 'left' or 'right' according to the opportunities of the moment."[13] Thus, political mythologies revolve around such major themes as the Golden Age (innocence lost, glorious patriarchal beginnings, the fall into modernity); victimhood, martyrdom, treason and conspiracy; salvation and the advent of the millennium; charismatic saviors (who can be heroic individuals, allegedly predestined classes, or biologically defined races); and ultimate bliss in the form of revolutionary chiliasm, when leader, movement, nation, and mankind become one, whether in life or death.

Myth remains a fundamental datum of the political world, especially in societies beset by discord, enmities, and problematic democratic traditions. Myth has the power not only to offer relatively facile explanations for perceived victimhood and failure but also to mobilize, energize, and even instigate large groups into action. For instance, the myth of Kosovo as the shrine of Serbian national identity, threatened by the "barbaric" Albanians (most of whom are Muslim) played a central role in the organization of anger and hatred during the destruction of Yugoslavia. The principal function of myth is not to describe but to imagine a reality in accordance with certain political interests.

Political myth is a partial invention, an exaggeration of certain authentic elements of the political space: its power comes precisely from its lack of conceptual timidity. What traditional doctrinaires may simply hint at mythographers turn into shocking statements, uninhibited by rational arguments to the contrary. Recall Houston Stewart Chamberlain or Joseph de Gobineau: neither of them was in any way intimidated by scholarly criticism of his racist fantasies. On the contrary, they treated these analyses as the ultimate proof that their theories were right. Metapolitics, as Pieter Viereck has shown, roots itself in this arrogance of political mythology, on the basis of which a certain group (the "Aryan race" or even the proletarian class) is endowed with transcendental virtues.[14] The nineteenth century, with its strange combination of scientism and romanticism, paved the ground for the constitution of the major mythologies that led to the totalitarian catastrophes of the twentieth century.[15]

Millenarian revolutionaries used the myth of the superior race (or class) to justify their lust for power and the establishment of ideocratic tyrannies (*Weltanschauungstaat*, as Hannah Arendt described Nazi Germany). Indeed, it was to a large extent the myth of historical predestination, the investment of history with providential powers, its substitution for God, and the identification of the charismatic savior with the sense of history, that led to the tyrannies of certitude in our century.[16] Political myth is thus part of modernity, an illustration of the role of ideological delusions in the justification of unprecedented experiments in social and racial engineering. Such experiments were based on the assumption that the ultimate utopian vision justifies even the most cruel and sordid means. But as Isaiah Berlin has written, their basis was a preposterous and ultimately murderous belief in the plasticity of human nature and the conviction that a "final solution" to all human predicaments could be devised:

> The possibility of a final solution—even if we forget the terrible sense that these words acquired in Hitler's day—turns out to be an illusion; and a very dangerous one. For if one really believes that such a solution is possible, then surely no cost will be too high to obtain it: to make mankind just and happy and creative and harmonious for ever—what could be too high a price for that? To make such an omelette, there is surely no limit to the number of eggs that should be broken. . . . Some armed prophets seek to save mankind, and some only their race because of its superior attributes, but whichever the motive, the millions slaughtered in wars or revolutions—gas chambers, gulag, genocide, all the monstrosities for which our century will be remembered—are the price men must pay for the felicity of the future generations.[17]

Political myth was used by the ideological condottieri of our century to legitimize all sorts of violence, exclusion, mass extermination, the Gulag and the Holocaust. Thanks to myth, twentieth-century tyrants could think and act "big"—moral concerns being of course just philistine limits. It was indeed the blinding power of the Aryan myth that cauterized the moral sense of the Nazis and allowed them to organize the genocide of the Jews in the name of a "superior cause." Thanks to eschatological myths individuals can feel superior and ultimately unaccountable; myth not only explains everything but also excuses the worst abominations. National socialism was indeed a pathology of racial universalism.[18] Hitler's willing mass killers were convinced that their actions purified humanity.[19] Stalinism was the pathology of class warfare. Marx's religion of the proletariat as the messiah class of history was transformed into a recipe for the destruction of all sources of private property, primarily that of the peasantry, resulting in the Ukrainian great famine, the genocide of the "kulaks," and the Great Purge.

Nationalists of all stripes have used mythologies to construct boundaries and deny equal rights to their fellow countrymen. For instance, the myth of the Dacian past has been used by Romanian nationalists to deny Hungarian claims on the cultural heritage of Transylvania; the issue gets lost in the mists of the pre-Christian history, and the debate loses any rational content. Romanian nationalists invoke a passage in Herodotus according to which the Dacians were the bravest among Thracians, but forget to refer to other lines in the same text according to which they also considered agricultural work to be humiliating and found idleness as a most pleasant experience.[20]

Now, as we prepare to enter the new millennium, salvation is once again on the top of humanity's agenda. Old certainties have fallen apart, traditional ideologies and political dichotomies have lost their meaning. In politics, we cannot make real sense of the old-fashioned distinctions between Left and Right. The revolutions of 1989–1991, with their post-ideological and anti-utopian flavor, have annulled these conventional demarcations so much indebted to the legacies of the French political spasms of the late eighteenth and nineteenth centuries.

Humanity is once again confronted with such issues as the value and desirability of technological progress, the role of parties in democratic politics, and the possibility of new forms of human organization beyond parties, nations, or ethnic states. New waves of nationalism flow on the Old Continent and new millennial expectations have taken shape, often informed by time-honored chiliastic fantasies. Not only in Europe and the Middle East but in the United States as well, groups and movements have emerged that deplore and denounce liberal democracy in the name of the rights of nature; of organic and vital communities; of tribal identity, and the like.[21] America's far-right militias share with the Persian ayatollahs, with Jean-Marie Le Pen and his National Front, and with Russian demagogue Vladimir Zhirinovsky a deep hostility to the principles of tolerance and equality. Moreover, they share a belief in the mystique of hidden forces, of occult groups that master the world and pursue their nefarious agendas in order to enslave free individuals and establish some satanic tyranny.

In times of great transformations, conspiracy theories thrive. The "Protocols of the Elders of Zion," arguably the world's most infamous forgery, fabricated by the Czarist Okhrana (secret police) at the end of the nineteenth century, for example, has been reprinted and distributed in the new European democracies by extremist groups convinced that all evils are in one way or another related to a Jewish plot to run the planet.[22] In their frantic urge to unmask diabolical conspiracies, radical rightist groups reiterate the fantasies of the nineteenth-century racist maniacs. In the past, the myth of a secret alliance between the revolutionary left and the world financiers (a pact between the communist and the capitalist internationals, between "Comintern" and "Cap-intern") was used to explain economic and political turmoil. Now, as the com-munist order has collapsed, vindictive voices are heard that resurrect another old myth: the collusion between liberal democracy and Jewish plutocracy. Political mythologies are thus part and parcel of the collective imagination of fin-de-siècle East and West.

In the former communist countries, such myths perhaps tend to be more powerful and visible precisely because of the weakness of liberal and demo-cratic traditions; people tend to harken back to old doctrines and visions, and have little patience for rational interpretations of the dramatic changes that have so quickly affected their lives. Political myths have the power to satisfy this thirst for immediate understanding; causalities are simplified or invented, im-ages are presented in a vivid, metaphorical way, and the individual can discover sources for reassurance and psychological security. Furthermore, myths are not mutually exclusive. Some that are past-oriented (such as the Golden Age of felicity and unity threatened by the capitalist order; the splendor of the village as opposed to the destructive forces of industry) or that exalt nature and, of course, the noble savage intersect with the search for the redeemer, the charis-matic savior, and new versions of revolutionary millennialism.[23]

Such conspiratorial myths operate on the assumption that there is a hidden meaning, a secret cause of all phenomena: the enigmatic powers of the enemy are turned into the explanation for defeats and presumed dangers. In the case of Serbian nationalists, the role of the Catholic Church in the destruction of Yugoslavia is taken for granted. Because Croats are Catholic, and the Church is a universal organization, the myth claims that Croats enjoyed decisive sup-port from the West (especially from Germany) in their quest for indepen-dence. Furthermore, the same myth combines Catholicism and Islam in the figure of an anti-Serbian, that is, anti-Orthodox, conspiracy. Needless to add, this vision has stirred responsive chords among Slavophiles in Russia, always ready to believe in the existence of Western lobbies ready to use any instru-ment, including Muslim fundamentalism, to ruin the prospects for Russia to become the Third Rome.[24]

Myths of Revolution, Myths of Restoration

Were the revolutions 1989–1991 defeated? Can the "velvet restoration" bring these societies back to the status quo ante?[25] From my perspective, the posi-tive results of the breakdown cannot be overestimated: a system based on duplicity, schizophrenic relationships of the individual to reality, dictatorship over human needs, memories, and hopes, and the almost complete control of the party/police state over human activities has disappeared. One of modernity's main avenues, the dream of social engineering bound to force humanity into a perfect order, devoid of fear, grief, and doubt, came to an end.[26] It is thus much too early to engage in lamentation about the inescapable moral debacle of the post-communist era. Adam Michnik once told me that the many years he spent in dissident activities taught him that history knows no absolute determinism.[27] Still unknown are the political, social, and cultural configurations in the former communist states in a decade or two. We know, however, that human beings need frames of reference. They need relatively stable images with which to identify, galvanizing figures of a better order, and explanations for perceived or real failure. In other words, humans need political myths.

Of all the political thinkers associated with the Marxian tradition, none has preserved more actuality, at least at this juncture of cognitive anarchy, than the French thinker Georges Sorel. Writing at the turn of the century, he understood better than so many of the official socialists of his age that individuals do not engage in politics for the sake of Cartesian demonstrations but for vivid, attractive, magnetizing images that can structure their mental world. He was wrong, to be sure, about the all-embracing value of the myth of the general strike. No less mistaken was he regarding the sanctifying, cathartic virtue of proletarian violence. But one thing he did understand correctly, and this intuition was clearly non-Marxist: the power of myth as a discourse or story about origins, movement, and direction, a source of pride for the disenfranchised and a balm for the humiliated self.[28] Myths are not banal descriptions of the desired society but calls for action. In the words of Sorel: "A myth cannot be refuted, since it is, at bottom, identical with the conviction of a group, being the expression of these convictions in the language of movement; and it in consequence unanalyzable into parts which could be placed on the plane of historical descriptions."[29]

Sorel's ideas had a major influence on two revolutionaries of radically different persuasions in this century, the fascist Benito Mussolini and the Leninist Antonio Gramsci. Both insisted on the paramount role of myth in modern politics. Although Lenin publicly scorned Sorel, he shared with the French writer a hatred for bourgeois values and the cult of violence. Sorel, in turn, applauded the Bolshevik uprising, lambasted the Western attempts to isolate Soviet Russia, and even concluded an article entitled "In Defense of Lenin" with these dramatic words: "Cursed by the plutocratic democracies which are starving Russia I am only an old man whose life is at the mercy of trifling accidents; but may I, before descending into the tomb, see the humiliation of the arrogant bourgeois democracies, today shamelessly triumphant."[30] Isaiah Berlin sums up Sorel's philosophy of political myth as a major paradigm for understanding our age: "For Sorel, the function of myths is not to stabilize, but to direct energies and inspire action. They do this by embodying a dynamic vision of the movement of life, the more potent because not rational, and therefore not subject to criticism and refutation by university wiseacres. . . . The function of myth is to create an 'epic state of mind.'"[31]

The transition to post-communist order has brought to the fore a number of unexpected political and cultural phenomena. Among these, the resurgence of deep-seated anti-modern sentiments and the revolt against liberal values are disquieting precisely because they appeal to large groups of bewildered individuals. The initial euphoria that accompanied the disintegration of communist regimes has been followed by malaise, widespread exasperation, fatigue, a general sense of exhaustion. Some of the famous dissidents of yore declare that what they have been witnessing in the first half-decade of post-communism is not what they fought for. This book focuses on the political psychology of post-communism and explores, in an intellectually comparative way, the new East European discourses that are trying to articulate responses to the moral disarray of individuals in times of historical fracture. My approach is thematic rather than geographic, inviting the reader to discover how similar *fantasies of redemption* (atonement and escape or flight from reality) operate concurrently in different countries. To achieve my goal, I do not take the country-by-country approach. Others have done so, and I strongly recommend their works.[32] Events and concrete developments are examined only to the extent that they highlight motivations for the emergence of certain political mythologies.

This book is not about everyday politics in post-communist societies, but the spiritual reactions to the discomfitures of the transition. The main hypothesis is that these societies are still in search of a new axis mundi, because traditional identities have fallen apart, and new mythologies have emerged to inspire unity in a despairingly fragmented body politic. As the Leninist authoritarian order collapsed, societies have tended to be atomized and deprived of a political center able to articulate coherent visions of a common good. In some respects, the "landscape after the battle" is more depressing than the times of communist rule: adventurers, charlatans, and racketeers have replaced the dull, morose members of the nomenklatura—or worse, they are the same persons. Nostalgia for the relative security and social predictability of the communist times is rampant.[33] The first post-communist elites often have been seen as corrupt, amateurish, greedy, rapacious, and so on. In all these countries, former dissidents have been vilified. Their criticism of the status quo, once celebrated and admired under communism, is now seen as utopian. The calls by Václav Havel, Sergey Kovalyov or Jacek Kuron for a politics rooted in morality and civic solidarity are perceived as sentimental exhortations with little relevance for the turbulent times of transition. Ironically, advocates of economic neoliberalism, presumably informed by the ideas of Scottish Enlightenment, concur with the proponents of ethnic collectivism in the supercilious deprecation of the former dissidents, and deride the latters' vision of a civil society and their yearning for living in truth as a "new moralism."[34]

The new political myths have had a galvanizing power that is linked to their claim to be all-explanatory. Thus my approach does not treat myth as a necessarily mendacious vision of reality but as a narrative that is able to inspire collective loyalties, affinities, passions, and actions. The value of myth is that it mobilizes and energizes the infrarational segments of political behavior. Its propositions do not make sense because of rational coherence, but in spite of it.[35] For instance, viewed from the United States in the mid-1990s the idea that there was a Croat plan to restore the Ustasha pro-Nazi regime was obviously a paranoid exaggeration, but this delusion was believed by a number of active and powerful Serbian leaders. Their belief system had acquired a dramatically different shape under conditions of war, ethnic cleansing, and hysterical populism.

My underlying hypothesis is that the post-communist political and intellectual world will remain a battlefield between different, often incompatible myths. Countless exculpatory mythologies have emerged in post-Leninist regimes, from narratives of mass national resistance to communism to visions of universal complicity. They all tend to minimize the heroic meaning of the dissidents' efforts: if everybody was an anti-communist, why should former dissidents be celebrated as moral examples? And, vice versa, if nothing could have been done against the system, and everyone believed in its eternity, maybe dissidents were what the communist propaganda claimed them to be: neurotic, self-absorbed individuals, manipulated by Western intelligence agencies.

Often focused on the past, the new mythologies are actually discourses about the present and especially the future of post-communist societies.[36] This book examines the major political creeds in question. The book first proposes a framework to explain how political myths operate and then a comparative approach to the following four themes.

1. Salvationist Mythologies and Authoritarian Expectations

Addressed in Chapter Two, this theme deals with the impact of the Leninist heritage on the new political experiments. I argue that the revolutions of 1989 included a latent anti-liberal, communitarian component that was to develop in later years. The discussions on liberalism have been abstract and speculative in the absence of a real middle class, especially as an inefficient but dominant state bureaucracy has been more inclined to promote corporatist deals than to foster genuine competition of ideas and interests. I discuss the psychological barriers to an open society, the main vulnerabilities of the new pluralist governments, the role of corruption (including moral corruption), the rise of the new networks of power and influence, and the relationship between political myth and elite legitimation.

2. Messianic and Demonizing Mythologies: The Nationalist Temptation

This theme focuses on the varieties of nationalism in post-communist societies, including the strange alliance between neocommunists and ethnic fundamentalists. The question is whom do these symbols and myths appeal to, who is "in" and who is "out"?

I examine the nature of radical nationalism in the rise of new authoritarian groups and movements, discussing this phenomenon in the light of the mythology of the enemy and foreign threat. The complementary myth explored in these pages is the narcissistic vision of one's ultimate victimization and the ongoing competition between East Europeans to emphasize their unique predicament and ordeal under communism or fascism. I discuss nationalism as an ambivalent project: on the one hand, it is associated with modernity and the cultural awakening of ethnic groups; on the other, in its chauvinistic and exclusive versions it represents a rebellion against the very principle of modernity.

Chapters Three and Four discuss anti-Semitism, anti-capitalism, anti-liberalism, and anti-Westernism as the main ingredients of the new populist radicalism. Such mythologies are analyzed as responses to the perceived crisis of the still-infant parliamentary democratic system and to the lukewarm Western readiness to accept the new democracies into the Euro-Atlantic structures. I do not claim that they will triumph but rather that they are real threats to the emerging pluralist institutions and values. Indeed, in most of these countries a psychology of panic and fears of spying seem to be contagious. Many individuals feel an intense sentiment of exclusion, uprootedness, and nonbelonging to the new democratic order.[37] In the words of one of the greatest students of political myth, Emile Durkheim; "When society suffers, it needs to find somebody to blame for its malaise, to take revenge on for all its disappointments."[38]

3. Mythologies of Vengeance: Decommunization and the Myth of Political Justice

How to handle the former secret police files, officers, and agents? What to do with the former communist bureaucrats? My discussion in Chapter Five explores different strategies of decommunization, from the Polish "thick line" with the past adopted under the Mazowiecki government to the "lustration" (screening, purification) laws and their effects in the Czech Republic. I also examine the German approach to the former Stasi officers and informers. In some countries the rhetoric of decommunization served as ammunition for new forms of radicalism: in Poland, for instance, populist and conservative parties have used it in their efforts to destabilize political institutions and delegitimize the liberal segment of the new political class. In Romania, revolutionary expedience was invoked to justify a judicial farce that led to the execution of Nicolae Ceauşescu and his wife in December 1989, but left most of the old regime's structures basically intact. Vindictive and moralizing, the rhetoric of decommunization championed by the anti-Iliescu opposition failed to generate mass support and had to be toned down. In the same vein, the staunch anti-communist language of the Bulgarian Union of Democratic Forces in the early 1990s alienated many voters and even had the perverse effect of bringing the post-communists back to power. In its radical form, the myth of decommunization maintains that only by instituting retroactive justice, bringing former communist leaders to trial, or barring them from holding public office for a certain amount of time, will these societies be able to exorcize their demons. It is a vengeful myth whose fulfillment would presumably create a community of presumed just avengers versus a minority of villains and rascals. It is based on the assumption that the communist society was divided into two main groups: them and us. It hyperbolizes the resilience of the former communists and obfuscates the true dangers faced by the new democracies. Indeed, the main risk these days is not the restoration of the communist ideocracy but the resurgence of the old system's authoritarian and malignantly corrupt practices.[39]

4. Redemptive, Reactionary and Restorative Mythologies

Chapter Six discusses the marginalization of former dissidents in post-communist politics, the role of critical intellectuals, and the controversial legacy of anti-politics. I focus my analysis on such personalities as Václav Havel, George Konrád, Jacek Kuron, Adam Michnik, and others who formulated the discourse of dissent in the universalistic language of civil society and human rights. At this level I discuss the myth of anti-communist resistance and the growing attacks on those who were involved in this resistance. I agree with Adam Michnik that this is a period when the "prudent people with clean hands" get the upper hand and can deride the efforts of those who had engaged in the building of the "parallel polis."[40]

The deeper question therefore is to what extent these were genuine revolutions. And, no less important, were they, as many observers thought, "revolutions of the intellectuals," moral insurrections against ideologically based police states? Was the dissidents' refusal to endorse a politics of vengeance and resentment the cause of the ex-communists' electoral victories after 1993? My response is that it is precisely their commitment to the values of tolerance and individual rights which guarantees the long-term validity of the critical intellectuals' concept of freedom as well as their political relevance. To put it briefly: intellectuals do need to stay in politics for the liberal revolution truly to succeed in the countries of the former communist empire. Indeed, as Jeffrey Isaac points out, the greatest relevance of the so-called "anti-politics" as proposed by the dissidents is hermeneutical or interpretative: "Even if anti-political politics currently had no evident influence whatsoever, it would still remain relevant as a crucial historical moment of the recent past."[41] The hour may belong for some time to populist adventurers or pragmatic bureaucrats, but none of these can provide the moral inspiration, the transcendent values so badly needed for citizens to live in dignity and self-respect.[42]

The Collapse of Sovietism and the New Vacuum

Marxism as an oracular doctrine may be dead, but the need for political myths is alive. Far from being the science of social change lionized by its partisans, Marxism was a secular eschatology whose main function was to give an answer (even if a mystified one) to the predicament of the historically wounded, neurotic individual.[43] Alienation can be surmounted here and now, Marx proclaimed prophetically. Even the enemies of this grandiose fantasy had to admit its extraordinary galvanizing force.

Lenin's Bolshevism transformed the original gnosis into a sociology of power and revolution. Revolutionary Russia became the palpable utopia in which Marxism-Leninism functioned as "one of the most effective mobilizing ideologies and legitimating belief-systems in the history of parties, states and societies."[44] Revolutionary zeal was the driving force that inspired flaming and obstinate chiliastic beliefs from Havana to Beijing, and from Moscow to Paris. As Leninism became a world system, its denizens were imbued with a political faith that sacralized the future and imposed on individuals complete, heroic dedication to the fulfillment of extraordinary transformational tasks. The *Sturm und Drang* of the Leninist romanticism faded away, however, under the impact of bureaucratic constraints, especially after 1956, when Stalin's myth was dismantled by Nikita Khrushchev. A turning point in the history of world communism, Khrushchev's attack on Stalin inaugurated an era of doubt, heresy, and open revolt. The Leninist dogma lost its original mesmerizing power and appeared as just a hypocritical device used by corrupt bureaucrats to legitimize their monopoly on power: "Mass murder did not undermine conviction, but the squalor of the Brezhnev years did have such an effect. When the *nomenklatura* killed each other and accompanied the murderous rampage with blatantly mendacious political theatre, belief survived; but when the *nomenklatura* switched from shooting each other to bribing each other, faith evaporated."[45] Tedious, infinitely boring, indeed a world without surprises, the decaying Leninist order was also one where routinized behavior implied no risk. Rulers and ruled seemed united in this sentiment of historical ennui. By the end of the 1980s, so all-pervasive were moral and economic failure that even Soviet ideologues decried this last stage as stagnation.

The twilight of Leninism coincided with the rediscovery of the values of freedom, citizenry, responsibility, and dignity in the project of a resurrected civil society and the experimentation of a non-Machiavellian form of politics, often called "anti-politics." In more than one respect, the revolutions of 1989 resumed the original project of Enlightenment in that they repudiated any form of mental or institutional absolutism and called for a nonideological and nonmanipulative treatment of the individual.

But has political pluralism been achieved? Instead of genuine parties, we see charismatic or pseudo-charismatic figures migrating from one group to another, with little interest in defining their ideological choices. This is the ground for the neoauthoritarian calls for "law and order," nostalgia for Stalin, and expectations of a strongman to get rid of the parliamentary chatter. Not only the angry masses but also some of the most sophisticated pundits see the future of Russia (and not only Russia) dominated by a figure inspired by Chile's Pinochet or Portugal's Salazar.

Transitions from the old order are going to last for a long period of time, with many convulsions, setbacks, and frustrations.[46] Perhaps the only safe prediction is that some of the post-communist countries will develop stable democratic institutions and join the European and Atlantic political, economic, and military structures. Others will persist in a hybrid semi-liberal, semi-authoritarian order that combines populism and nationalism as forms of expedient legitimation based on mass enthusiasm.[47]

Can we simply treat the past communist experience as completely exhausted? Or rather should we identify its relics in the belief systems of the post-Soviet age? What was the relationship between the Leninist experiments and the strategy of modernization? Can one say together with Hungarian philosopher G. M. Tamás that the revolutions of 1989 included a strong anti-modern component, that they voiced a strong yearning for communitarian, organic values, presumably denied by Leninist "developmentalism"—appallingly ruthless, but nevertheless effective?[48] Answering these questions means taking into account the diversity of Leninist legacies in different countries. The ideological vision and the role of the secret police was hardly the same in Poland and Hungary, on the one hand, and Romania or Albania, on the other. Some Leninist regimes were more permissive than others, some communist leaders were less fanatic than others. János Kádár was not Erich Honecker, neither was general Wojciech Jaruzelski a died-in-the-wool, firebrand Stalinist like Nicolae Ceaușescu. Even in the former USSR there were differences between Lithuania, with its reformist wing of the Communist party headed by Algirdas Brazauskas, and Ukraine, where former ideologue Leonid Kravchuk discovered the advantages of nationalism only after the collapse of the imperial center—he became the first president of independent Ukraine and then a fierce champion of Ukrainian sovereignty.

These different heritages, as well as the cultural traditions of the pre-communist times, explain the advances of some countries in contrast to the sluggishness of others. Clericalism, militarism, national fundamentalism have loomed large in many of these countries, and this is not simply because of the "return of the repressed past," as it were. Even as the Church lost much of its previous influence in Poland, there was a growing temptation to radicalize its critique of its traditional enemies: secularism, atheism, licentiousness, and amoralism.[49] The past matters, of course, but the need to use it for purposes of legitimation, is linked to the uncertain status of the new elites, still devoid of enough legal-procedural authority and reluctant to accept political compromises with their opponents.

Filling the Political Vacuum

At the end of this most tumultuous century (the bloodiest and most violent ever) we have come to realize the precariousness of our human condition, the limits of our knowledge, and the absurdity of any grandiose project to restructure the world. However, this awareness creates a spiritual vacuum, a dissatisfaction with an environment dominated by technology and bureaucratic effectiveness (or ineffectiveness). The unsparing skepticism so characteristic of "post-modernity" and "post-history" leaves the individual with a sense of despondency and a profound need for identification with a creed, religion, community, militia, and so on. This sentiment was acutely expressed years ago by Martin Heidegger in his famous exclamation: "Only a God could save us!" With its logic of fragmentation and disruption, "post-modernity" (I prefer to speak of late modernity) has placed the individual in the middle of an axiological turmoil. But ambivalence does not mean total relativism. The repudiation of claims to absolute truth does not amount to the dissipation of truth into mutually subversive but equally valid discourses. What is right and what is wrong—or, in Immanuel Kant's words, what can man [humans] hope?—remains an essential question even for the citizen of the satisfied Western world.[50]

The universalistic redemptive paradigms have gone bankrupt in our century of institutionalized terror and infernal barbarism, it is true—but who would dare to predict that humans will willingly abandon their aptitude for social dreaming in favor of piecemeal political adjustment to a rational reality? On the other hand, the triumphalist portrayal of our civilization as the culmination of historical progress tends to neglect the fact that this world is constructed on renunciations of all sorts, and that progress itself is a questionable proposition. Thus, Walter Benjamin warned that unless a messianic viewpoint remains with us, humanity risks sliding into atomized uniformity and barbarous regimentation. Modernity appeared to Benjamin as pregnant with the most dangerous, catastrophically destructive trends: "There is no document of civilization which is not at the same time a document of barbarism."[51] Political myth, as a fantasy of a better world, cannot be simply discarded as infantile daydreaming. Although some myths are exclusionary, vindictive, and potentially disastrous, others are favorable to dialogue and a commitment to a free community of equal individuals. It is always a matter of interpretation and, as in the case of Jean-Jacques Rousseau's general will, the same myth can be used for expansion or limitation of one's freedoms and responsibilities.

The question I raise, which is essential for the validity of the liberal project in societies with a non- or even anti-liberal past, is whether the new mythologies will be assets or hindrances from the viewpoint of a democratic transition. Why is such a question important? Because all societies need foundational myths, and this is a fact of civilization no one can or should deny. On the other hand, if civil society is to function, it has to overcome the hostile forces of collective identities, corporate segmentarism, and any form of ideocratic authoritarianism.[52]

At the same time, one cannot see the project of civil society as intractably benign. There is a tendency to level out individuality, there is a risk of the tyranny of the majority, and no less important, there is a danger that the public sphere will be atomized and that culture and opinions will be homogenized. Furthermore, one can ask whether the very project of civil society is not the fruit of a peculiar Western intellectual and political development, and the result of several centuries of search for a normative framework for human rights justified by the old-fashioned idea of God-given natural rights. In the same vein, civil society, even in the West, has met strong rivals, among which exacerbated nationalisms and the new racisms are the most vehement.

In all the communist states, the dominant political culture was made up of different, often conflicting subcultures: from the more or less avowed ultranationalists within the party and the secret police, through reformers and semi-liberals, to the marginal dissident communities. Indeed, the interpretation of post-communist ideological landscape has to keep in mind that old adage *ex nihilo nihil*: much of the nationalist pathos is not just the resurrection of interwar right-wing trends, but the prolongation of a xenophobic subculture that lingered under communism (both within and outside the party). The predestined role of the nation state has in the Orthodox religion its supporter: Mother Russia, Mother Romania, and Mother Serbia appear as the ultimate value, and anybody who falters in the full support for it is declared a traitor, including those priests who call for a reassessment of the relationship between secular and religious authorities.[53]

Despite Leninism's decline, the utopian reservoir of humanity has not been completely exhausted: refurbished ideologies have resurfaced, among them populism, chauvinism, and traditionalism of different shades.[54] The ghost of the future conjured up by young Karl Marx in the *Communist Manifesto* has been replaced by revamped specters of the past, summoned into the present by disconcerted political actors, unable to come to terms with the hardships of the democratic project and the challenges of modernity. To the soulless "Europe of butter" they counterpose, together with Aleksandr Solzhenitsyn, the myth of the original communal democracy of the agrarian societies.[55] In short, the end of communism, the revolutions of 1989, and the ambiguous legacy of anti-politics have created a world full of dangers, with traditional lines of demarcation completely disintegrated, and new forms of radicalism simmering under the carapace of pseudo stability.

A major theme of this book is that many of the discussions going on in East and Central Europe regarding the status of the intellectual in politics and the role of the intelligentsia in formulating both positive (consensual) and negative (confrontational) agendas for the nation bear upon trends that affect the West as well. What happened in the former Yugoslavia should be ominously instructive: it was, after all, a group of stellar intellectuals, writers, philosophers, and anthropologists who spelled out in 1986, in the notorious Memorandum of the Serbian Academy of Sciences, a blueprint for ethnic cleansing and paranoid nationalism. But intoxicating effects of this nationalist fever, the most powerful opponent of liberal values, are not limited to Europe's Southeast. As Jacek Kuroń, one of Poland's most thoughtful intellectuals and political figures, put it: "The crisis we face is foremost a crisis of ideas—we now lack universal ideas of the kind that mobilize hearts and minds, of the kind without which no civilization could exist. Is this not why, in various parts of the globe, particularistic or nationalist ideas and religious fundamentalism are gaining ground? After communism collapsed, we expected a Westernization of the Orient, but it is the West that is being orientalized."[56]

One _____

Resurrecting Utopia: Ideology versus Mythology

> The past is an essential element, perhaps *the*
> *essential* element in these ideologies. If there is
> no suitable past, it can always be invented.
>   (*Eric Hobsbawm*)

WHAT IS the difference between myth and ideology? Is there a difference between myth and ideology? A short answer would be that a myth proposes a story, whereas ideology has its roots in systematic ideas. But don't stories have their roots in ideas? The story told by the myth—in this case the political myth—is rooted in beliefs, aspirations, deep expectations, hopes, frustrations, illusions, and disillusions. All ideologies do have a mythological core, but in addition they build up conceptual edifices. As John Girling put it: "'Myth' is fusion of concept and emotion; a passionate desire to achieve a primordial objective. 'Ideology' represents the agglomeration and systematization of both emotional and conceptual elements."[1] Radical ideologies tend to be especially interwoven with mythology in that they emphasize the possibility (or even urgency) of a complete break with the chain of historical development, a somersault into a fully liberated world.

Myth deals less with the world as it exists than with its unfulfilled potential. In the words of literary critic Northrop Frye, "Man lives in two worlds, the worlds traditionally called the worlds of nature and art. We live in an actual world, our physical environment in time and space, and this is the world studied mainly by the natural and physical sciences. At the same time, we keep trying to create a culture and civilization of our own. This represents the world we want to live in, as well as the world we are creating of our environment. It is where our values and desires and hopes and ideals belong, and this world is always geocentric, always anthropocentric, always centered on man and man's concerns."[2]

Myth emerges precisely because of this discrepancy between the real world and the world of our aspirations: "It is obvious that the basis of the world we want to live in is mythological."[3] Myths propose another reality, beyond history, and their success depends on their plausibility. If they make sense for those supposed to believe in them, myths succeed in their most important task: to endow the individual with a sense of identity and an orientation in the disjointed world.

Indeed, myth responds to the quest for identity, community, foundations, and meaning in one's existence: "We want a human community that will conform to our hopes and ideals and our sense of what might be; we need a knowledge of our environment that will give it foundations and keep it from being a castle in the air."[4] In the past, for the denizens of the communist world, the myth of the classless society could serve such a purpose. We should not delude ourselves: Leninist regimes were based on terror, but also on mobilization and enthusiasm. If there is a nostalgia for the lost times of "heroic mobilization," this is linked as much to the sense of lost unity and disappeared community as to the current disaffection with democratic pluralism and market economy.[5]

The endurance of nationalism is a testimonial to the persistence of myth as a major vector of our spiritual situation. This chapter examines myth versus ideology as an explanatory paradigm for the political and moral disenchantment characteristic of post-communist societies. They are both expressions of this crisis, as well as attempts to resurrect utopia. They both try to structure the mental world and to change the existing realities. The myth is thus both a form of contemplation and a call for action. A classic definition of mythological structures comes from ethnologist Bronislaw Malinowski, who described myth not as a symbolic allegory but rather as a "direct expression of its subject matter; it is not an explanation in satisfaction of a scientific interest, but a narrative resurrection of a primeval reality, told in satisfaction of deep religious wants, moral cravings, social submissions, assertions, even practical requirements."[6]

From students of mythologies we have learned to be cautious about judging political myths in terms of good and evil. Which is not to say that we should refrain from assessing their meaning and impact; obviously conspiratorial fantasies are inimical to liberalism, and so are narratives of perpetual victimization. Simply exposing their inconsistency is not enough, however. One needs to discover what these myths try to explain, what passions and anguish they appeal to, and why they enjoy credibility.

Like all political myths, nationalism is ambiguous. It depends who is delivering the nationalist message, or what voice uses it, so to speak. For liberal intellectuals, to be sure, nationalism has little redeeming virtue. It is a discourse of parochialism, it is limitative, self-absorbed, incapable of promising universality. But for the nationalist militant of the Third World revolutionary movement, it is a religion, or better said, it is a *ratio moriendi*, a reason to die. Think of the Peruvian Sendero Luminoso (Shining Path) guerrillas with their ideological blend of Maoism, Inca nationalist mythology, and deep hatred of liberal institutions and values.

Acknowledging the importance of myth does nothing to diminish the significance of ideology. More than in any other period in human history, individuals in the twentieth century were tempted by the promises of revolutionary messianisms having their roots in the grandiose teleological fantasies imagined by prophets who mostly wrote their manifestoes during the previous century. From these builders of philosophical systems to our century's ideological sleepwalkers, constructors of empires erected on ideological quicksands, the continuity cannot be denied. It is a simplification, of course, to see a direct lineage from Karl Marx to Bolshevism and to Stalin's reign of terror.[7] On the other hand, it would be dishonest to exonerate the founder of historical materialism from responsibility for the transformation of his theoretical legacy into a doctrine of "universal bondage" (Leszek Kolakowski).[8]

In the same vein, Benito Mussolini's glorification of empire, nation, and state cannot be separated from the strong counter-Enlightenment traditions of the nineteenth century, including the romantic political school and the ultramontane repudiation of democratic principles. Indeed, il Duce did not leave any ambiguity about his revolutionary rejection of the liberal status quo when he declared in 1926: "We represent a new principle in the world; we represent the exact, categorical, definitive antithesis of the whole world of democracy, plutocracy, freemasonry, in short the whole world of the immortal principles of 1789."[9] Political myths have been artfully used by revolutionaries of both extremes, convinced that the ends could justify any means. The myth of revolutionary class warfare helped Lenin, Stalin, Mao, and Fidel Castro to establish their ideological experiments. No less spellbinding, the myth of the superior race, inherited by Hitler and Alfred Rosenberg, the main Nazi doctrinaire, from the Social Darwinians and the political romantics of the nineteenth century, served as justification for the extermination of whole human groups.

At the other end of the spectrum, the myth of resistance and liberation from totalitarian domination served the liberal democracies to preserve their morale and to refuse to give up to the neobarbarians. The functions of myth, however, in totalitarian versus nontotalitarian systems are crucially different: in ideological dictatorships, myth penetrates every part of the social fabric, motivates and orients mass enthusiasms, generates fanatic regimentations and no less fanatic persecution of dissenters. In democracies, its power is curtailed by the existence of communities of reflexive communication, the rational organization of political structures, and the universality of legal arrangements.

In other words, the most glaring impact of political myth can be detected in the experiences of the two totalitarian systems of the twentieth century, communism and fascism, with their single-minded belief that human history had an end, and that this end could be identified by the insightful genius of the charismatic leader. But even these mythologies were exaggerations, distortions of ideas and obsessions functioning in the democratic universe.[10] Both fascism and communism stemmed from the turbulent reservoir of passions and uncertainties generated by the breakdown of the old European order during the French Revolution and its aftermath. Indeed, it was the French revolutionary drama that foreshadowed much of the following excesses perpetrated in the name of popular will, national self-determination, or universal freedom. Even Immanuel Kant, horrified as he was by the cruelties of the revolutionaries, could condone them in the name of the superior value they were conducive to, namely, the autonomous man: "One must be free in order to learn how to use one's powers freely and usefully. To be sure, the first attempts will be brutal, and will bring about a more painful and more dangerous state than when one was under the orders, but also under the protection of a third party. However, one never ripens into reason except through one's own experiences, and one must be free in order to be able to undergo them."[11] These ideas were carried to troublesome extremes by political mythographers convinced, together with the Jacobins, that liberty (as they defined it) should be denied to its enemies (St. Just's famous dictum: "pas de libertés pour les ennemis de la liberté!"— no liberties for the enemies of liberty!).

Everything Old Is New Again

Myth and magic are phenomena that belong to both archaic and modern societies. The Third Reich, Stalin's Russia, Fidel's Cuba cannot be understood in the absence of the myth of the leader, of the Party, of the Fatherland, of the revolution. At the same time, developed industrial democracies have their own mythologies, constellations of compelling ideas and emotions that organize collective passions: "law and order," "family values," "manifest destiny," "equal opportunity," "technological progress," or "new world order." Such constructions of the mind inspire intensive positive or negative attitudes simultaneously. Political mythologies are not atemporal archetypes, existing outside the environment of human history. They react to and evaluate existing forms of human organization, legitimize or expose political structures, and often propose either past or future-oriented alternatives.

Myths also provide an emotive standard by which to judge a changing reality. Should the latter be too obviously at variance with the myth, then believers in the myth have a powerful instrument at their disposal "to enforce 'ideal' standards in conformity with the myth."[12] For instance, the myth of an "originally humanist Marxism," supposedly betrayed by Lenin and Stalin, helped the critical Marxists of East-Central Europe—the "revisionists"—formulate their rejection of bureaucratic socialism, and contributed to the dispelling of the official hierophany.[13] Similarly, the Trotskyites and other oppositionists attacked Stalin in the name of the ideal patterns of an "original Bolshevism" that the general secretary had allegedly abandoned in his quest for absolute power. The odyssey of perestroika and the meaning of Mikhail Gorbachev's tantalizing endeavor to revise the foundations of Bolshevism cannot be grasped unless we see them as part of a search for the resurrection of the heroic cultural ethos of the revolutionary beginnings.

In late nineteenth-century France, the deep divisions between democratic republicans and conservative traditionalists exploded in the mythology of the Dreyfus Affair. The rhetoric of both sides, as Michael Marrus has shown, was impregnated with self-serving and mutually exclusive stories: 'they spoke to the entire nation, or at least claimed to do so; and they travelled on newly created channels using the most up-to-date technology in print and illustration. . . . Myths provided instant, ready-made answers to the questions raised by the Affair; they linked sometimes banal developments in a complex sequence to deeply held ideals; and they stimulated the powerful passions associated with Alfred Dreyfus and his cause."[14]

Indeed, when societies tend to lose their center and polarize themselves along belligerent lines, myths not only try to explain reality but also act upon it and even supplant it. As Frye wrote, the mythological universe is made up of human hopes and desires and anxieties.[15] Individuals become entrapped in the mythological discourse, accept its axiomatic premises, and refuse to question its allegations. Demagogues, tribunes, and prophets emerge who can articulate collective hopes and anxieties in aggressive ways. These are mythologists who know how to stimulate fears and ecstasies, illusions and redemptive expectations. An illustration of this is the resurgence in contemporary United States of anti-"Big Government" sentiments and their exploitation by different political actors.

The ideologies of communism and fascism held in common a belief in the plasticity of human nature and in the possibility of transforming it in accordance with a utopian blueprint. Both Marxism and fascism have inspired unflinching loyalties, a fascination with the figure of the perfect society, and romantic immersion in collective movements promising the advent of the millennium. Fascism was historically defeated during World War II but, as we have seen in recent years, its echoes continue to resurface each time conditions deteriorate and individuals find themselves under unbearable psychological constraints.[16]

Beyond its historical context, there is a psychological and social matrix to which fascism responds: the rejection of modern institutions and practices, the repudiation of reason, the cataclysmic celebration of soul against intellect, and so on.[17] The attraction of significant sectors of the Western intellectual left in the middle 1990s toward the writings of Carl Schmitt, who was the legal theorist of the Third Reich, at least until 1936, is not simply a cultural fashion. Its roots are to be found in the common dissatisfaction with liberalism and the yearning for a solution that would avoid the "mediocrity" of parliamentary democracy.[18]

Meanwhile, in the former communist societies the shock of modernity, the difficult adjustment of individuals to the collapse of traditional communities and solidarities, and the inner tensions of the still fragile democracies have engendered popular and some intellectual interest in "recovered" history and myth instead of liberal ideas and institutions. Among the most forceful myths have been the myth of the nation, of the heroic past, and of the victimized community, and the simultaneous glorification and stigmatization of the West. Not unlike the Western anti-liberal thinkers,[19] East European political mythmakers, both between the world wars and after the collapse of communism, looked backward and were inspired by the visions of an homogenous community presumably ruined by the advent of modernity.[20]

Political mythologies are not ideologies, but they share with ideology the appearance of a coherent narrative. As they are often described, myths are stories, but they have an enchanting power, and they tend to favor the emotional elements rather than the rational ones. Especially in times of dramatic transformations people experience frustration and uncertainty about the future and the breakdown of well-established patterns of conduct and expectations. In such times there is the temptation among disparaged, dispossessed, and alienated individuals to espouse a mythological construct, or an Armageddon-like salvationist paradigm, which historian Norman Cohn has described as the central phantasy of revolutionary eschatology: "The world is dominated by an evil, tyrannous power of boundless destructiveness—a power moreover which is imagined not as simply human but as demonic. The tyranny of that power will become more and more outrageous, the sufferings of its victims more and more intolerable—until suddenly the hour will strike when the Saints of God are able to rise and overthrow it."[21]

Political ideologies claim to offer systematic responses to human questions about the best organization of societies. This pretense is indeed the crux of what we may call ideological hubris: the firm belief that there is one and only one answer to the social questions, and that the ideologue is the one who holds it.[22] By projecting a certain model as superior to any other and predicting that society will eventually move in that direction, ideologies are often political teleologies. Their arrogance is matched only by their coercive impetus and exclusive rejection of any competitor. Ideologies are all-embracing and all-explanatory: they refuse dialogue, questioning, doubt. In this respect, liberalism is an ideology only in name: with its incrementalism and skepticism regarding any ultimate solutions to human problems, it lacks the soteriological, apocalyptic power of radical visions of change.

In the 1960s, Daniel Bell and others announced the extinction of the older ideological impetus.[23] Industrialism and consumerism, no less than general disappointment with the disasters provoked by radical universalisms or radical particularisms, have made traditional ideologies (i.e., secular religions) obsolete, they said. What has happened in reality does not entirely confirm this assessment: radical ideologies have continued to inspire collective movements of protest, though in a less coherent and methodical way than in the past. Think of 1968 social movements in Europe and the revolutionary wave of the 1970s in Latin America. With the breakdown of Leninism, however, a crucial threshold was crossed. The revolutions of 1989–1991 dealt a mortal blow to the ideological pretense according to which human life can be structured in accordance to scientific designs proposed by a general staff of revolutionary doctrinaires. Some acclaimed these revolutions precisely because they were nonteleological and nonideological. They were anti-utopian precisely because they refused to pursue any predetermined, foreordained blueprint. With the exception of some nebulous concepts like "civil society," "return to Europe," and "popular sovereignty," these revolutions occurred in the absence of ideology.

In spite of its hazy connotations, or precisely because of them, the idea of civil society energized large human groups and allowed them to pass the system-imposed threshold of fear. What succumbed during that unique moment of human emancipation was the most vainglorious utopia in history. As Norberto Bobbio writes, the revolutions of 1989 have completely "upturned" the communist utopia:

> It is a utopia which, for at least a century, has fascinated philosophers, writers and poets . . . ; which has shaken whole masses of the dispossessed and impelled them to violent action; which has led men with a high moral sense to sacrifice their own lives, to face prison, exile and extermination camps; and whose unquelled force, both material and spiritual, has at times seemed irresistible, from the Red Army to Mao's Long March, from the conquest of power by a group of resolute men in Cuba to the desperate struggle of the Vietnamese people against the mightiest power in the world. In one of his early writings—why should we not recall it?—Marx defined communism as "the solution to the enigma of history."[24]

Indeed, what came to an end in 1989 was not history but rather the oracular pretense that history has one sense and that a certain group has the privilege to identify it and impose its conclusions on the whole of humanity.

At the very core of Marxism one finds a millennialist mythology, a social dream about a perfect world where the ancient conflict between man and society, between essence and existence, would have been transcended. More than anything else, Marxism represented a spectacular invitation to human beings to engage in a frantic search for the City of God. This human adventure has failed, but the deep needs to which Marxism tried to give an answer have not come to an end. Now that the Leninist order has been overthrown, the moral landscape of post-communism is marred with moral confusion, venomous hatreds, unsatisfied desires, and endless bickerings. This is the bewildering, often terrifying territory on which political mythologies make a return.

People of the former communist world, from Tbilisi to Prague, and from Vladivostok to Tirana, have been exposed to the same Leninist experiment.

One may of course smile at the naïveté of Sidney and Beatrice Webb, who thought that Sovietism really represented a new civilization. But one cannot deny that it embodied an ensemble of habits, norms, attitudes, and emotions deeply inculcated in individual psyches. In addition, the powerful cultural legacies of Leninism rested on a pre-Leninist past that for many of these countries was not one of liberal values. East Germany, for example, had not experienced any democracy since the destruction of the Weimar Republic by the Nazis in 1933.[25] One can thus extend Umberto Eco's analysis of fascism to communism's inheritance: "even though political regimes can be overthrown, and ideologies can be criticized and disowned, behind a regime and its ideology there is always a way of thinking and feeling, a group of cultural habits, of obscure instincts and unfathomable drives."[26] Even if communism as an ideologically driven autocracy is dead, what remains is a nostalgia for the equality, solidarity, even fraternity that the Bolshevik model simulated.[27] This is the ground on which successor mythologies can emerge.

Post-communist fascism is of course one of these. When people are scared of the avalanche of risks, they look for solace in their past, which is often idealized. People listen to the mythographers who tell them that their present agonies are abnormal, that they are just the result of the "plots" fomented by aliens. They try to find a refuge in tradition and in the exaltation of primordial roots. Indeed, the post-communist world is the optimal territory for the rise of new varieties of fascism that would fuse leftovers of the Bolshevik model and psychological features of fascist salvationism.

The buds of this fusion can be detected in most, if not all, post-communist societies. The new mythologies inherit from Leninism its Manichean simplicity, while eliminating the systematic form. They are deliberately vague, protean, easily revisable. The ludicrous statements of Russian demagogue Vladimir Zhirinovsky's—chairman of an antiphrastically called Liberal Democratic party—about deporting whole groups, reconquering the Baltic states, and restoring the empire through military force should not be dismissed as simple buffoonery (although there is a clownish element in his performances); such statements stir responsive chords among many demoralized and outraged former Soviet citizens who still do not see how was it possible for their great Fatherland to have fallen apart. Similar rhetoric ensured the mass appeal of Gennady Zyuganov and his Communist Party of the Russian Federation.[28]

The end of communism has left individuals with a sense of loss: even if they hated their cage, it offered at least the advantage of stability and predictability. Like former prisoners, they now have freedoms but do not know exactly what to do with them. Under these circumstances, they are ready to espouse the rhetoric of the tribe with its emphasis on group identity and community values. The neuroses of the transition period, the collective fear of a general collapse, the closing of the historical horizon and the anger at the new economic barons, the *nouveaux riches*, no less brazen and amoral than Balzac's characters in *La comédie humaine*, nourish sentiments of revolt, distress, and intolerance. There is a need to find scapegoats, to identify those culpable for the ongoing sorrows. The political myth of lost and reconquered ethnic unity serves precisely this purpose: to explain defeats and alienation and reassure the individual that he or she has a place within the *volkisch* community.

Under these conditions, the easiest way to find the scapegoat is to look for those who do not belong (ethnically or religiously), the inner enemy, the potential traitors, the intruders, the "cosmopolitans." Traditionally, this role was assigned by the xenophobic imagination to the Jews: essentialized as internationalists, linked to modern institutions, to the rise of financial capital, to money and banks, and to communism and radicalism. They appear as the embodiment of what the nationalist mind fears the most. In the new mythologies, the Jews and the liberal intellectuals are unified in the figure of nihilist foes of the country's imperial status. The October Revolution is presented as a German-Jewish plot against Russia. For a Romanian, Hungarian, or Slovak chauvinist, the Jew (or the Gypsy) is by definition inferior. Even their economic success is an indication of some devious machinations. Hence the insistence on origins and the obsession with purity. Hence the need for Russian chauvinists to demonstrate that Lenin was of Jewish origin, and that his whole Politburo was nothing but a disguised Sanhedrin. Thus, the whole twentieth century was nothing but a battle between the occult force of the Jewish (liberal) experts in dissolution and the defenders of national, organic values. Any rational questionings of the mythological premises of such views are immediately denounced. The exclusionary mythologies operate on the semantic sterilization of the discourse and the anesthetization of critical faculties. They are obsessed with homogeneity, unity, and purity.

The new exclusionary mythologies, in addition, attack any expression of doubt about the predestined mission of the nation. The normal and understandable need for identity and belonging is turned into an absolute. Critical intellectuals who refuse to join the national chorus of self-congratulation are accused of treason. In Croatia, for example, writer Slavenka Drakulić and sociologist Vesna Pusić have been bitterly attacked for having criticized the new tribal nationalism.[29] When the country is presumably surrounded by vicious enemies, when internal fiends constantly conspire against the nation's very survival, any expression of disagreement is by definition treacherous. These themes appear obsessionally in the discourse of the "black-red" coalition in Russia: the war in Afghanistan was lost, nationalist writer Aleksander Prokhanov thunders, because of domestic traitors.[30] As in Weimar Germany, post-Leninist Russia is replete with pamphlets denouncing the "stab in the back" that led to the Soviet empire's end.

The new mythologies are characteristically syncretic: they combine a nostalgia for the social osmosis of the communist state (the myth of equality) with the celebration of authoritarian, even fascist traditions. Think of the Russian red-brown coalition's glorification of both Stalin and the late Czar Nicholas II. What the two had in common, the mythological story maintains, was the same commitment to Russian values and hostility to liberal cosmopolitans bound to destroy Russia.[31] Especially if they try to evoke cultural predecessors, these new mythologies, draw from the most unexpected sources: racist ideologues of the nineteenth century, romantic poets, Western Christian fundamentalists, and the whole subterranean tradition of European conspiracy theories (anti-Semitic, anti-Masonic, anti-Jesuit).

The new exclusionary mythologies execrate difference and alterity. They impose a vertical, strictly masculine, indeed phallocratic vision of the good society. Parliamentary governments are criticized for their impotence, softness, and failure to deal drastically with the enemies of the nation. The persecution of sexual minorities is accompanied by a condescending, patriarchal treatment of women. The Russian Nazis or the members of the Pamiat society are proud of their black uniforms. They enjoy hatred as a most exhilarating experience. Their sentences are short. They don't need arguments. Complexity, as much as diversity, is their enemy. The simpler their statements, the better.[32]

All communities have a need to indulge in fantasies of origin, but when these references become monomaniacal nationalism becomes pathological. Colonized nations do need national pride as an incentive in their struggle for liberation. But once the old colonial bonds have been broken, civic virtues must be considered as part of the new national ethos. Otherwise, these countries continue to experience suicidal adventures and cyclical waves of patriotic hysteria. This is the type of tribal self-centeredness Eugène Ionesco analyzed in the aftermath of World War II when he wrote that Romania's tragedy had been nationalism: "Romania was and still is sick with nationalism. Nationalism has poisoned the whole culture and the Romanian soul. . . . Due to nationalism. . . . Romanian culture has been unable to attain the order of universal values and has remained a sick local culture. The problem of 'ethnic specificity' . . . has been, for Romania, a calamity as great as a permanent earthquake, or the alliance with Germany: it paralyzed every élan, it made impossible any opening, any exit, any detachment, any liberty, any kind of spiritual life."[33] It is possible to hear in this deeply disturbing passage—which one could safely extrapolate to most East European societies—another function of the vindictive myth: it not only mobilizes but paralyzes and traps. In Ionesco's own words:

> On my street, in a cold and bleak November [probably the bloody November of 1940 when the Iron Guard (fascist) thugs, then in government, murdered a number of prominent personalities including the country's foremost historian Nicolae Iorga], groups of legionaries, incarnating the whole bestiality and unlimited stupidity of mankind and the cosmos, were marching and singing I don't know what "song" (a

kind of roar) of iron, with words of ire and iron, spitting bile and iron, like branded beasts chained to one another. When you looked at their faces, which resembled each other so much that they seemed to be the same face in multiple copies, . . . you came under the grave impression that Romania was lost to humanity. As they advanced, an infernal night descended on the city's streets. . . . I did all I could to leave the country: there, anything might have happened. I could have died; I could have been infected; I could have become myself a dog; I could have been inhabited by the demon of the Legionaries. When I got out of the country I had the feeling that I had escaped a fire, an earthquake, a tidal wave or a whirlwind.[34]

Reading these lines may help us understand the intersection between myth and madness in contemporary Balkan politics, especially in the Yugoslav war. Nationalist chiliasms are indeed forms of "compensatory megalomania."[35]

No term of abuse is thus sufficient for the promoters of the new mythologies when it comes to denouncing the evils of liberal society. Pluralism is by definition a plot allowing profiteers to make it under the new regime. Parliamentarism is inept, effete, divisive. Organic community has been destroyed by the invasion of bourgeois modernity. The theme is not new. French nationalist writer Charles Péguy wrote at the beginning of the twentieth century: "We will never tire of repeating it. All evil comes from the bourgeoisie. All aberration, all crime. It is the capitalist bourgeoisie which has infected the people. And it has infected it with a bourgeois and capitalist spirit."[36] Clearly, for the intruder to be the poisonous factor the mythological "people" must be imagined as pure, untouched by the evils of industrial, mercantile civilization.

Modernity is noisy, corrupt, and corrupting. Bourgeois values, with their soulless, artificial, mechanic connotations, destroy the Ur-community, the brotherhood of origins. Nostalgia for the precapitalist agrarian communities of Russia motivates Solzhenitsyn, as much as yearning for the village values inspire nationalists from Serbia, Romania, or Hungary. It is like a return to Rousseau's dream of the perfectly unified community, in which the individual finds perfect shelter, being finally protected against the pitfalls of solitude. Good institutions, this view holds, are the ones that allow for the ego to lose identity in the transcendent collectivity. Once, such a community had been the "Party" with its "oceanic" mystique of fraternal solidarity. The Nation, in turn, is the substitute for the total community. In the nation one finds solace and security, a refuge from the vicissitudes of wild competition and ruinous selfishness.

Dealing with the post-communist perplexities, we have to discover the role of mentalities, their persistence in spite of the institutional breakup. Whatever its cruelties, and they were countless, whatever its barbarism, which was indeed abysmal, Leninism attacked the very foundations of the ancient communitarian cohesion. It did not create a sense of individual autonomy, but it did bring industry and urban life into most of these societies. The revolt against Leninism included a revolt against the distorted modernity it had ferociously imposed on these nations. Most citizens resented the Leninist commissar's iron fist, and his imposition of urban life, destruction of village life, aggression against pastoral, traditional values. Leninism, which was a Russian variation on the Western socialist dream of modernization, has profoundly and destructively shaken these societies. Hungarian philosopher G. M. Tamás provocatively argues: "The dirty work of modernization, which was done in England by *laissez-faire* liberalism and in Germany by the Prussian state and military industry, was performed in Eastern Europe and large parts of Asia by various versions of state socialism. What Stalin wrought—with labor camps, forced collectivization, mass deportations, and the ruthless exploitation and destruction of natural resources—is a gigantic, if terrible achievement."[37]

In most of these countries, during the interwar period, strong millennial movements of the extreme right had engaged in visceral attacks on pluralist democracy. The Romanian Iron Guard, with its spiritualist pageants and cult of heroic death, was only the most visible among them.[38] And the aftermath of Leninism's collapse has witnessed the resurgence of communitarian, neoromantic mythologies of belonging and origins.

The Next Utopia?

The question therefore is what polity will the East European nations choose? Will they choose the problematic, dubiously created modern society as it emerged as part of "socialist industrialization," or will they return to the cult of autarchic community and profoundly anti-Western sentiments? Will the romantic-populist forces that have been resurrected in post-communist societies get the upper hand, or will they be defeated by the partisans of Westernization and liberal modernity? The socialist nebulous dream of reconciling modernity and community failed. Part of the anti-communist rhetoric half a decade after the collapse of communism concealed in effect a secret fear: that the post-communist polis would continue communism's onslaught on rural, communitarian, and traditional values. Hence, the immediate successor societies have experienced immoderate calls for punishment and the rise of neopopulist, often anti-Western movements of anger. G. M. Tamás exaggerates only slightly when he writes, from a liberal perspective: "Our traditions are strongly anti-individualistic; fear of political spontaneity is present all along our political spectrum. The dissolution of the late-communist state gave birth to a unique—and it now appears all too brief—moment of liberty, innovation, and diversity. Now once again we have indoctrination, mindless militancy, anti-Western and anti-capitalist xenophobia, and revolutionary disregard for the law—all brought to us by movements that shouted themselves hoarse calling for human rights just a few years ago."[39] Given the presence of these new or not so new mythologies and their tremendous impact, one wonders whether the past can be overcome or whether it is an albatross around these societies' necks that will ruin any effort to create genuinely open societies.[40]

In the information age, with the burgeoning of the Internet, it is hard if not impossible to erect walls to communication. The regimes that succeeded the communists combine various features, some of them liberal, other semi-authoritarian. Presidentialist tendencies, for example, have emerged in Albania, Belarus, Croatia, Poland, Romania, Russia, and Serbia.[41] But the revolutions of 1989–1991 released enormous civic energies, and one cannot see all these efforts to recreate public spheres as mere neo-Jacobin experiments in majoritarian tyranny. The liberal project, or the Enlightenment agenda associated with modernity, is indeed in danger in post-communist societies (and not only there).[42] But vibrant forces strongly committed to pluralism and a free market also exist. Whatever one may think of the Russian elites in the mid-1990s, they tend to be consensual in their espousal of a Western-style economic model. And this is true for the East European elites as well.

This is a time when these societies have to make decisive choices: either to embrace the values of individual autonomy, accepting an order based on tensions, contradictions, and risk, or to reject modernity in the name of collective dreams of salvation. The first choice is anti-utopian; the latter neoutopian.

To avoid any misunderstandings, political mythologies and utopian fantasies are not necessarily exclusive and harmful. They also provide the "social glue" any collectivity needs to ensure its legitimacy and self-pride. When conventional identifications fall apart and old belief systems become vacuous, there is a normal tendency for symbolic compensation. If we look into the case of Russia in the mid-1990s, the need for new mythologies is more than obvious. What was the spiritual effect of perestroika? It hit the final nail in the coffin of the mythocratic system which was Leninism. All the main mythologies were dramatically shattered and eventually given the lie: the myth of the Communist party as the incarnation of historical wisdom; the myth of the working class as the predestined group intimately linked to the project of ultimate social justice, freedom, and equality; the myth of World War II as a collective struggle of all nations of the Soviet Union for survival against Nazi attack; the myth of the Soviet industrial and military achievements; the myth of "democratic centralism" as a superior form of political organization, and so on. Once de-Stalinization reached its climax in the late 1980s, it became clear that socialist internationalism has been just a smoke screen. The party was nothing but the springboard for cynical careerists, and its history had been marred by countless crimes and atrocities. The October Revolution was not a mass uprising against an autocratic regime, but a Machiavellian coup d'état organized by the dictatorial, militaristic sect of the Bolsheviks against a weak liberal government. And so on.

The mythological foundations of Sovietism foundered under the burden of the gigantic edifice of lies. But what attachments can the individual develop or maintain when faced with this historical "rubble," to use Solzhenitsyn's term? What has remained of the Soviet identity? A number of failed dreams, broken hopes, and an excruciating sense of shame. In Russia (and in other former Leninist countries as well) the disappearance of the old identifications was followed by a sense of nonbelonging.[43] As in post-World War I Germany, there were many who felt excluded, "singularized," anathematized. This emotional constellation explains the readiness to follow apostles of new millennialisms and dispensors of immediate gratifications. These societies got rid of the old authoritarian institutions, but they remained hostage to their memories, fears, even neuroses. It is true that the old political fear, the specter of the Gulag vanished. But the risk of an authoritarian relapse and the advent of a new dictatorship did not. The Russians have experienced new feelings of loss and insecurity: what traditions can they rely on to secure property rights and the irreversibility of the democratic changes? In the words of Richard Pipes, "Russia has no democratic past to go back to. After Hitler, Germany could go back to Weimar. What do the Russians have to go back to—their great writers?"[44]

In all the societies exiting from communist dictatorship, the need for stability and normality endures. But the meaning of these terms differs from one group to another. As unemployment rises and living standards plummet, many feel an attraction for easy solutions and convenient explanations for their dismal condition. Although it is true that people have overcome the fear of the secret police, they may not be protected from the new mafias, corruption, and the old political barons turned new economic robber barons.[45] Liberalism, as it takes shape in East-Central Europe and the former Soviet Union, remains indebted to a cult of pragmatic opportunities, technocratic effectiveness, and rationality that many individuals find unsatisfactory.

What future remains for religion in these societies? What bonds will keep the community together in the new liberal order? The critique of the Western values formulated by Solzhenitsyn in the 1980s has found echoes among many intellectuals from the region: it is not simply capitalism that is challenged or denied but also the absence of an exhilarating vision that would preserve the connection with the sacred. The major weakness of liberalism is, according to this view, its coldness. This search for the transcendent—"not by bread alone"—is a call that comes from the beginnings of civilization and voices a need for deep spiritual values. Some of these values surface in the elusive discourse of myth.

The return of political myth is thus an expression of the crisis of modernity. It is more visible in societies where the project of Enlightenment was derailed or simply rejected. Post-Leninist regimes, with their extremely personalized politics, social disruptions, deep anxieties, and decline of authority are fertile ground for the rise of these mythologies. In the East as well as in the West, technology and pragmatic procedures alone cannot answer deep human psychological needs. Myth is the glue of society. Its denial cannot last forever. Political parties are increasingly distrusted and uninspiring, and there exists a pressing need for new forms of activism. This explains perhaps the growing popularity of terms like "civil society," "grassroots democracy," and "new social movements": they express the wish to recover civic dignity, and participation, and the possibility of a political project that reconciles truth with effectiveness.[46] Whether these terms represent new political myths or utopian projects no one knows.

Two _____

The Leninist Debris, or Waiting for Perón

> The clearest fact is that we are living in a time of
> transition, but whether we are going toward liberty
> or marching toward despotism, God alone knows
> precisely.
>
> (*Alexis de Tocqueville, 1831*)

LEFT, RIGHT, CENTER: these notions have strange and elusive meanings under post-communism. Using interpretive Western paradigms creates false analogies and explains little, if anything. The abuses committed in the name of the Marxist faith in the former Soviet Union and East-Central Europe engendered apprehensions toward any explicitly socialist program. This explains why post-communist leftist leaders have gone out of their way to emphasize their commitment to the free market, private property, and political pluralism. Poland's President Aleksander Kwasniewski (a former minister of youth under the communist regime in the 1980s) or Hungary's prime minister Gyula Horn (a former Communist minister of foreign affairs) have insisted on their commitment to democratic consolidation, and disassociated themselves from any form of neo-Leninist radicalism.[1] At the same time, nostalgia for the benefits of the socialist welfare state is rampant. It has become increasingly obvious that large social strata resented communist ideology without detesting the state socialist guarantees of security and stability. Yes, there was scarcity, but there was no unemployment, and there was also a feeling that the future was predictable within an unchangeable universe. The return of the post-communists is thus not a restoration of the old order but rather an expression of malaise and frustration with the first stage of the revolutionary changes when politics was dominated by the former dissidents. Adam Michnik gave a poignant explanation of this regional trend, relating it to the widespread disaffection with Lech Walesa's politics of emotion and perpetual confrontation:

> Lech Walesa paid for his mistakes—this is obvious. But he also paid for the great changing of the world that he initiated. Like Winston Churchill, he won the most difficult of wars and lost the election. Did those who voted for Aleksander Kwasniewski vote for the return of the Polish People's Republic? For Soviet domination, single-party dictatorship, a state-controlled economy? I believe this would be

an absurd thesis. They voted for normalcy, stabilization, and peace. Kwasniewski managed to present himself as a contradiction to the authoritarian, plebeian and coarse Walesa, a modern, self-composed, and conciliatory politician, a politician of the future, and of "a shared Poland."[2]

This chapter focuses on the political psychology of the transition from state socialism, the shifting meanings of the conventional political distinctions between "Left" and "Right," and the persistence of paternalistic and authoritarian mentalities and habits inherited from the Leninist past. One-party systems, mass parades, ideological rituals, and monumental architecture celebrating the "glowing tomorrows" were once the rule from Moscow to East Berlin. Post-communism, instead, presents the individual with unique opportunities of affirmation, and the risks of failure and self-destruction. Freedom means assertion of diversity and individuality, and many people have not easily adjusted themselves to this ambivalent situation.[3] In the words of Václav Havel:

> The fall of communism destroyed this shroud of sameness, and the world was caught napping by an outburst of the many unanticipated differences concealed beneath it, each of which—after such a long time in the shadows—felt a natural need to draw attention to itself, to emphasize its uniqueness, and its difference from others. This is the reason for the eruption of so many different kinds of old-fashioned patriotism, revivalist messianism, conservatism, and expressions of hatred toward all those who appeared to be betraying their roots or identifying with different ones.[4]

On the one hand, there is exhilaration and excitement over the regained freedoms. On the other, individuals find themselves demoralized, lost in the new political and economic chaos. There is nobody to take care of them, to plan their future, and protect them against what they perceive as threatening, uncontrollable forces. This is the cause for an idealization not of the communist forms of coercion but of the old system's egalitarian promises. The political parties that succeeded communism have had to come to grips with this schizoid social psychology, and have often acted in contradiction with their own ideological claims: in Hungary, for instance, the government run by the former communists (in concert with the Alliance of Free Democrats, a liberal party dominated by former dissidents) initiated, in March 1995, a reform of the welfare system more drastic than anything advocated by the liberal parties.

Seven years after the upheaval, the former Sovietized world is confused, disconcerted, rudderless, nervous, and exasperated. The old paradigms are exhausted, the new ones are still inchoate. On the one hand, there is longing for calm and normalcy. On the other, there is nervousness and exasperation with the all-pervasive corruption, cliquishness, and political fragmentation. It is as if there is a yearning for a new figure of the future, an expectation of a true revolution that would put an end to all the current ordeals and anxieties.

A Need for New Concepts and Categories

The old mythologies of the left and the right require a drastic overhaul in the light of the major changes in these countries. What has remained of the Marxist pledge to install a classless society? What is one to make of the astounding transmogrifications of the former communist potentates (presumably leftists) into robber barons, successful bankers, and free-market zealots? Is populism indeed left or right? Or liberalism? Do democratic socialist ideals still have a future in the former Leninist societies? Or rather are all ideologies extinct and have these countries entered, together with the West, a post-utopian age? Will the social hybrid made up of mafia and former apparatchiks that is now running the show in so many of the former communist countries eventually turn into a new, law-abiding bourgeoisie?[5] Can one speak of liberal politics in countries where the middle class is still in the bud, unemployment is skyrocketing, social norms are broken, and political parties are more often than not vehicles for personal promotion and influence in the name of privatization? Nothing is foreordained in this unfolding drama called transition from state socialism. Today's opportunities may be tomorrow's pitfalls. As British philosopher Karl Popper often said, "the future is entirely open."[6]

Even after the demise of Marxism, the last grandiose historical narrative, individuals need to believe in something. Nature abhors a void, and so do the post-communist societies. Political creeds, liberal, nonliberal, or anti-liberal, continue to orient them, to generate passions, emotions, and polemics. Public opinion is extremely volatile, and the same majorities that one day favor fierce anti-communist politicians can bring the born-again socialists back to power the next day. Later, as people become disenchanted with the pace of reforms, they may support other varieties of politics, including the populist demagogy of anti-establishment prophets.[7]

The appearance of an intellectual proletariat, obsessed with conspiracies and specialized in producing impatient slogans, is a salient feature of the post-Leninist political cultures. They appeal to the losers of the transition, for whom "aliens" are guilty of causing all their troubles. An illustration of this logic is embodied by Miroslav Sladek, a former communist censor converted to far-right politics and the leader of the Czech Republican party. Indulging in outrageous racism, he appealed to his supporters to rally against Gypsies, whom he described as "inferior," "animals," and simply "subhuman." Before the country's breakup in December 1992, Sladek cultivated the dream of "Greater Czechoslovakia" and accused the West for its failure: "We won't allow another Munich! Havel, Klaus, and Meciar have sold us to the Germans. The West is afraid of united Czechoslovakia. Today we have the best chance ever of becoming the world's fourth superpower after the United States, Russia, and China."[8]

An anti-elitist, anti-communist, and ethnocentric politician, is Sladek just an exponent of the traditional right? Or does he speak for the rise of a new radicalism, mixing traditional xenophobic themes with lingering Leninist reflexes? In the same vein, Corneliu Vadim Tudor, the chairman of the Great Romania party, does not tire of inveighing against corruption and the role of "foreigners" (Jews, Hungarians, and Gypsies) in the country's presumed bankruptcy. At the same time, each issue of *România Mare* (the party's weekly) extols ad nauseam the memory of the late dictator Ceauşescu and publishes panegyrics about the pro-Nazi marshal Ion Antonescu, who was executed as a war criminal in 1946. Former Romanian president Iliescu avoided a true break with the extremists, inviting several nationalist parties (including Tudor's), to become members of the government coalition.[9] Representatives of the Romanian National Unity party, a vehement anti-Hungarian group linked to the ultra-chauvinistic Vatra Românească (Romanian Cradle) movement created in March 1990, gained control over the ministries of Education and Justice. Theirs is a new version of radicalism combining themes of left and right in a baroque, often unpredictable alchemy. Such parties, which exist in most of the post-communist societies, share a number of political attributes: hostility to pluralism and diversity; cultivation of an idealized and self-congratulatory historical tradition; xenophobia and bigotry against minorities; a neoromantic, often irrational glorification of premodern, nonurban values; and strong reservations about, and often direct enmity toward, private property and the market.

The fact that exponents of this populist-authoritarian trend tend to direct their criticism toward ethnic minorities should not be reduced to traditional scapegoating. What is at stake is the vision of their countries' future: Western (capitalist and democratic) or anti-Western (authoritarian and ethnocentric). This point is clearly made by Katherine Verdery: "Whereas intolerance of Gypsies suggests problems related specifically to the market, anti-Semitism suggests a broader hostility to things of "the West," including democracy and private property, as well as markets; and it embraces themes of concern to a broad array of groups, distressed either at past injustices under socialism or at present dislocations. To say that one dislikes Jews is easier and less revealing than to say one dislikes democracy or international lending institutions. One can make this statement employing Jews as a symbol even if there are few actual Jews around."[10]

On the one hand, these parties declare their commitment to European values and the need to join such structures as NATO and the European Union. On the other, they do their utmost to denounce any form of criticism of the resurgent authoritarianism and xenophobia. To a greater or lesser extent, this trend exists in most post-communist countries. In August 1995, when Hungarian-born American financier George Soros dared to express reservations

about Slovakia's readiness to join the European institutions, the Slovak government declared him persona non grata. This happened despite Soros's consistent record of support for the development of Slovakia's educational and
public policy infrastructure. Prime Minister Vladimir Meciar went so far as to
award a top journalism award to an anti-Semitic magazine well known for its
anti-Soros cartoons. No less symptomatic was an incident involving two hundred Slovak intellectuals who circulated a petition decrying the absence of
tolerance in Slovakia—the Ministry of Culture spurned them as "a bunch of
people who hate anything that is Slovak."[11]

The East European situation, regardless of the hegemonic self-congratulatory narratives, will remain for the foreseeable future part of the ideological
age: symbols, myths, rationalized miracles, liturgical (ethno-eligious) nationalisms, and teleological pretense have returned after the short-lived "post-
modern" interlude of the revolutions of 1989.[12] With these have also come
frantic displays of emotion, unreason, hostility, anger, and unavowed, unbearable shame. These are the politics of rancorous marginality, "cultural despair,"
and convulsive impotence that the nascent democratic (dis)order can barely
contain.[13] The fate of Yugoslavia tells much about the infinite capacity of elites
in these societies to reinvent fallacies and insanities of the past in the attempt
to maintain and expand their hold on power. The latter-day explosions of
hatred are not just a return to a kind of recurrent wild tribalism but rather the
exploitation of ancient fears and vengeful fantasies by cynical elites ready to
use any means to foster their supremacy.

Political adventurers like Bosnian Serb leader Radovan Karadžić, the poet-
psychiatrist who was charged with the crime of genocide in 1995 by the international court in the Hague, have shown immense ability to use myth as a
dangerous weapon.[14] In Karadžić's mind, Bosnian Serbs are not simply fighting a war for territorial control and expansion, but a genuine crusade against
Islam, "Europe's last anti-colonialist war." He argues that their struggle is justified by the Serbian sacrifices in the past and their refusal to be subjected once
again to persecution. This is indeed the ideology of preemptive genocide.[15]

The Yugoslav debacle is simply an example of a worst case scenario for
other countries in the region. Since "forewarned is forearmed," it is better to
look into such pitfalls and avoid them than be certain of the "ultimate liberal
triumph." Indeed, we deal here not with the strength but the fragility and
vulnerability of liberalism in the region; the backwardness, delays, and distortions of modernity, and the rise of majoritarian, neoplebiscitarian parties and
movements.[16]

Fantasies of redemption abound in all the post-communist countries, and
explain the electoral successes of aggressive demagogues like Russia's Gennady Zyuganov, Romania's Gheorghe Funar, or Hungary's Jozsef Torgyan.
Zyuganov's rise to prominence cannot be separated from the post-imperial
malaise experienced by so many Russians. As mayor of the Transylvanian city

of Cluj and chairman of the Romanian National Unity party until 1996, Funar consistently banked on chauvinistic, anti-Hungarian sentiments among Romanians. Torgyan is the leader of the Smallholders' party who has managed to outrun in popularity the government of former communist Gyula Horn by combining staunch nationalism and an open criticism of the post-World War I Trianon Treaty. Like his peers in Russia, Serbia, or Romania, he resorts to the symbolism of the "Great Fatherland," amputated by mischievous or insensitive foreigners.[17] Whereas other Hungarian parties treat the legacies of the twentieth century as an inescapable reality, Torgyan has raised his voice to criticize the West for its alleged treason. Irresponsible demagogues have an advantage over realist politicians because they do not need to worry about the implications of their hateful, often bellicose statements.[18]

In March 1996, the Independent Smallholders party organized a mass protest demonstration in Budapest against the "corrupt" and "non-Hungarian" (socialist and liberal) government coalition. On that occasion, Torgyan used inflammatory rhetoric to depict his country's alleged destruction by the "antinational forces": "The Liberal-Bolshevik danger that is threatening our country at present is greater than any other danger to date because in the past few years the country has suffered greater damages than the total damages in World War II, owing to the Bolshevik takeover of power and extension of this power to property. They have made more than 70 percent of the national assets disappear. You must see that they have done so to paralyze the acting power of the Hungarian nation." Torgyan concluded his hateful diatribe using the Nazi-style biological clichés about the need to preserve ethnic purity: "We, however, cannot be paralyzed. We are Hungarian. In the spring, the Hungarian manually clears away the vermin. Let us also clear away the vermin."[19] Similar statements can be heard from Romanian, Croat, Serbian, or Polish experts in national self-aggrandizement.

Critical intellectuals, who were so involved in subverting the communist pretense of cognitive infallibility, have clearly lost much of their political impact. In general, one notices the retrenchment of universalistic, supranational discourse and the prevailing role of the new rhetoric of identity and collectivity; again, this is not the "privilege of the East." German sociologist Wolf Lepenies captures these phenomena when he writes:

> The unexpected fall of the communist regimes has been fatal, not only for Western governments but for Western intellectuals as well. . . . The responsibility of both politicians and intellectuals has increased. The task before them is to reflect upon values capable of guiding the world, and to formulate convictions that are livable and instructive for the global market economy. In the face of this challenge the strategies of retreat followed by intellectuals today loom large. Instead of trying their utmost to fortify the achievements of the liberal constitutional state and support economic policies that regulate the strength of the market by socially peaceful means, intellec-

tuals are retreating from the modern age. . . . We are now experiencing the return of regional loyalties and the rebirth of ethnicity.[20]

The search for new eschatologies is simply more visible in the East, where all social tensions are exacerbated and where the individual senses the tragic breakdown of old identities with more acuity. Cultural legacies are invoked to justify contemporary political choices. In all these countries, political movements have emerged that proclaim their affinities with the interrupted interwar traditions. And these traditions were not predominantly liberal: the region's political culture includes intense anti-Westernism, feudal romanticism, anti-capitalism, and even anti-industrialism, all sentiments that preceded communism. In pre-World War II Romania, Croatia, or Hungary, homegrown fascism resented capitalism and money-related activities as alien, corruptive, and destructive of national identity. These movements were defeated or silenced, but much of the archaic, anti-modern nostalgia to which they appealed has remained. The phenomenon is worldwide: the return of neoromantic, anti-capitalist mythology is part of the universal uneasiness with the boring, cold, calculated, *Zweckmässig* rationality of what Max Weber described as the "iron cage"; prophets and demagogues (often the same persons) who implicitly or explicitly denounce the heritage of the Enlightenment and exalt all varieties of "metapolitics" do have audiences in the West as well as in the East. The former region, however, is better protected: institutions function impersonally, and procedures are deeply embedded in the civic cultures based on social trust.[21] In the post-communist world, both civil and political societies are only incipient.

The Leninist decline has accompanied a general breakdown of the established framework of political arrangements and accepted "rules of the game" in the West, as well. How otherwise can we interpret the Italians' almost nihilistic rebellion against the status quo? Foreseeing these new waves of rage, Gianni De Michelis, Italy's foreign minister until 1992, wrote in 1993 that the Perot phenomenon in the United States was linked to an overall revolt against conventional party politics, in Italy and elsewhere. Such a transition transcends the simple "sweeping away of the scoundrels" and bears upon a genuine political "great transformation": "we are witnessing the explosion of a long-obsolete model of liberal democracy that can no longer accommodate our dynamic, complex societies with their sophisticated electorates of vast diversity and highly differentiated interests."[22] It is thus tempting to believe that the major difficulties in the articulation of ideologically differentiated political platforms in Eastern Europe are connected not only to the absence or weakness of clear-cut interest groups and lobbies, but also to the atrophy of the Western sources of inspiration for such endeavors. After all, the onslaught on democratic values in East-Central Europe during the 1920s and 1930s coincided and was to a large extent inspired by similar attacks in the West, where large segments of the intelligentsia execrated liberal values and contributed to the weakening of democratic institutions.

Nowadays, as Jacques Rupnik suggests, things are essentially different: the major distinction from the interwar period "is linked to the status of democracy and the international situation. The experience of totalitarianism and especially its failure have paradoxically contributed to reinforce the attachment to democracy in Eastern Europe. But first and foremost it is the international environment that has changed: in the 1930s, the failure of democracy in the East was part of its breakdown on the continent as a whole. Today, the existence of a prosperous and democratic Western Europe could contribute to making the difference."[23] The famous law of political synchronization of the East and the West may this time play against the revival of ideological politics.[24]

On the other hand, it is precisely the exhaustion of traditional worldviews that is conducive to ennui and yearning for alternative visions. For example, although the post-communist region is a secularized world, the search for the sacred, the New Age mystique, and religious revivalism are contagious. No less attractive are ideas that reject modernity, capitalism, parliamentarism, and exalt force, contempt for minorities, and action for action's sake.[25] The cult of *novus dux*, the providential savior, is still limited to relatively small parties, but one should not forget how fast this fascination with the leader can grow under conditions of mass anguish.[26]

It is thus important to see why, in achieving the overthrow of Sovietism, many of the countries in Eastern Europe have not achieved democracy or political stability. Although arguments can be made that democratic stability cannot happen without massive inflows of Western economic aid, my point is that a lack of capital is not the determining factor in the region's future. More important is the debility of social capital, the loss of emotional ties of solidarity between the members of the political community, the weakness, decline, or inertia of civil society, and the overall erosion of any source of authority. Viktor Kulerski, a former prominent Solidarity activist, diagnosed suspicion, envy, and hatred as the main features of a post-communist neurotic syndrome. These resentful attitudes make individuals blind to the real choices and opportunities: "Not only do we have a skewed view of the world, the world itself is becoming skewed as a result of our manner of perceiving it. We live in a warped world of our own making, a world where we take our dreams and delusions for reality. We see threats where none exists and security where danger lies. We put our trust in swindlers and thieves as we reject and slander individuals of good sense and good will."[27]

Kulerski's jeremiad is perhaps overstated, but it would be hard to deny that he highlights real features of the post-communist collective anxieties and aggressiveness. There are several complex internal factors that make the fall of communism in Eastern Europe an uncomfortable victory indeed, and these factors are discussed below.[28]

No society is completely hostage to its history, however, and the democratic experiments in post-communist societies are still in their early stage. Indeed, with all the predicaments and setbacks, the spiritual situation in Europe (and in Eastern Europe in particular) remains fundamental to the attempt to try reinvent politics. As Julia Kristeva insists, "The collapse of communism in Eastern Europe, which calls into question, beyond socialism, the very basis of the democratic governments that stemmed from the French Revolution, demands that one rethink that basis so that the twenty-first century not be the reactional domain of fundamentalism, religious illusions, and ethnic wars."[29]

The remainder of this chapter highlights the uncertainties of this political drama, under eight rubrics that outline the possible fractures, delusions, and pathologies, and the still untested freedoms and new forms of human solidarity.[30]

1. Where We Came From: Coping with the Leninist Heritage

It was Karl Marx who, in the *Critique of the Gotha Program*, clearly indicated that any new society will carry its birthmarks for a long time. In the case of post-communist countries, these birthmarks include the habits, mores, visions, and mentalities associated with the sectarian and militaristic faith called Leninism. Amazing as it may seem, the "new man," the Homo Sovieticus, extolled by the communist propaganda had become real: not in the sense announced by Trotsky's utopian dreams, which envisioned the average communist man as more gifted than Aristotle and Goethe, but rather as an individual hostile to risk, to fair competition, and to pluralist values.[31]

Not only did people listen to the official communist parlance but many internalized it. Collectivistic, panic-ridden, mobilizational rhetoric sounds familiar to them. It is enough to analyze political discourses of people so different as Boris Yeltsin, Ion Iliescu, Sali Berisha, Slobodan Milošević, Aleksandr Lukashenko, Franjo Tudjman and even Lech Walesa with his calls for a "war at the top," in order to recognize the persistence of a certain intolerance so characteristic of the Leninist logic of monopolistic truth.[32] Needless to say, these people adhere to different philosophies, but they all share an authoritarian political style and the rhetoric of revolutionary transformation. As former Solidarity advisor and celebrated dissident Karol Modzelewski wrote:

> The authoritarian threat hanging over post-communist Europe concentrates primarily around the presidency; one sees this not only in Moscow and Minsk, but also in Warsaw. True, the dictatorial weed that risks growing here has profound roots. The authoritarian temptation is inherent in the great social tensions that have accompanied the neoliberal transformation of the economy. But the threat for democracy also flows from the legacy of a relatively recent past. Several decades of arbitrary and

irresponsible power did shape attitudes, mental structures, and mechanisms still present among cadres of the military, police, and public administration. This legacy has no ideological color. It matters little that Walesa, contrary to Jaruzelski, is an anti-communist; it is not ideology that matters, but the model of power."[33]

As Leninists used to revere the "class viewpoint," many post-communist leaders now worship the ethnic nation as the ultimate reservoir of hope and the main source of individual dignity. True, some politicians pay lip service to liberal values, but their true commitment is to a vision of politics that subordinates the individual to the interests of the nation state (as defined by them, of course). Instead of valuing statesmanship and compromise, they play on neurotic sentiments of victimization. National consciousness is thus manipulated to legitimize nationalist practices of discrimination against minorities. That the psychological background of certain populist leaders is often marked by deep traumas is of course an important element. But more important than the fact, for example, that both of Slobodan Milošević's parents committed suicide has been the readiness of so many Serbian officials and intellectuals to endorse his policies.[34]

At first glance, one sees emerging democratic institutions and free democratic elections in East and Central Europe.[35] The affliction called "Balkanization" has so far plagued only the former Yugoslavia and has bubbled up in some areas of the former Soviet Union like Abkhazia or Chechnya. Some authors believe that the democratic "habits of the heart" have set solid roots among politicians. In reality, however, democracy remains vulnerable and superficial, coexisting with strong populist, nationalist, and authoritarian trends.[36] Constitutional pluralism is marred by its very universalistic formal ism, by its coolness and lack of magnetizing virtues. It is based on procedures, not on emotions. Whereas individuals long for reassuring stories of glory and redemption, democratic regimes offer them endless debates on laws and regulations. Furthermore, the masses are fed up with politicians whose unique objective is to get rich as fast as possible and leaders who practice the cynical politics of deception as often as the old communists. Eastern Europe's descamisados yearn for some providential leader to come and tell them that the nightmare is over, that all riches belong to them, and that all their misfortune has just been the result of devious foreign conspiracies.

As in the 1930s, when society was deeply split, the post-Leninist syndrome of despair is conducive to outbursts of militant anti-democratic activism and vibrant expectations of salvation. In Romania between the wars, Iron Guard marchers were chanting: "Let the Captain make a country like the holy sun in the sky." Corneliu Zelea Codreanu, the Guard's Captain, was killed by King Carol's police in 1938, but the fanaticism of the Guard outlived his death, leading to the horrible pogroms of 1940–1941. A Nazi slogan put it very clearly: "Our program consists of two words: Adolf Hitler!" Simplicity, ruthlessness, and violence become virtues, as the *novus dux* allures the masses into the new millennium of honor and grandeur. Did not Hitler proclaim in front of his ecstatic votaries as early as 1924 that he was the "new light," the apostle that had seen the revelation? "It is the miracle of our age that you found me, and that you found me among so many millions of individuals. And the fact that I found you, this is the chance for Germany."[37]

Democracies are not prepared to provide such fantasies of ultimate regeneration. Recently born and still inexperienced, Eastern Europe's democracies have had difficulty adjusting to pressures aimed at subverting and obliterating the project of modernity (by which I tentatively understand the construction of politics in an anti-absolutist, individualistic and contractual way).[38] In many of these countries, reasserted presidentialism and statism are reminiscent of Latin American (Peronista-style) experiments in corporatism and authoritarian monopartidism.[39] Corporatism, after all, has a long tradition in the region. During the 1930s, Romanian economist Mihail Manoilescu was among the most influential theorists of revolutionary-nationalist corporatism. Such ideas seem to come back with a vengeance in the discourse of fundamentalist populists of various stripes. Their appeal in the 1990s, like fascism's in the 1930s, is linked to their ability to "combine resentful nationalism with a plausible theory of economic development that emphasized authoritarianism, mass mobilization of the population, and the retention of supposedly traditional, pure, non-Western values."[40] And the growing political appeals and uses of myths and the omnipresent selective memory (and forgetfulness) have led to the resurrection of historical phantoms, such as Admiral Miklos Horthy, Iron Guard "Captain" Corneliu Zelea Codreanu, Marshal Ion Antonescu, and Ustasha leader Ante Pavelić.

The achievements of East Central European societies cannot be simply dismissed: since 1989 they have evolved from authoritarian, ideologically monistic, extremely centralized and bureaucratically corrupt regimes toward proto-democratic forms of political and economic organization. To focus exclusively on their difficulties during the transition period is to miss the drama of social and political experimentation in that region. To deny the dangers is, on the other hand, myopic and in the long run disastrous. Furthermore, what is at stake is the validity and the very possibility of the liberal democratic paradigm in traditionally authoritarian societies.[41] Even if we do not wish to indulge in historical fatalism, the unpleasant fact remains that very few of these countries can invoke serious and reliable liberal traditions. Instead of being the outcome of natural growth, modernity was experienced as an externally induced shock. The political culture of the region was beset by chauvinism, anti-Semitism, distrust of intellectual free thinkers, and the celebration of the nation. And then, under communism, all these authoritarian instincts were further strengthened and encouraged: any form of alterity was persecuted, any germ of independent thought was denounced as subversive. The more subservient an individual, the better his or her chances to succeed.

The region has thus inherited a combination of pre-communist and communist forms of authoritarian monolithic thought: even the most adamant anti-Leninists today do obey to the logic of "whoever is not with us is against us." This is the profound meaning of Adam Michnik's rebuff of "anti-Communism with a Bolshevik face," a symptom he diagnosed among the most vocal proponents of radical decommunization.[42] For generations, these people have been deprived of the chance of dialogue, their ears have been exposed to the monotonous rhythms of the official propaganda, delivering again and again the same trite platitudes. And now, suddenly, they hear so many voices, so many discourses, each one competing with each other, each one disputing the others. No wonder that there is a widespread nostalgia for uniformity, monologue, and comforting unity. In Eastern Europe the past is endowed with the value of harmony. The present is decried because of its heterogeneous messages, perceived as chaotic, confusing, troublesome. Not without melancholy, one can ask: what do Benjamin Constant, John Stuart Mill and Alexis de Tocqueville have to say to the denizens of the post-Leninist world?

Can the revolutionary promises, which at least during the period immediately following 1989 were predominantly civic and "cosmopolitan," be constitutionalized?[13] What are the chances that these countries will rid themselves of their legacies of autarchy, obscurantism, "tribalism," and resentments, and safeguard the recently acquired areas of autonomy?[44] Thus formulated, these issues bear upon the future of the region as well as on that of the whole of Europe and international security in general. Or, to recall Ken Jowitt's apposite warning: "Liberal capitalist democracy has aroused a heterogeneous set of opponents: Romantic poets, Persian ayatollahs, the Roman Catholic Church, and fascists. For all the real and massive differences that separate these oppositions, one can detect a shared critique. Liberal capitalist democracy is scorned for an inordinate emphasis on individual materialism, technical achievement, and rationality . . . [and] for undervaluing the essential collective dimension of human existence [and the] human need for security."[45]

2. The Power of Magical Thinking

Intellectual stupor, moral disarray, and yearning for the "magic savior" are symptoms of the post-communist culture of disillusionment. The end of the Soviet Union as the absolute Other, the essentialized, eternally conspiring figure of an alternative system, has left the West without a clear-cut symbol of the enemy. In the East a whole institutional universe has fallen apart. In some ways the consequences of this breakdown can be boiled down to what pop psychology calls "magical thinking."

The moral identity of individuals in post-communist societies has been shattered by the dissolution of all the established values and "icons." There are immense continuity gaps in both social and personal memory: the same arguments that ensured one's career before 1989 played the opposite role after that watershed year. Being well connected with party bureaucracy and the secret police was a sign of political trustworthiness in any of these countries, ensuring not only social success but also a relative economic prosperity. The same background became, at least initially, a liability after the revolutions. Too many moral zigzags, too many political somersaults have created a sense of deep cynicism among the citizens. There is very little public trust and only a vague recognition of the need for a shared vision of the public good. Responsibility for personal actions, risk taking, and questioning of institutions on the basis of legitimate claims for improvement are still embryonic.[46]

Obsessive self-pity, the absence of empathy, the inability to mourn with the others and to understand their plight are indicative of a general collective self-centeredness that constructs fences around the in-group and elaborate, manufactured images about the "Other." Even when expelled from the Krajina region in Croatia in 1995, Serbs resisted being resettled in Kosovo, among the "inferior" Albanians. In turn, Albanians see the coming of Serbian refugees as part of an old plan to alter the ethnic structure of the region (whose population of 2 million is 90 percent Albanian).[47] As Michael Ignatieff once argued, this exclusive national arrogance is a latter-day expression of what Freud called the "narcissism of minor differences."[48] As the Czech philosopher and former Charter 77 activist Martin Palous has pointed out, the prospects for democratic development depend on civic awareness of the real stakes involved in the ongoing political struggles.[49] The stakes are obscured by ambiguities of the left-right polarization in post-communist regimes, which are linked to the ambiguity and even obsolescence of the traditional taxonomies. The references to the "Left" (in its radical version, at least) are opportunistic gestures rather than expressions of genuine commitment. As Adam Michnik lucidly put it: "The issue is not whether one is left or right of center, but West of center."[50]

Liberal values are thus seen by some as left-oriented simply because they emphasize secularism, tolerance, and individual rights as against different varieties of radicalism, including "civic" or "ethical," clericalism, or even theocratic fundamentalism. At the same time, radical-authoritarian trends are often disguised as pro-democratic when they surface in Russia, Ukraine, Bulgaria, Romania, and Slovakia, for example. These lingering reflexes and habits inherited from Leninist and pre-Leninist authoritarianisms continue to exist, and can be detected at both ends of the political spectrum (the "right" and the "left"). This explains the rise of the new alliances between traditionally incompatible formations and movements. In Russia, this takes the form of the Stalino-nationalist coalition, with its own tradition of National Bolshevism (or "Bolshevism of the extreme right").[51]

Political corruption, economic frustrations, and cultural despair are the ingredients for the rise of mass phenomena of panic, belief in miracles, millennial expectations, pseudo chiliasms, and sectarian magic. This was, for instance, the case of the "Caritas" pyramid scam in Cluj, Romania. For about two years, between April 1992 and May 1994, over two million Romanians put all their savings into the hands of a self-appointed savior. Cluj became the equivalent of an El Dorado, a magnet for financially gullible pilgrims. The mastermind of the whole operation was one Ion Stoica, a Brasov accountant, formerly involved in illegal currency exchanges. The principle was simple, using what Westerners have long known as the "chain letter." Stoica announced that every single player in the Caritas "mutual aid" society would get back eight times the amount of his or her invested sum. He was called the "new Messiah" who had descended to earth to "rescue Romanians from poverty," God, and the "Pope." Romanians and Hungarians alike rushed to throw their money into Stoica's obscure dealings. I was told of cleaning ladies who became millionaires in a matter of weeks. The rector of the University of Cluj, distinguished philosopher Andrei Marga, refused to play the game. He is still living off his salary. His secretaries did play and got rich. After operating for two years, the game was stopped by the Romanian government. Eventually Stoica was arrested, and charged with embezzlement, but no compensations were paid to the countless losers.[32]

In reality, Caritas had been an operation engineered by local elites with the assistance of Gheorghe Funar, the notorious nationalist mayor of Cluj, with the cooperation of the secret police. Rumors had it that it was a form of money laundering for the Italian mafia. After 1992, Romania replaced Yugoslavia as a major highway for weapons, drugs, and other dirty trades. As writer William McPherson reported, booklets were circulated that praised Stoica for his presumed patriotic performance. One of them, signed by an Orthodox priest, elaborated on the salvationist meaning of Caritas: "But how could Clujeans be happy, or Transylvanians, if they had neither food nor money to buy food . . . ? Who made himself happy? Only foreigners in our land! . . . The Caritas phenomenon has come as a divine phenomenon, not only for men, that they should have money and happiness, but as the salvation of the Romanian people."[53]

What matters more than the money, however, was the mass psychosis, the readiness of thousands of Romanians and Hungarians to endow a charlatan with the attributes of a demigod. Under post-communism, when social trust has been so low, individuals were paradoxically eager to buy the most fantastic promises. Social malaise and anomie have fed gullibility and self-illusionism. Magical thinking allows the individual to abandon the sense of responsibility, surrender his or her autonomy of will to crackpots and adventurers. As long as the state of law is still embryonic and corruption is pandemic, magical thinking offers easy ways to externalize guilt, demonize the outsiders, and create a false but galvanizing sense of community.

3. Remembrance of Things Not Quite Past, or Even Nonexistent

In post-communist societies, history is redefined and used by elites to suit their current interests. This applies both to the post-communist parties, eager to whitewash their historical responsibility for past tragedies, and to their opponents, eager to present the revolutions of 1989–1991 as a complete break with the Leninist times, a historical cleavage that separates the realm of "totalitarian night" from the realm of freedom. The 1995–1996 discussion on the legacy of the Polish People's Republic indicates precisely this ongoing struggle over the past: on the one hand there are those who admit that forty years of history cannot be simply written off, and on the other there are those who maintain this absolute break. The latter, among whom are famous anti-communist intellectuals like Gustaw Herling-Grudzinski, Zbigniew Herbert, and Jan Novak-Jezioranski, consider the four decades of "People's Republic" to have been an historical anomaly, and overstretch the Arendtian definition of totalitarianism to apply it to the defunct Leninist regime in that country. In fact, the issue is not the past but the present; by making the whole experience of ancien régime look grim and frightening, they want to delegitimize the post-communist Alliance of the Democratic Left that managed to achieve impressive electoral successes in both the 1993 parliamentary elections and the 1995 presidential ones.[54]

Less paradoxically than at first glance, there is a growing nostalgia for the old regime and the revival of "reactionary rhetoric."[55] But for such a development to take place, ideological zeal and utopian-eschatological motivation are needed. A true counterrevolution needs a blueprint that romanticizes the ancien régime. True, Petru Lucinski in Moldova, Algirdas Brazauskas in Lithuania, Leonid Kuchma in Ukraine, Aleksandr Kwasniewski in Poland, Ion Iliescu in Romania, Kiro Gligorov in Macedonia, Vladimir Meciar in Slovakia, and Slobodan Milošević in Serbia are all former communists. But they are not neocommunists, to the extent that this would mean a commitment to a certain political and economic vision inspired by the doctrines of Marx and Lenin. The danger is not that once in power they would restore concentration camps for political opponents, cut off relations with the West, and dismantle the free-market economy. They are rather cynical pragmatists, chameleonlike survivors, ready to espouse any creed with lightning speed, and believe it at least temporarily, if only it upholds their stay in power.[56] These people will not revive communism, but they can perpetuate a climate of cronyism, cynicism, and contempt for law.

For a genuine democratic left to emerge, its proponents need to rethink the reasons for the communist debacle and assume their intellectual and moral responsibility. Although he focuses on Latin America, Mexican political scientist Jorge Castañeda captures well this post-Cold War dilemma: "The left found itself in a no-win situation. Either it stuck to its guns—which were not really its own, but were foisted on it—and defended the undefendable; a state-run, closed, subsidized economy in a world in which such a notion seemed totally obsolete; or it turned around and supported the opposite, apparently modern, competitive, free-market course. In that case it ended up imitating—or being assimilated by—the right and losing its raison d'être."[57]

Between recantation and impersonation, the successor formations to the Leninist parties have to cope with a widespread sentiment of disaffection with socialist rhetoric.[58] The cases of Russia's communists headed by Gennady Zyuganov and Milošević's Serbian Socialist party are emblematic for the trend toward the cooperation between radical nationalist forces and those who are nostalgic for bureaucratic collectivism. The foundation of this trend is the ideological vacuum created by the collapse of state socialism, with populism being the most convenient and frequently the most appealing ersatz ideology.[59] Simply marching with Stalin's portrait is not an expression of Stalinism, but rather one of disaffection with the status quo, perceived as chaotic, anarchic, corrupt, politically decadent, and morally decrepit. Especially in Russia, where this disaffection is linked to the sentiment of imperial loss, the cultural despair can lead to dictatorial trends. Anti-liberal collectivistic trends exist in Bulgaria, Hungary, Poland, Romania, Serbia, and Slovakia (such as populist, anti-Semitic writer István Csurka's "Hungarian Life and Justice Party" or the aforementioned Torgyan and Vadim Tudor).

The distortion of the past is not limited to the communist period, and has produced some truly bizarre effects. The rehabilitation in Romania, for example, of Marshal Ion Antonescu (a most outrageous example of political insensitivity and historical amoralism), is accompanied by eulogies of the marshal's persecutions of the "ungrateful species of cheaters and exploiters."[60] The need for protection, for authority, for "order and rigurous discipline," and the yearning for the "Father" (cruel, brutal, but always present) explain why thousands of Romanians went on January 26, 1996, to lay flowers on Ceauşescu's tomb. As in the case of yearning for Stalin's days of certitude, there is increasing nostalgia in Romania for Ceauşescu's days of equality (even if only in misery).

Social demagogy and populist exploitation of mass discontent represent one face of the post-communists' tactics. The elections in Belarus have brought to power in 1994 Aleksandr Lukashenko, a demagogue ready to promise everything to everybody. A former Communist party member and state farm manager, Lukashenko combined in his campaign anti-corruption with anti-capitalism, and offered only vague responses to the truly painful problems that his country has confronted.[61] In 1995, Lukashenko continued to make anti-Western and anti-capitalist statements and went so far as to express admiration for Adolf Hitler. In 1996, he expressed support for the restoration of the USSR and indicated that he would be a possible presidential candidate.

Similar demagoguery assured the electoral victories of ex-communists in Bulgaria, Serbia, and Slovakia. The political comeback of the "comrades" is the result of their ability to blend social populism with ethnic radicalism. The in-group orientation of this rhetoric, the self-congratulatory visions of one's own historical past as against the other's stirs responsive chords among the disconcerted masses, in the same way that Third World dictators (from Perón to Fidel Castro) have often managed to come to power by manipulating anti-Western and anti-American emotions among their populations.

In post-communist Russia, one of the main paradoxes is the emergence of a Nazi movement in a country where virtually every family had somebody murdered by the Germans during World War II. But, the revival of the anti-Semitic myth functions almost miraculously by explaining the inexplicable, and reassuring with its hypnotic power those ready to hear that reality is the opposite of what the evidence shows. According to this paranoid view, World War II was imposed on Hitler by the Jews and their agents, including the Freemasons and the Vatican, throughout the Western world. Alexander Barshakov, a 41-year-old former engineer turned leader of the neofascist "Russian National Unity" movement, considers the Holocaust a diversion "created especially to conceal a Jewish-inspired genocide which killed 100 million Russians."[62] The uses of vindictive and scapegoating mythologies appear quite clear in this example: communism is attributed to the Jewish conspiracy, the Jew is endowed with a diabolical dual identity: supporter of money/destroyer of money; enemy of religion/Vatican ally; nihilistic adversary of the capitalist status quo/the most committed and perfidious defender of the bourgeois order). These irreconcilable qualities are unified through reference to that allegedly overarching Jewish characteristic: the ambition to dominate, control, and exploit the gentiles. All White Guard literature (or, in Romania, Iron Guard) is unearthed and recirculated to explain how Jews such as Lev Trotsky, Grigory Zinoviev, or Lev Kamenev conspired against the stronghold of Christianity, symbolized by Czarist Russia. Stalin's most atrocious crimes are primarily attributed to Lazar Kaganovich, the only Jewish member of the dictator's inner circle. As for Stalin's own anti-Semitism, this is seen as an illustration of his bona fide Russian patriotism, so different from the "rootless cosmopolitanism" of the early Bolsheviks.

To put it briefly: historical legacies have become symbolic weapons used by different political actors to justify their vision not only of the past but also of the present and the future. In the name of the need to know the past, new legends are manufactured by prophets of hatred. New alibis are devised for authoritarian, xenophobic, and exclusive policies. After the evisceration of truth during the communist period, many post-communist intellectuals and politicians have engaged in exercises meant less to highlight what did really happen than what they think should become the new historical orthodoxy.[63]

4. Protean Politics: Fluidity of Political Formations

With a private sector and entrepreneurial class still in the making, political liberalism, democratic individualism, and the civic culture associated with them are under siege.[64] Political parties in most of these countries are coalitions of personal and group affinities rather than collective efforts based on the common awareness of short and long-term interests: hence fragmentation, divisiveness, political convulsions, and instability.[65] Think of the avatars of the Democratic Union in Poland or the Free Democrats in Hungary: although headed by famous liberal intellectuals and counting among its leaders some of their countries' brightest minds, none of these parties managed to establish strong bases outside the major cities. They have remained, in more than one respect, discussion clubs.

The distances between political parties are often minuscule, and only personal vanities can explain why an individual decided to join one particular party instead of another. True, Hungary's FIDESZ (Federation of Young Democrats) distinguished itself by its nonconformist style, remarkable legal expertise, and the decision to keep the age of thirty-five as an upper limit for party membership. Its ideological program, however, was not very distinct from the Free Democrats. Consequently, after a brief period of immense popularity, FIDESZ lost momentum and in the 1994 elections suffered a major defeat. Eloquence, glamor, and wit turned out to be insufficient to ensure political longevity. One of the problems FIDESZ faced was its reluctance to engage in an alliance with the party to which it was ideologically closest: instead of attacking the conservative populist Magyar Democratic Forum, FIDESZ leaders spent a lot of time disassociating themselves from the Free Democrats.

In most of these countries, pre-communist political formations have failed to surface as major actors. Instead, the new formations have found themselves at a loss in indicating to their potential supporters what their main values were and, for that matter, what their major disagreements consisted of. The post communists succeeded in overcoming their initial state of despondency and stupor, and used their organizational skills and mobilizational techniques effectively. In the Polish and Hungarian cases, they played the card of consensus. In Romania, they pretended to be revolutionaries while preserving much of the old order. The anti-communist opposition, however, although in power for sometime in many post-Leninist states, lacked political skills and imagination. With the exception of Poland, none of these countries had entered the post-communist age with a mature political counterelite. This is the main cause for the ongoing fragmentation, divisiveness, and lack of a common notion of public good.

One reason for the rise of populist, potentially fundamentalist movements is the perception that the civic-romantic stage of the revolution is over and that currently the bureaucracy is intent upon consolidating its privileges. The strong attacks against Alekander Kwasniewski in Poland (and also Prime Minister Gyula Horn in Hungary) as "protectors of the establishment" are an expression of a search for a second revolution. Kwasniewski's or Horn's policies can, of course, be questioned. The issue, however, is the recognition of the institutional dignity of the parliaments and the elected offices. If it gathers momentum, this anti-establishment, plebeian trend could jeopardize the still precarious pluralist institutions.

Political reform in post-communist societies has, in general, not gone very far in creating and safely protecting countermajoritarian institutions such as independent media, a market economy, or relatively durable political parties. These institutions would diminish the threat of new authoritarian experiments by protecting the right to heterodoxy and diversity.[66] The main dangers are the formulae linked to statism, clericalism, religious fundamentalism, ethnocentrism, and militaristic fascism.[67] The key question is linked to the risk of further political polarization in the region, with the more developed states (Poland, Hungary, Baltic states, the Czech Republic) fostering an institutional culture of impersonal democratic procedures, but with the southern tier (the Balkans) and most of the successor states of the Soviet Union moving increasingly toward more or less benign forms of authoritarianism. The time-honored distinction between Central Europe (as the "abducted Europe") and Eastern Europe (as a collection of insecure, traditionally nationalist and economically backward states, unable or unwilling to internalize Western values) seems thus to be actual again.[68]

5. Crises of Values and Authority

The weakness of the political parties is primarily determined by the crises of values and authority and the no less widespread skepticism regarding a culture of deliberation. The existing formations have failed to imagine the ingredients needed for a consensus to generate "constitutional patriotism." Instead, there is the feeling of a "betrayal of the politicians" and a quest for "the new purity." This is the rationale for István Csurka's "radical revolutionism" as well as the political resurrection of the former Communist parties. This also explains the magnetizing power of Russian political groups opposed to Yeltsin's reforms and the lightning ascent of Zyuganov and his restored Communist Party of the Russian Federation.

But those who come to power through playing on disillusionment also fail their supporters. What is the meaning of the left-right dichotomy when the ex-communists often carry out programs as merciless for their supporters as for the execrated free marketeers? In the words of a disaffected Polish citizen: "I voted for the communists, but they cheated and lied to us. It's much worse under the former communists than it ever was under the center-right governments."[69]

We are dealing here with the same impotent fury against the failure of the state to behave as a "good father," part of a patrimonial legacy characteristic, to different degrees, of all these societies. Peter Reddaway correctly labeled this yearning for the state as a nostalgia for the protective "nanny."[70] For instance, it is not for Ceauşescu that Romanians are expressing their regrets, but rather for the age of predictability and frozen stability, when the party-state took care of everything. For many, the jump into freedom has turned out to be excruciatingly painful. Think of the thousands and thousands of educators in all these countries. In the former GDR, most teachers were replaced by Westerners. But in the other countries, the same people who used to lecture on the universal truth of "scientific socialism" are now praising the virtues of a market economy. Their own mental universe is shaken. All they used to stigmatize is now valid, all that was valuable less than ten years ago is now the symbol of oppression and infamy. The ideological collapse of Leninism has led to confusion, uncertainty and moral relativism.

6. No Justice, No Peace

Can these societies recover without coming to terms with the communist past? Could corrective, or retroactive, justice ever work? In reality, and for reasons that will be examined in another chapter, decommunization as a political myth failed, even as a catalyst for genuine historical debate. Think of Russia, where much ado about the "trial of the old party" has not resulted in anything significant, beside the perverse effect of Zyuganov's amazing popularity. Demagogy, overblown rhetoric, the continuous indulgence in scapegoating as well as in fictitious boundaries between "martyrs" and "criminals" undermine the legitimacy of the existing institutions and allow the rise of ethnocentric crackpots. This repression of public discussion is bound to fuel discontent and frustrations, thus encouraging demagogues and mafiosi.[71]

Instead of lucid analyses of the past, new mythologies are created to explain the current predicament: foreign conspiracies, the "endangered national interest," vindictive references to the need for "purification through retribution." In the Czech Republic, for instance, rightist groups have obsessively claimed that the Velvet Revolution was in fact a conspiracy fomented by Freemasons, the CIA, the KGB, and the Mossad. In Poland, it is frequently believed that the resurrection of the former communists is an indication that the revolution was just a smokescreen to ensure their conversion into the new capitalists.

Former Securitate colonel Filip Teodorescu was directly involved in the savage repression of the anti-Ceauşescu demonstrators in Timişoara in December 1989. Released from prison after a short term, he published a memoir full of surreal stories about foreign plots bound to destroy Romania's sovereignty. Another ex-intelligence officer, Pavel Coruţ, specializes in the production of a series of novels that combine Thracian-Dacian mythology, Orthodox

symbolism, science fiction, and the exaltation of the Securitate as the stronghold of Romanianness. The Securitate officers are portrayed as supermen, always outsmarting the vicious conspiracies fomented by foreigners, primarily
Hungarians who want to dismember the country and take Transylvania back.
In one of these novels he even claims that the cradle of European civilization,
a kind of pre-Aryan nation, was located in the Carpathian mountains.[72] The
cross, later appropriated as a symbol by Christianity, was their major identity
sign. Coruţ's novels sell hundreds of thousands of copies and, in spite of their
ludicrous fabrications, many people take them at face value, as historically
verified arguments. The alleged anti-Romanian conspiracy involves a strange,
mysterious sect, called the "bubuls": they are indeed the masters of this world,
and it was only because of the heroism of the Securitate Dacian hero, a post-
communist James Bond, that these horrible scenarios did not succeed.

Obscuring the past does not help these societies understand where they
come from. Letting the former tormentors and hacks enjoy the benefits of a
democratic order without expressing any repentance is both frustrating and
demeaning. On the other hand, their conversion to free-market entrepreneurship is certainly less dangerous for the liberal future of these societies than
any attempt to institutionalize collective punishment. Daniel Chirot rightly
emphasizes the disastrous outcomes of endeavors meant to assign collective
guilt to whole human groups:

> The great political atrocities of the twentieth century have been based on the assign-
> ment of collective guilt to one community or another, explained in historical terms
> to energize populations to action at critical turning points. The Jewish Bolsheviks,
> the bourgeois, the kulaks, the Muslims, the Croats, the Tutsis—whoever—are de-
> picted according to historical mythologies that explain how they are the source of
> evil and it is only just that they be punished. Further, because "they" are criminal,
> not to destroy them and their families becomes the ultimate danger because "they"
> will fracture "our" unity, defeat "our" noble goal, and ruin "our" community.[73]

It is ironic that this warning also applies to the fate of the former communists, who wrought so much havoc in the name of "class justice." But commitment to this individualistic approach is precisely the indication that the post-
communist order may be truly liberal rather than crudely and mindlessly
"anti-communist."

7. The Absence of a New Political Class

Democratic consolidation involves what political scientist Giovanni Sartori
calls the "taming" of politics, a normalization of the political climate so that it
stops being a "warlike affair."[74] Delays in the coalescence of a political class
significantly distinct from the old communist nomenklatura are linked to the

weakness of a democratic core elite; political values remain very vague, programs tend to overlap, and corruption is rampant.[75] This is particularly dangerous in Russia, where there is a conspicuous absence of political competition between ideologically defined and distinct parties. The public mood is then inclined to see privatization as the springboard for the rise of a new class of profiteers: a transfiguration of the old political elite into a new, economic one.[76]

To enjoy credibility, the new elites have to demonstrate that they are different from the old ones. Their legitimacy is linked as much to their professed espousal of democratic values as to their ability to live up to their pledges. This is precisely the missing point in most of these countries: although everybody speaks about constitutionalism and democracy, there is little consensus on the meaning of these terms. Instead of new and clean hands, people notice the perpetuation of the old elites with new masks. In Russia, the case of Aleksander Yakovlev is emblematic: first an ideologue under Brezhnev, then ambassador to Canada, he became Gorbachev's chief doctrinaire and a fervent proponent of perestroika. Later, he broke with Gorbachev, resigned from the Communist party (in 1990), and joined the Yeltsin camp. Between 1993 and 1995, he served as chairman of the government-controlled television. For many disappointed Russians, the political survival of people like Yakovlev is an indication that no revolution took place.

Cases similar to Yakovlev's can be documented in other political groups as well, with former ideological apparatchiks converted to the new discourses in favor of free market and pluralism. Think of the prominent role played in Boris Yeltsin's entourage by Aleksandr Korzhakov, the former chief of his personal guards, a former KGB officer whose sole political credential was his personal loyalty to the Russian president.[77] Another case: in 1995 the Russian prime minister, Viktor Chernomyrdin, created a new party named "Russia Is Our Home." Chernomyrdin is a former Brezhnev-era technocrat who also served as minister of gas industry under Mikhail Gorbachev. His main political asset is the promise of stability. Supported by the "Big Eight," Russia's most powerful bankers, he turned the new party into the "party of power." Dull and uninspiring, Chernomyrdin represents the continuity of the political and economic elites within the country's ruling forces. Meanwhile, the radical reformers are in deep disarray, and "red" and "brown" alliances offer even less hope for real change.[78]

The persistence of the old elites can be identified in most of the post-Leninist countries, from Georgia to Macedonia. In some of these emerging democracies former party leaders are now presidents. The situation in such countries as Albania, Bulgaria, Croatia, Russia, Ukraine, Serbia, and Slovakia, sometimes recalls a sad line in Giuseppe de Lampedusa' novel *The Leopard*: "In order for nothing to change, everything had to change"—at least in appearance. The problem is not so much the political background of these new leaders, al-

though this factor obviously matters, but rather their style, and their attempt
to establish networks of influence and control that may eventually stifle the
democratic process. One can conclude that although democracy appears to be
on the way to consolidation in Central Europe, where new political elites have
been recruited from both former oppositional and ruling forces and have radically broken with authoritarianism, the situation is still fluid and uncertain in
Russia, Ukraine, and most of the Balkans. In these countries, liberal democracy remains problematic and one notices the crystallization of a national-
populist consensus.[79]

8. Individualistic versus Communitarian Values

Will the post-Leninist societies become liberal democracies or will they look
for other models? Will collective visions and loyalties prevail over the affirmation of individual rights, including the right to assess *individually* the meaning
of these rights? As Croat political scientist Vesna Pusić put it:

> In single-nation states it is senseless to equate national self-determination and indi-
> vidual self-determination. National self-determination is a collective feature; just like
> class self-determination, it does not guarantee the freedom of the individual in all its
> peculiarities and variants. . . . The right to make political decisions may be temporar-
> ily delegated to the state. But it is impossible to delegate the right to choose one's
> own lifestyle, the right to public activity, the right to political association, or the right
> to freedom of opinion. These rights disappear if they are not tied to the individual,
> or controlled by the individual. Not because an individual would use them more
> rationally than a nation, but because availing of these rights is in itself an objective
> of democracy."[80]

Politically, the most important sectors to be reformed are the legal and the
military ones: as long as property rights are not fully guaranteed, economic
reforms cannot really succeed. Strategy is as important as tactic, and the will
to reform is as important as the articulation of concrete goals. As Václav Havel,
Adam Michnik, and other authors have consistently stated, the conflict takes
place between the advocates of the homogenizing (mythologically instituted
and constructed) nation state, aiming to create an ethnically pure community,
and those who believe in the right to diversity, to think and act autonomously.
Both sides use political archetypes, or myths, to advance their agendas, and
the conflict between these views will define the post-communist condition
for the foreseeable future. Although opinion polls in the whole region indicate strong support for democracy, awareness of rights is still low, and so is
the degree of tolerance for minorities.[81] Many who claim to favor democracy
actually support new forms of fundamentalism viscerally inimical to liberal
individualism.

In Poland, but not only there, this opposition takes the form of a struggle between the proponents of a liberal, secular republic and those who believe that the Church as a national institution has the right to impose political values. Although clericalism is still a marginal trend, many Poles find disturbing the Church's insistence on religious education in schools and the efforts to issue strict anti-abortion legislation. To be sure, there are enlightened sectors within Polish Catholicism that do not share the vision of an organically united nation under God. But there are also strong sectors who conceive the role of the Church in terms of a moral crusade for the "reconquest of Poland" by the "true Catholics." In their endeavors to wrench the country from the hands of "leftists," they define Polishness exclusively on the basis of a common religious identity. Their ideology is imbued with the belief that "the Church knows no limits." Some authors consider the rise of such religious fundamentalism as a major threat to nascent liberal democracies.[82]

To deny the need for rootedness would be a major error: individuals are not free-floating islands. Liberalism, however, is not the atomizing paradigm portrayed by its adversaries. Its content is primarily related to the sovereignty of the individual, including the essential right to engage in free economic and political initiatives. Moreover, liberalism questions the pretense of collectively imposed notions of truth, valor, honor, and dignity. Especially in societies that have only recently escaped the constraints of tyranny, equality under law and protection from state or other "sacred" institutional intrusion into the private sphere represent not only the core of liberalism but also its ultimate moral justification. To use a term proposed by Judith Shklar, this is a "liberalism of fear," to the extent that it is fully aware of the abominations engendered by the coercive and despotic abuses of public power.[83]

Conclusion

These eight threats to democracy as a whole make the general landscape, in many respects, one of disenchantment. Dispirited political cultures are plagued by the rise of new collectivisms, the marginalization of the former heroes, and more recently the return of the former communists. Adam Michnik's term for this general trend is "the velvet restoration." He sees it as inevitable, assuming it may help these societies avoid Jacobin-style "second revolutions." He may be right, but on the other hand one should not forget the causes of the 1989 breakthroughs: the Communist elites had failed abysmally in creating utopia. Without their ideological legitimation, they were completely lost, and had eventually to give up power. The former communists now do not have anything novel or exciting to offer in terms of ideological resources, unless they combine ethno-nationalist rhetoric with a sense of communitarian vision and promises of social tranquillity.[84]

Unlike Ceauşescu's nationalist socialism in Romania, Kadarism in Hungary was not xenophobic, but they both included strong egalitarian and collectivistic components, whose resurrection in the post-communist discourses are not surprising. When other ideological devices turned out to have become obsolete, communist regimes played on the chord of national pride. They insisted that, thanks to Leninist policies, their societies had escaped economic underdevelopment. In 1995, even Fidel Castro toned down Marxist rhetoric and focused his propaganda on nationalist, anti-North American motifs.

It is not my purpose in this chapter to put forward apocalyptic scenarios for post-communist societies. More than one possible future can be reasonably canvassed, and the likelihood of the worst-case scenario, with Eastern Europe run by neofascist, paranoid dictators engaged in ethnic cleansing and foreign aggressions, is somewhat dubious.[85] Although a tempting exercise in political thought, cataclysmic forecasts are much too hyperbolic and defy evidential demonstration. But the potential for ethnocratic or theocratic experiments still exists. Antiliberal, xenophobic groups and movements do not have to gain total power over the state to inflict harm on people, destabilize democratic politics and free markets, and influence the discourse of major parties.

Again, the most obvious and horrific example of staunch nationalist discourses and ethnocentrism being used by elites interested in nothing but power is the dissolution of Yugoslavia, a country that "had neither a velvet revolution, nor a velvet divorce."[86] Indeed, what Yugoslavia experienced was a combination of bloody counterrevolution and no less bloody divorce. The Yugoslav disaster should not be regarded as an isolated aberration; the exploitation of real or imaginary griefs, collective wounds, panic, and insecurity, are real ammunition for prophets of hatred and envy in all the post-communist nations. The feelings of betrayal, especially in Russia, and the populist belief that the West's ambitions are dictated by greed and contempt for the less modernized nations of the East are motifs used and abused by the neopopulists throughout the region.

Zbigniew Brzezinski has identified the rise of "metamyths," what I call *fantasies of salvation*, as a salient feature of our times. Brzezinski accurately sees these myths as a "an irrational but compelling blend of religious impulse to seek salvation, of the nationalist self-identification as being superior to outsiders, and of utopian social doctrines reduced to the level of popular slogans."[87] And nowhere do Isaiah Berlin's thoughts on the rise of nationalism in what might be called "battered societies" more appropriately apply than in the devastated moral landscape of post-Bolshevik Russia and post-Titoist ex-Yugoslav states. In these worlds of disarray, there is propitious ground for the most eccentric discourses of resentment. Under such conditions, when myth replaces analysis in the formulation of political goals, even a voice like Aleksandr Solzhenitsyn's,—authoritarian and definitely illiberal—appears reasonable when compared to the vociferous, albeit still marginal rhetoric of the radical right. Xenophobic nationalism, combined with neo-Darwinian, Nazi-style racism, are part of the rise of the vindictive, pseudo-chiliastic mythologies.

I use the term "pseudo-chiliastic" because the salvation these myths promise is one based on exclusion and marginalization of the very category of otherness. It is not a universalistic call for the unity of mankind in the glory of redemption but rather a call to achieve self-esteem by destroying and stigmatizing those who are different. The purity of the race, allegedly tarnished by aliens, gays, or cosmopolitan vermin, are themes that emerge in the discourses of new political movements from Zagreb to Bucharest, from Budapest to Saint Petersburg.

Such neonationalist prophets, movements, and proto-parties appeal to the general feeling of abandonment and alienation that seem to be the hallmark of the post-communist psychological condition. This seems to be increasingly the case in Russia, where half of the respondents in one 1994 poll perceived themselves as "offended, lied [to], and exploited."[88] Furthermore, if one listened to Pamiat founder and leader Dmitri Vasiliev, outbursts of unmitigated, rabid anti-Semitic and anti-Western rage would be the norm: "It is not necessary to be Jewish to be a Jew. Anyone who helps Jews encroach on others' traditions is a Jew. Everybody in power is a Jew, or their wives are." And how should Russians cope with such threats to the social health? Vasiliev has a direct, frighteningly unabashed answer: "Jews have inflicted humiliation after humiliation in Russia. You must kill them, it's the only solution. It's filthy business."[89]

Looking at these words a number of disturbing questions arise: what happened to the ethical, transnational project of "civil society" and "Central Europe"? Was the celebration of dissent the result of the Western intelligentsia's narcissistic projection more than the expression of home-grown intellectual and moral trends? How can one account for the rise of the communitarian paradigm that simply reconverts and reshapes the same values that underlay the defunct communist project? How can these societies reconcile their predominantly nonliberal political cultures with the yearning to belong to Europe? No less significant is the interpretation of cultural fault lines in Europe.[90] Do the Balkans belong to "the West," or are they irretrievably part of the "rest"? A Polish newspaper apparently referred to the continental Southeast as "Turkish Europe." And then, one could legitimately ask, what is Russia: "Tartar Europe"?[91]

In a provocative piece, Nicholas Eberstadt noticed the demographic mysteries of post-communism: a cataclysmic decline of population growth combined with soaring rates of mortality. Is the death of communism such a traumatic experience for individuals that they alter radically their most intimate patterns of conduct? But then, as Eberstadt admits, in the Czech Republic, arguably the most advanced in moving toward a market economy and a plu-

ralist order, the collapse of the old regime has not had the same type of ominous demographic impact.[92]

After the extinct period of "legitimation from the top," it seems that in most
of these countries nascent legal-procedural legitimation is paralleled (or countered) by something that could be called *legitimation from the past*.[93] The more
inchoate and nebulous this past, the more aggressive, feverish, and intolerant
the proponents of the neoromantic mythologies. But one cannot see the eastern part of Europe as the only candidate for embracing mythological fallacies.
Instead, we should admit that we deal with a resilient, persistent form of
barbarism that is situated in the very heart of modernity. As George Steiner
wrote about this "mono-identitary discourse" (what I call the homogenizing
instinct), "Nationalism is the venom of our age. It has brought Europe to the
edge of ruin. It drives the new states of Asia and Africa like crazed lemmings.
By proclaiming himself a Ghanaean, a Nicaraguan, a Maltese a man spares
himself vexation. He need not ravel out what he is, where his humanity lies.
He becomes one of an armed, coherent pack. Every mob impulse in modern
politics, every totalitarian design, feeds on nationalism, on the drug of hatred
which makes human beings bare their teeth across a wall, across ten yards of
waste ground."[94] Ethnic fundamentalism is the reification of difference, the
rejection of the claim to common humanity and proclamation of the national
distinction as the primordial fact of human existence.[95]

Three _____

Vindictive and Messianic Mythologies:
Post-Communist Nationalism and Populism

> It seems to me that those who, however perceptive
> in other respects, ignored the explosive power gen-
> erated by the combination of unhealed mental
> wounds, however caused, with the image of the
> nation as a society of the living, the dead, and those
> yet unborn (sinister as this could prove to be when
> driven to a point of pathological exasperation) dis-
> played an insufficient grasp of reality.
> (Sir Isaiah Berlin)

No POLITICAL DREAM has proved to be more resilient, protean, and enduring in this century than nationalism. A comprehensive and potentially aggressive constellation of symbols, emotions, and ideas, nationalism can also offer the redemptive language of liberation for long-subjugated or humiliated groups. Conductor Leonard Bernstein used to say that whatever statement one makes about Gustav Mahler's music the opposite is equally true. This is the case with nationalism, as well. It is often described as archaic, anti-modern, traditional-ist—in short, reactionary. Other interpretations see it as a driving force of liberation, an ideology of collective emancipation, and a source of human pride. Whatever one thinks of nationalism, its ubiquitous presence at the end of this century is beyond any doubt. The problem, therefore, is to find ways for reconciling it with the democratic agenda.[1]

The roots of contemporary nationalism can be traced to the early days of the ideological age: the myth of the nation was created by historians, poets, and philosophers in the era when nation states appeared to be the political units par excellence. Take for instance, Polish nationalism of the nineteenth century, comprising romantic, salvationist, and redemptive components; deprived of statehood, Poles cherished an idealized vision of national community unified by unique traditions of heroism, martyrdom, and sacrifice. During that romantic stage, being a Pole was primarily a state of mind, not a biological determination. Referring to this persistent though not unique component of Polish nationalism, Andrzej Walicki wrote, "The dominant form of the Polish national ideology became romantic nationalism, conceiving nations as moral entities and agents of universal progress: a nationalism passionately believing in the brotherhood of nations and in the potentially ethical nature of politics, whereby it was hoped to put an end to such political crimes as had culminated in the martyrdom of Poland. The most extreme and best articulated form of romantic nationalism was religiously inspired romantic messianism, which saw the Poles as the chosen nation, the spiritual leaders of mankind and the sacred instrument of universal salvation."[2]

During the twentieth century, this variety of Polish romantic nationalism was increasingly challenged by a new concept of the nation rooted in common ancestry and ethnic bonds, primarily developed by Roman Dmowski, the founder of Polish modern, integral nationalism. But the myth of Poland's unique status within the international community and its predestined mission has continued to impregnate both political discourse and practice, from Pilsudski to Solidarity.

Poles are not unique, of course, in celebrating this special link between their national destiny and the salvation of mankind. As formulated by Fyodor Dostoevsky, Russian nationalism also had a strong messianic dimension: "If a great people doesn't believe that the truth is only to be found in itself alone (in itself alone and in it exclusively)," Dostoevsky wrote in his novel *The Possessed*, "if it doesn't believe that it alone is fit and destined to raise up and save all the rest by its truth, it would at once sink into being ethnographical material and not a great people."[3]

The nationalist myth owes its galvanizing power to its unique blend of scientific and emotional claims. But the problem is how to define nationhood; liberals emphasize the civic bonds, whereas militant nationalists focus on ethnic purity based on common origins and presumed common destiny. The former favor dialogue, tolerance, and inclusion, the latter champion assimilation, segregation, or exclusion of those with different ancestries. The competition between these visions cuts across every political community and constitutes one of the most tenacious contradictions of modernity. Furthermore, each camp is not homogenous. In post-Leninist countries, one encounters among the illiberal nationalists former communists, socialists, neofascists, traditional conservatives, and populists committed to the search for a "third way" between communism and capitalism. What do all these groups have in common? Most likely, their hostility to democratic, liberal, modern values, plus a common conviction that individuals should relinquish their rights in favor of collective aspirations and interests. In the same vein, the liberal or civic approach to nationalism is held by Christian Democrats (as in the case of Slovakia), liberal democrats, and even former communists converted to the values of an open society (as in the case of Hungary and Poland). Liberalism in this context does not mean a suppression of ethic differences and group identities, but an institutional and cultural effort to diminish and organize these distinctions "just enough to increase the chances for peaceful coexistence and mutually beneficial cooperation."[4] But radical nationalism opposes precisely these values of cooperation, tolerance, and dialogue.

These two paradigms are related to prevailing values, traditions, and the development of civic institutions and mentalities. This explains why liberal values seem to get the upper hand in Central Europe, whereas the Balkans have been prone to ethnic strife, populist collectivism, and plebiscitary democracies. True, liberal and illiberal versions of nationalism exist in all these countries, but their impact in Romania and Serbia is different from that in Slovenia and the Czech Republic.[5] The problem is to see how the political and cultural elites use the existing symbolic capital to suit their tactical goals. The ultimate competition in the region is between those formations that share a civic-based conception of nationalism and those who adhere to exclusionary ethnic nationalism. In most of East and Central Europe, in fact, ethno-nationalism has fundamentally altered the left-right ideological spectrum.[6]

The end of communism and the new era of international ethnic conflict that followed the Cold War have made radical nationalism the main competitor to liberalism and civil society. Its main strength comes precisely from its ability to become a substitute for lost certainties; it caters to painful collective anxieties, alleviates angst, and reduces the individual to one lowest common denominator: the simple fact of ethnic belonging.[7]

Ethnic nationalism appeals more often than not to primary instincts of unity and identification with one's own group. Especially in times of social frustration, foreigners tend to be demonized and scapegoated. A Ukrainian nationalist, for instance, would see Russians (and/or Jews) as forever conspiring against Ukraine's independence and prosperity. A Romanian one would regard members of the Hungarian minority as belonging to a unified body perpetually involved in subversive and irredentist activities. A Croatian militant nationalist would never trust Serbs, whereas Serbian ethnic fundamentalists would always invoke Croatia's alliance with Nazi Germany as an argument against trust and ethnic coexistence. Estonian, Latvian, or Lithuanian nationalisms are colored by the memory of the Soviet (and previously Russian) occupations of the Baltic states.

National discourses serve not only to preserve the sense of ethnic identity but also to "reinvent the tradition," regenerate the historical mythology, infuse a transcendental content into the sense of national identity. In the words of a contemporary Lithuanian writer,

> As the nation enters history, the word of the poet must acquire the properties of a narrative discourse, must grow to become a myth that could in some ways function like those of epic Greek antiquity, when they gave the people a soul, an identity liberated by time. . . . The present situation of the Baltic States requires a new approach to the myth of nationhood, one that would cut through the bourgeois sentimentalism of a small country and the reveries of the romantic era to reach back to the roots which were there at the dawn of history and before.[8]

It is usually intellectuals who generate discourses that justify nationalist identifications and projections; then, in turn, the mobilized masses give these discourses the validation of practical realities. With their shattered identities and wavering loyalties, the masses of the post-communist world offer fertile ground for delusional xenophobic fantasies to thrive. Thus, national homogenization becomes the battle cry of political elites for whom unity and cohesion are the ultimate values. For Croatian president Franjo Tudjman, for instance, it is only the intellectuals supportive of the "national spirit and self-determination" who deserve the name of intelligentsia. All others, he maintains, are just "pharisees."[9] A continuous invention of enemies and hatreds aggravates the climate of insecurity and makes many honest individuals despair about the future of their societies.

The new constitutions adopted in the post-communist states locate the source of state sovereignty in the majority ethnic nation, rather than in the individual citizen. They potentially discriminate against minorities; for instance, more than one-third of Estonia's population was barred from participating in the 1992 elections. Anthropologist Robert Hayden calls this variety of post-communist reification of the ethno-nationalist domination *constitutional nationalism*.[10] Constitutions are used to enshrine the sovereignty and privileges of the dominant nation, whereas the minorities' complaints are treated as anti-national behavior. In Romania, for instance, an education law adopted in 1995 forces ethnic Hungarian school students not only to take mandatory Romanian language and literature classes but also to take Romanian history and geography lessons in Romanian. Political commentator Andrei Cornea describes this approach as "the mentality of the main resident" that invests Romanian language with a liturgical authority.[11]

This chapter examines the dynamics of post-communist nationalism, the tension between liberal and illiberal definitions of national community, and the intellectual struggles over which type shall prevail in each country. Contemporary ethnic nationalism is seen less as a resurrection of the pre-communist politics of intolerance—though it is that, as well—than as an avatar of the Leninist effort to construct the perfectly unified body politic. This "return of history" is an ideological reconstruction meant to respond to present-day grievances rather than a primordial, inescapable destiny of these nations cursed to fight with and fear each other.[12] Whether this post-communist nationalism will become civic or will turn into vicious chauvinism is too early to forecast.[13]

Communism and Nationalism

With its internationalist vision, Marxist communism strove to overcome the limitations of national consciousness. "The proletarians have no homeland," the founding fathers of the doctrine proclaimed in the *Communist Manifesto*.

They were wrong, and internationalism turned out to be a utopian program.[14] In reality, as the collapse of the German left has shown twice in this century (first in 1914, then after Hitler's takeover in 1933), proletarians do have a homeland and they are ready to die for it as willingly as the members of any other social group. During World War I, the cult of la patrie et les morts (the fatherland and the dead) was more than a poetic metaphor: it provided millions of French people with the belief that fighting the Germans was a sacred cause. In the same vein, pan-German nationalism combined with pseudo-scientific racism served as a main ingredient for Hitler's doctrine of imperialist expansion.

At the same time, Joseph Stalin's appeal to Russian nationalism and Hitler's scorn for the Slavic "inferior race" enhanced the enthusiasm of the Red Army and the Russian people in the anti-fascist struggle (the "Great Patriotic War.") Stalin articulated war goals in terms of national survival, and even some of the most adamant anti-Bolsheviks closed ranks behind the "little father of the peoples" to defend the holy Russian soil. In 1948, it was nationalism that helped Josip Broz Tito build up the anti-Stalinist consensus in Yugoslavia and the ideology of "national communism." Democratic national ideals inspired Polish and Hungarian revolutionaries in their anti-Stalinist struggles in 1956. Nationalism has been the force that led to the breakup of last colonial empire, the USSR.[15] No less significant, it has been the legitimation for Third World self-appointed saviors to posture as "national redeemers."[16]

Some communist dictators understood that their stay in power would be guaranteed by resort to nationalist rhetoric. Romania's Nicolae Ceauşescu and Albania's Enver Hoxha knew how to present their autarchic regimes as reincarnations of millennia-old dreams of independence. The whole propaganda system under Ceauşescu was set in high gear to present him as the reincarnation of the Dacian and Thracian tribal chieftains who had resisted Roman invasions. In 1987, Serbian communist leader Slobodan Milošević used nationalist slogans to foster his power. As Tito's legacy disintegrated, Milošević turned into a hyper-nationalist demagogue, abandoned Marxist tenets, and unleashed his struggle for the creation of Great Serbia. He postured as a resurrected Prince Lazar, the Serbian hero who had died in the Kosovo battle of 1389 opposing the Ottoman Empire's expansion. Similarly, Franjo Tudjman, a Croat communist general, broke with Titoism in the 1970s and espoused militant nationalist symbols, including some linked to the Ustasha, pro-Nazi regime (whom he had fought against during World War II). This choice paid off. In 1995, Tudjman was the extremely popular president of an independent Croatia, successfully pursuing his strategy of building a nationally homogenous state by expelling Serbs from areas they had inhabited for centuries.[17]

Whether these leaders believe the nationalist myths they operate with is less important than that such discourses offer the ordinary individual the sentiments of pride, security, and unity so coveted in times of traumatic disloca-

tion. As the Marxist utopian creed faded away, nationalist discourses have
(re)entered the scene, ready to fill in the apparent ideological void.[18] Precisely
because the social space appears ominously unpredictable, with weak civil
societies and still inchoate political parties, individuals invest their aspirations
for solidarity and belonging into the nation. Moreover, the celebration of the
community as the ultimate reservoir of human dignity is usually associated
with the exaltation of military virtues, the cult of the state, and the persecution
of independent thinking.[19]

Post-communist nationalism is intimately linked to the Leninist legacy.
Marxist internationalism was nothing but an empty slogan in most of Eastern
Europe. How many of the Bulgarian, East German, Russian, or Romanian citizens nourished feelings of fraternal solidarity with the Angolan guerrillas, or
the Chilean, Greek, Portuguese, or Spanish communists? How many believed
in the myth of the Warsaw Pact as a community of equal brotherly states? It is
now obvious that ideology and a number of political goals shared by the oli-
garchic elites in these countries were not sufficient to create an internationalist
popular consciousness. Instead, under the veneer of the official slogans,
nationalist passions continued to smoulder and even irrigate the Leninist
regimes. Zbigniew Brzezinski noticed this unification of Leninist style and
nationalist themes in the communist experiments:

> though it proclaimed itself to be a doctrine of internationalism, communism in fact
> intensified popular nationalist passions. It produced a political culture imbued with
> intolerance, self-righteousness, rejection of social compromise and a massive inclina-
> tion toward self-glorifying oversimplification. On the level of belief, dogmatic com-
> munism thus fused with and even reinforced intolerant nationalism; on the level of
> practice, the destruction of such relatively internationalist classes as the aristocracy or
> the business elite further reinforced the populist inclination toward nationalistic
> chauvinism. Nationalism was therefore nurtured, rather than diluted, in the commu-
> nist experience.[20]

This synthesis of unavowed national ambition with ideological monism explains the intensity of nationalist passions in the post-communist world: ethnic exclusiveness is a continuation of the Leninist reductionist hubris, of its
adversity to anything smacking of difference. Anti-liberalism, collectivism,
and staunch anti-intellectualism blend together in the new discourses of national self-aggrandizement. At the same time, the recollection of the times of
oppression under the communist regimes is used to bolster a sense of uniqueness. Suffering is often exploited to justify a strange competition for the status
of most victimized nation. No less important, because communism was seen
by many as a dictatorship of "foreigners," contemporary radical nationalism is
also intensely anti-communist. Ironically, the nationalist zealots are often former communists for whom the internationalist veneer of the old ideology had
always been an embarrassing and shallow ritual.

What Is Nationalism?

The literature on nations and nationalism is dauntingly diverse. For some authors, nationalism is primarily an expression of insecurity, the exacerbated rationalization of unbearable inferiority complexes. They see nationalism as the most vibrant channel able to give vent to feelings of frustration, discontent, exclusion, and wrath, especially among communities that have long experienced historical humiliations. This often results in national martyrologies that fuse self-pity with self-idealization, and even in a "cult of failure." In the words of Polish writer Andrzej Bryk: "Modern Polish history has been a story of nearly constant defeat and internal failure. A defeated people lives by myths, clings to myths. Apologetic and martyrological visions of national history only mirror an incurable romantic despair. Poles thus look at their history in terms of "honor" versus "shame" because categories of victory or national success are largely beyond the modern Polish consciousness and any of the institutions that shape it. Honor seems to Poles the only reliable justification of the national existence."[21]

Other scholars insist that nationalism can play the role of a positive search for collective identities, especially among populations long deprived of independent forms of political organization. Nationalism is therefore not essentially hostile to civic and liberal values. Admitting that tensions cannot be always avoided between liberalism and nationalism, Yael Tamir proposes a normative concept of liberal nationalism: "the liberal tradition, with its respect for personal autonomy, reflection, and choice, and the national tradition, with its emphasis on belonging, loyalty, and solidarity, although generally seen as mutually exclusive, can indeed accommodate each other. Liberals can acknowledge the importance of belonging, membership, and cultural affiliations, as well as the particular moral commitments that follow from them. Nationalists can appreciate the value of personal autonomy and individual rights and freedoms, and sustain a commitment for social justice both between and within nations."[22]

Some writers argue that nationalism is the main underpinning of nations, that it precedes and allows for national formation, and that without nationalism nations could not exist. Ernest Gellner, for instance, insists that nationalism "invents nations where they do not exist."[23] Benedict Anderson defines the nation as an imagined community, but not in the sense that it is unreal or false: "It is *imagined* because the members of even the smallest nations will never know most of their fellow-members, meet them, or even hear of them, yet in the minds of each lives an image of their community. . . . Communities are to be distinguished not by their falsity/genuiness, but by the style in which they are imagined."[24] The key point is that nations are not simply invented but imagined on the base of shared perceptions, feelings, memories, and desires for sameness. Thus, the ideological myth called nationalism is not the creator of the nation: this would mean that it had a demiurgic power no ideology or myth can have. What this mythology of origins, foundation, belonging, and destiny does is create the sentiment of unity among otherwise disparate groups and individuals frequently (but not always) related by a shared territory, common ancestry, linguistic identity (or strong similarity), and cultural legacies (symbols, religion, folklore, mores).

Nationalism turns belonging to a nation into a status symbol: one becomes a participant, an actor in the historical evolution of the community, an inheritor of all the past experiences, and a producer of legacies for the next generations. Nationalism justifies identity, and reassures the individual that feelings of solitude, defeat, and alienation can be superseded through immersion in the larger community. Nationalism is thus a matter of belonging, fraternity, and solidarity. It is also one of differentiation, alterity, and eventually exclusion.

Isaiah Berlin, one of the wisest students of the intellectual and moral dilemmas of this century held that nationalism is more often than not, and especially in our age, a response to degradation and a search for dignity. "Nationalism is an inflamed condition of national consciousness which can be, and has on occasion been, tolerant and peaceful. It usually seems to be caused by wounds, some sort of collective humiliation."[25] In a similar vein, Liah Greenfeld, the author of a path-breaking study on nationalism, sees it as a road to modernity: *National identity is, fundamentally, a matter of dignity. It gives people reasons to be proud.*"[26] At the same time, Greenfeld carefully introduces a crucial distinction between the two versions of nationalism: one individualistic, liberal, and civic-democratic, the other aggressive, collectivistic, and marked by social and ethnic *ressentiment*. The former characterizes societies where modernity amounted to the development of strong civil societies; the latter, it seems, tends to prevail in nations with a delayed and problematic modernization, such as Germany, Russia, and most of East-Central Europe.

Other authors are reluctant to recognize that nationalism contains any potentially positive quality. One of them, British historian and political scientist Elie Kedourie, presciently wrote in 1992, several months before his death: "The disintegration and failure of socialism in the Soviet empire and its satellites has not meant the disappearance of the ideological style of politics—far from it. As we can see it has produced, in a revulsion against socialist tyranny, a revival or recrudescence of nationalism—that other ideological obsession."[27] For Bogdan Denitch, an American democratic socialist theorist, nationalism defined as a form of exclusive communitarian politics is responsible for the resurrection of Eastern Europe's political ghosts. The politics of nationalism, he writes, "are dangerous because, by definition, they exclude a number of subjects of the new nation states from full citizenship which is limited to the

national community. . . . As such it [nationalism] stands in fundamental opposition to liberal notions of *individual* as distinctive from *collective* rights; the
community is posited as the relevant unit when it comes to rights, to grievances which need to be addressed, and to representation."[28] In other words,
nationalism as a celebration of the ethnic community, or the people, is the
most powerful post-communist political myth.

The mythical structures of nationalism are often bonded to those of populism. Populism is a larger discourse that integrates nationalism in a structure
of expectations and demands for protection from the drastic changes imposed
by political and economic modernization. This "national-populism," argues
French political scientist Michel Wieworka, is a response to deep-seated and
excruciating fears of failure. It is not inherently anti-modern, but it expresses
the yearning among many strata for not being excluded or abandoned during
the ongoing seismic transformation: "Populism ensures the amalgamation of
unsatisfied social demands with fears linked to the risk of exclusion and social
breakdown. . . . Populism therefore has a mythical structure that tends to
reconcile a positive valuing of modernity and a rejection of what modernity
implies in terms of destructuring."[29]

The breakup of the monolithic ideology of state socialism created a new
burden of reality and, as T. S. Eliot once wrote: "Human kind cannot bear
very much reality" (*Murder in the Cathedral*). In the past, the individual could
identify the party with the source of all unpleasantness, hardships, and harassments (or, vice versa, with all achievements and heroic exploits). This exter-
nalization of evil (or of good) was psychologically reassuring: it offered a clear-
cut (even if misleading) distinction between "them" and "us." A higher or
lower degree of complicity was denied thanks to this fictitious split between
the public and the private spheres.[30] In the post-communist world, the disappearance of the old "Other" created a need for the construction of a new one.
As Katherine Verdery noticed: "Senses of self had been built up and repro-
duced for decades knowing that the enemy was the Communists. Until new
modes of self-constitution arise, we might expect a transformation of Communism's us-them into that other dichotomous social organization, ethnic distinction. Thus, persons self-constituted against a Communist Other now stand
against an Other who is ethnic."[31]

Nations are presented by nationalists, almost universally, as victims of foreigners, and in East and Central Europe, the former communist regimes are
described as having been engineered by aliens to serve foreign interests. Minorities, especially ethic ones, are thus the perfect candidate for the targeted
figure of the enemy. Russian nationalists, including some of the most gifted
fiction writers belonging to the "Siberian School," have not tired of blaming
the Jews for the Bolshevik destruction of traditional values and structures.
Needless to add, some of the most frantic propagandists for such dark visions

are former communists themselves, including a number of former communist intellectuals. Writing primarily about the tragic events in his native Yugoslavia, American poet Charles Simic strikes a depressing note when he observes: "The terrifying thing about modern intellectuals everywhere is that they are always changing idols. At least religious fanatics stick mostly to what they believe in. All the rabid nationalists in Eastern Europe were Marxists yesterday and Stalinists last week."[32] There may be some exaggeration in this statement, but think of the readiness of intellectuals like once-critical Marxist philosopher Mihajlo Marković or novelist Dobrica Cosić to endorse Milošević's nationalist rhetoric.

Several years before the end of communism in Europe, Joseph Rothschild argued that "ethnonationalism, or politicized ethnicity, remains the world's major ideological legitimator and delegitimator of states, regimes, and governments."[33] Nationalism provides the most energizing of the identity myths of modernity, a myth more powerful and vivid than Marxist socialism, liberal universalism, or constitutional patriotism; but is it a fundamental threat to the emergence of politically tolerant structures? Are these societies hostages to their past, doomed eternally to re-enact old animosities and conflicts? One needs to distinguish between varieties of nationalism: the inclusive versus the exclusive, the liberal versus the radical, or, as Yael Tamir proposes, the *polycentric* versus the *ethnocentric*.[34] I propose here a minimal typology of nationalism in post-communist societies.

Civic nationalism recognizes individual rights as fundamental for the construction of a liberal order and locates the sovereignty of the people in the defense of individual rights for all members of the political community, regardless of ethnic origin and any other differences.[35] It is a "soft" form of nationalism rooted in the democratic traditions, be they conservative, liberal, or social democratic. This vision allows for nationality to be acquired, and rejects the "genetic" definition of ethnic belonging. It tends to be characteristic of a number of prominent political and cultural figures in East and Central Europe, including leaders of the Civic Alliance party and the National Peasant Christian and Democratic party in Romania, the Federation of Young Democrats (FIDESZ) and the core of the Magyar Democratic Forum in Hungary, Poland's Union of Freedom, members of Jan Carnogursky's Christian Democratic party in Slovakia, important segments of the Rukh movement in Ukraine, and so on. It is not xenophobic and stresses the need for inclusion and tolerance of minorities. Especially in countries with a turbulent history, this trend should be seen as a constructive development. It offers the individual a minimal sense of security and of belonging to a community in times of dashed illusions and axiological tremors.[36]

A characteristic of this form of national affirmation is its primarily cultural-civic dimension. Anti-communism is often a major element, and since in Ro-

mania, Serbia, and Slovakia communism and chauvinism were intimately in-
tertwined, this trend has shown an increased sensitivity to the plight of ethnic
minorities persecuted by xenophobic communists. Liberal nationalism recognizes the preeminence of the moral person, the elective dimension of personal
identity, and refuses to see the individual as a prisoner of his or her communal
belonging. In a certain sense, to the extent that it does not exalt the superiority
of the national ideal over any other one, and does not sacralize the nation as
the ultimate and indisputable source of human identity, liberal nationalism
can be seen as "post-nationalist." It values reflection over emotion, and it insists on the autonomy of human will and choice.[37]

Liberal nationalism is not the self-absorbed cultural nationalism that historians have long associated with East European societies. Its positive possibilities should be stressed in our times of nationalist furies and ethnic cleansings,
when whole cities are bulldozed and hundreds of thousands are forcibly expelled from their homes and turned into superfluous populations of un-
wanted refugees. Ernest Renan's classic definition of the nation is worth being
remembered in this respect for its intense, unabashed humanity: "The existence of a nation is . . . a daily plebiscite, just as that of the individual is a
continual affirmation of life. . . . A nation has no more right than a king to say
to a province: 'you belong to me; so I will take you.' A province means to us
its inhabitants; and if anyone has a right to be consulted in the matter, it is the
inhabitant. It is never to the true interest of a nation to annex or keep a country against its will. The people's wish is after all the only justifiable criterion,
to which we must always come back."[38]

Hans Kohn gave the classic interpretation of the constructive, predominantly civic and political Western nationalism as opposed to the Eastern cultural nationalist tradition: "Nationalism in the West arose in an effort to build
a nation in the political reality and struggle of the present without too much
sentimental regard for the past; nationalists in Central and Eastern Europe
created, often out of myths of the past and the dreams of the future, an ideal
fatherland, closely linked to the past, devoid of any immediate connection
with the present, and expected to become sometime a reality."[39] One should
correct this approach by recognizing that sentimental treatment of the past is
not a specifically East European feature: think of the popular French recollec-
tions of the "Great War," or the ritualization of the monarchic institution and
its rites in Britain. The point is that Western intellectuals have been more
critical of their countries' traditions and have frequently exposed sentimental
false memories as self-serving mythologies, whereas their peers in the East
have been among the most enthusiastic manufacturers of national legends of
glory and victimization.

In post-communist societies, precisely because of the experience of the homogenizing efforts of the Leninist party/state, liberal nationalism promotes the
rights of particularity and diversity. It is to be detected in different political

formations, from left to right. One finds liberal nationalist views and activists as much among former communists as among the former dissidents. Unfortunately, this trend has been less effective and influential than other, less benign versions of nationalism.

Ethnic, less liberal, or illiberal nationalism encompasses various trends whose common feature is a collectivist interpretation of the nation, an exaltation of tradition and traditional institutions, a cultivation of heroic mythologies of the past, and a distrust of Western liberal values as "alien" to the local communal ethos. By postulating the common will of the "people" as the supreme national value, this version of nationalism paves the way for authoritarian experiments. It is always a minority that claims to be in the know, to have the right (or mission) to interpret this collective will, and to impose its vision of the less "enlightened" masses. One can think in terms of three varieties of this sort of nationalism.

1. *Conservative nationalism* is often associated with Christian democracy and folk traditionalism. Although its proponents formally recognize the importance of individual rights, they tend to exaggerate the role of the past, the influence of the Church, and the nefarious impact of Western mass culture and liberal institutions. In many cases, these groups and parties praise pre-modern values, especially the agrarian communal bonds, and lambaste the role of financial capital and industry in destroying the pure ethno-religious community. Whether they confess it or not, conservative nationalists have a serious grudge against liberalism, which they portray as soulless, atomistic, and mechanical. The sovereignty of the people as a whole prevails in this view over the rights of the individuals. An example of such conservative nationalist party is Croatia's Democratic Union. Initially a presidential party dominated by Franjo Tudjman and his close associates, the Union split in 1994 between a moderate ("centrist") faction, advocating integration with Euro-Atlantic structures and closer cooperation with the West, and a wing made up of "Croatia first-ists" whose concerns are to crystallize a uniquely distinct Croatian ethno-linguistic identity and contemplate ways of absorbing Bosnia and Hercegovina's Croatian majority areas into an expanded "Greater Croatia." Comparable cultural revivalist, neotraditionalist, "third-way" parties exist in Slovakia, Serbia, Hungary, Romania, Ukraine, and the Baltic States.

2. *Ethnocentric populism* has developed primarily in the Balkans, but is also notable in other post-communist countries, especially in Slovakia, Hungary, and Ukraine. Its background lies in the stressful coexistence of a beleaguered and still unarticulated civil society on the one hand, and the survival of the repressive institutions, including the secret police, on the other. One could speak of the "Belgrade syndrome" of populism, in which expansionist-militaristic policies and demagogic nationalism were used to preserve the political hegemony of the communist elite around Slobodan Milošević.

The former Serbian Communist party changed its name to "Socialist," but the Leninist hypercentralism remained the basis of state authority. The ruling party, the secret police, and the army represented the pillars on which Milošević could construct his personal nationalist authoritarian regime. His rhetoric offered simple formulas for those who resented the prospects of liberalization.

Milošević cultivated the idea that military solutions would solve the country's problems. To the entranced nationalist rally at Kosovo Polje in April 1987, he solemnly pledged: "No one must ever dare to beat you again."[40] Xenophobia and national megalomania merged in Milošević's bellicose rhetoric: "if we don't know how to work and produce, we Serbs will at least know how to fight."[41]

Features of this syndrome as it has developed in other post-communist societies can be found even in Russia, where strange alliances have emerged between national fundamentalists and those who are nostalgic for the Stalinist days of "iron discipline" and imperial grandeur.[42] Initially, in 1990, the new "Russian party" (a motley coalition of groups united by nostalgia for authoritarian methods and deep anti-Western and xenophobic feelings) even adopted the name of National Salvation Front (NSF) in order to emphasize its commitment to rescuing the beleaguered Russian national values.[43] In Romania, part of this syndrome was the wedding in 1994–1995 between the then presidential ruling party (the Party of Social Democracy) and the extreme nationalist and populist parties in the joint effort to promote the ideology of the radical, anti-Western, and anti-democratic factions of the Securitate and party bureaucracy. This ideology does not claim any continuity with the interwar extreme right, but does worship the notorious ally of the Nazis, Marshal Antonescu. It claims to be leftist, but its political lexicon is jingoistic, rabidly anti-Semitic, and viscerally anti-Hungarian.

Ethnocentric populism is neither left nor right: it handles political slogans without any concern about their long-term impact, and switches policies in accordance with the immediate interests of the power elite. Serbian journalist and democratic activist Nebojsa Popov calls this continuous change of political masks the "dramaticization of power" and accurately characterizes the ethnocentric populism as used by Milošević: "Populism's aim and symbol are huge—fulfilling the destiny of the nation as a whole, as a collectivity. The concept of the individual is foreign to it. For populism, history is a totality, the future is a totality. . . . The leaders change hats and costumes. Now they are pro-war, now they are pro-peace, now they are pro-private property, now they are pro-state property, now they like the U.S., now they hate the U.S., now they like Europe, now they hate Europe."[44] The ethnocentric populist leader allies himself with extremists, co-opts them into the ruling coalition, and then, when Western pressures intensify, he gets rid of the already useless former partners, posturing as a rational and reliable politician. Deep in his heart, however, he remains convinced that Western-style capitalism is neither possible nor desirable for his country.[45]

Ethnocentric populism is chauvinistic, and conspiracy-obsessed. Serbian academician Milorad Ekmećić, one of the country's most respected historians, points out that the Vatican and its weapon, Catholic nationalism, are "the Serbs' worst enemy in history because behind it stands the Church and its monopoly on truth."[46] In the same vein, Serbian Orthodox metropolitan Amfilohije Radovic maintains that "the lightning and thunder of the Catholic and Protestant West and the Ismaelite Islamic Middle East clash over the Serbian people."[47]

This form of extreme nationalism has a strong authoritarian element—it publicly advocates a military dictatorship to put an end to corruption and to the "democratic circus"—and is therefore linked to circles in the army, and the regular and the secret police. Think of the Serbian nationalists' fascination with the Chetnik militarist traditions, the Croat rehabilitation of the Ustasha, and the Romanian National Unity party's strenuous attempts to institutionalize Antonescu's cult. These movements look to the past for models to oppose democratic individualism. Democracy is condemned as being conducive to fragmentation and heterogeneity, as creating a state of anarchy that could lead to the disintegration of the unified ethnic body. Ethnocentric populist rhetoric exalts collective values, "homogeneity," "unity," and "absolute cohesion." Some ethnocentric populist formations like the Greater Romania party glorify the old regime; others, like Serbia's Radical party under Vojislav Šešelj or the Croatian Party of Rights, claim to be viscerally anticommunist. They combine, in fact, Leninist techniques of organization with fascist practices of mass mobilization and manipulation. Sometimes, they establish paramilitary units, as in Serbia, where political adventurers like Šešelj or Zeljko Raznatović (Arkan) were provided by the Milošević regime with resources to engage in mass murders during the offensives in Croatia and Bosnia. The resuscitation of the Chetnik tradition goes hand in hand with the rehabilitation of pro-Nazi collaborators while information about war crimes committed by Serbian forces is dismissed as propaganda fomented by anti-Serbian circles (Catholic, German, and Zionist). In addition to his title of president of the Serbian radical party, Šešelj proclaimed himself "Duke Chetnik." The Serbian national memory is purged of those elements that contradict this hyper-collectivistic, authoritarian vision. Important figures of the country's history who fought for democracy and human rights are decried as inimical to national survival. Speaking of human rights is considered a national betrayal.

This is not to say that ethnocentric populism has fully triumphed in Serbia. During the December 1992 elections, one-third of the electorate voted against Milošević and huge rallies took place in December 1996 to protest electoral frauds perpetrated by the ruling Socialist party. But the civic-oriented, democratic individualist forces are still marginal and confused, whereas the nationalists enjoy almost total control over repressive institutions, ideology, and media.[48]

The case of Serbia, extreme as it is, is not totally exceptional. In Romania, the umbrella movement for former apparatchiks who lost their "chapel" is Vatra Românească (Romania Hearth), created in March 1990, a few days before the bloody ethnic clashes in Tîrgu-Mureş. Later, Vatra created its own political party, the National Unity Party of the Romanians (PUNR), with a strong anti-Hungarian political platform. During the February 1992 elections, the PUNR-Vatra candidate Gheorghe Funar was elected mayor of Cluj, where he initiated a systematic campaign against the democratic parties and primarily against the Democratic Convention (which for several years included the Hungarian Democratic Union of Romania, a political alliance built along ethnic lines).[49] In many respects, Vatra appears as an anti-democratic and anti-monarchic movement—King Michael is described by Vatra propagandists as "non-Romanian."[50] Graphic artist Radu Ceontea was Vatra's first president. In a magazine interview, Ceontea gave a clear, albeit dire description of his Hungarophobic sentiments and fearful fantasies:

> I came from a pure Romanian village in the Mures Valley. My village suffered in every possible way under the Hungarians. My father was the village butcher, and my mother had four years of schooling. The only book I knew before my school text books was the Bible. Even as a small child I was told by my father not to trust Hungarians. He told me that "every single Hungarian carries a rope in his pocket." The cord with which they would strangle Romanians. All my life I have never trusted Hungarians, but I have maintained correct relations with them. I even learned their language to a certain extent. It is a horribly complicated language. In 1968, following the invasion of Czechoslovakia, I was afraid that the Hungarians would occupy Transylvania, so I fled to the Regat (Old Kingdom). Having seen that nothing happened, I went back to my native county in 1977.[51]

Similar stories could be heard from Serbian nationalists for whom ungrateful Croats, Muslim Bosnians, and Albanians are all conspiring to destroy their country. Thus novelist Dobrica Cosić, one of the main architects of the Serbian nationalist crusade that culminated in Yugoslavia destruction wrote regarding the alleged humiliation of his nation:

> Serbs were good and courageous soldiers in war, but they were bad and frightened citizens, weak builders of life. Thus, the majority nation in Yugoslavia fell to the level of an oppressed and imprisoned majority. . . . We have invested everything we were and had in the Yugoslav idea and in a common country. In return, we were stripped of our rights, suffered under political and economic hegemony, met only indifference toward our torments and sufferings, and today we are subject to severe hatred because we no longer wish to be a lowly obeisant mass of people.[52]

Note the repetition of the collective pronoun "we": the plight was collective; the redemption, the myth postulates, must be collective as well. In this strange alloy, the nomenklatura's salvationist rhetoric merges with the neofascist discourses of hatred to generate a sui generis authoritarian ideology of national collectivism. Add to this amalgam the idealization of rural values, adamantly opposed to "decadent" urban civilization. It is hard not to agree with sociologist Zagorka Golubović, who traced a correlation between rural origin, authoritarianism, and nationalism, and insisted that Leninist-style industrialization led to increased social tensions and a "ruralization of the towns."[53] The repudiation of democracy as inherently alien to the mystically defined national soul becomes an article of faith for the entranced ethnic fundamentalist. Thus, Dragoslav Bokan, an editor and film director, who led the White Eagles, one of the many private militias involved in combat, declared: "I told my fighters they were doing exactly the same as their ancestors did and their offspring will be doing. I don't believe in democracy because I don't believe any group at any time can change the course and goals of their ancestors by their own free will."[54]

3. *Nostalgic ethnocentrism* and *liturgical nationalism* are characterized by the ideal of "national democracy," or ethnocracy and the attempt to rehabilitate the interwar extreme right movements. The most visible example is the "Movement for Romania" under former student leader Marian Munteanu, one of the principal victims of the miners' violence in June 1990.[55] The values favored by this group are primarily spiritual, and they seem linked to the ideology of conservative-populist thinkers like romantic nineteenth-century poet Mihai Eminescu and interwar philosopher Nae Ionescu. The latter claimed that only individuals born Orthodox could claim to be truly Romanians, attacked the legacy of Enlightenment as "sentimental nonsense," and became the doctrinaire of a radical revolution against liberal modernity. This movement is programmatically vague regarding the form of government it advocates, but has voiced consistent distrust of the existing political movements and parties, which are seen as opportunistic, corrupt, intellectual, and non-Romanian in their lack of interest in the real problems of the Romanians. Sociologically, it appears as a generational movement of anguish and discontent, recruiting primarily among high-school and university students as well as recent graduates. For Munteanu and his movement, Orthodoxy is the essence of Romanianness: his "Movement for Romania" is committed to introducing mandatory religious education in schools and combating the effects of "Western secular materialism."[56]

In the same vein, one notices attempts to define ethnic belonging in terms of religious affiliation and a growing interference of the Catholic Church in Poland's political debates.[57] To be sure, the rise of ethno-religious fundamentalism in Romania is closer in both program and significance to similar movements in Serbia (both countries are predominantly Orthodox) than to the clerical-authoritarian trends in Poland. What these religious nationalist trends share, however, is the common dislike of liberal values, individual rights, secular education, and market competition.

When Nationalism Meets Mythology: Guilt, Pity, and Salvation

For many intellectuals in Eastern and Central Europe, the rise of nationalism in the aftermath of communism's collapse came as a surprise. After all, the "glorious revolutions" were, with exception of Romania, peaceful and gentle. Their dominant discourse was imbued with references to the universal rights of man and citizen. It was a rediscovery of the values of Enlightenment in a space once plagued by ethnic exclusiveness and authoritarian fundamentalisms. Then, as the euphoria of emancipation dissipated, and the costs of transition affecting large social groups rose, the appeal of the discourse of civil society and human rights subsided and these countries experienced a search for new ideas that would offer the intellectual and moral cement all societies need in order not to fall apart.

Actually, the appeals of the civil-society paradigm, during the first post-revolutionary stage, as championed and articulated within the dissident subcultures of the post-totalitarian order, were to a great extent not rooted in popular experience. The majority of the populations in East-Central Europe had not been involved in the anti-systemic activities and had not appropriated the values of moral resistance. The case of Solidarity was, of course, different, but even there the normative code of civic opposition failed to generate a positive concept of the "politics of truth." In reality, dissent, in most East-Central European societies, was a marginal and not necessarily popular experience. Those belonging to the "grey area" between government and opposition tended to regard dissidents as moral challengers, neurotic outsiders, Quixotic characters with little or no understanding of the "real game." As Hungarian philosopher and former dissident G. M. Tamás put it:

> The minority within the body politic which was aware of the "dissident activities," as they were called, felt ambivalent about them. This was because the dissidents challenged the notion that political reform was the only way forward. With the emphasis on "rights" and "liberties," they also challenged the dominant political discourse of interest and naked power. . . . The essence of dissent was, or so intellectuals in "reform dictatorships" believed, the Silent Reproach. According to them, dissidents were not so much telling the leaders of the regime to "Go to hell!", as saying "Shame on you!" to the majority of bystanders.[58]

The vision of civil society, with its repudiation of hierarchical structures and skepticism of any institutional authority, showed its limits in the morally fractured and ideologically fluid post-communist order. As conventional attachments and loyalties lost their meaning and as uncertainty spread, individuals looked for points of reference in which they could recognize themselves. This has been particularly true in those Balkan societies that never developed collective dissident efforts and had little tradition of liberalism and civil society. Without exaggerating the role of civil society in Central Europe, one has to admit that it was much more developed there than in Southeastern Europe. No Charter 77, Network of Free Initiatives, or Solidarity ever came into being in Romania, Yugoslavia, Bulgaria, or Albania. Once the Leninist regimes collapsed, there was too little "usable past" for the democratic liberal forces to cling to. In the words of Slavenka Drakulić: "The myth of Europe, of our belonging to the European family and culture, even as poor relations, is gone. We have been left alone with our newly-won independence, new symbols, new autocratic leaders, but with no democracy at all."[59]

The intensity of ethnocentric populism in Southeastern Europe, especially compared to the northern part of the post-communist map, is not simply the consequence of political manipulations exerted by skillful demagogues. To understand it one has to look into local traditions, the role of national religions (especially the Orthodox Church) and their attitude toward the state, the interpenetration between communism and Stalinism in the pre-1989 local political cultures and, in the cases of Romania and Albania, the extreme isolation from the outside world. Add to this the absence of any thorough examination of the pre-communist experiences, the mystification of the anti-fascist resistance, and the communist distortions of ethnic relations. In this respect, the Balkans exacerbate the cultural dilemmas of post-communism. Precisely because of the weakness of civic traditions and of liberal memories, these societies are different from their Central European neighbors. True, dissidents were always a minority in Hungary and Czechoslovakia, but they created a concept of freedom that was fundamental for the new, post-1989 polities. Balkan cultures, on the other hand, have always had a problematic relationship with the concept of universal individual rights, tolerance of alterity, admission of ethnic diversity, and full equality under law. This is not to deny the existence of liberal and pluralist traditions, but simply to acknowledge their precariousness.

One of the key elements in interpreting the rise of nationalism as a political myth in post-communist societies is the role of intellectuals and their relationship with the West. In Central Europe, there has always been a strong Westernizing wing among the national intelligentsias. The fact that, with few exceptions, mainstream contemporary Hungarian intellectuals have not drifted toward the populist right is connected to their acceptance of the most important lesson of the twentieth century, namely, that the main conflict has not been between communism and fascism but rather between collectivistic ideologies and liberal individualism. The sad consequences of endorsing one or another ideocratic pathology has not passed unnoticed in Central Europe, whereas the same can hardly be said about the Balkans. True, in each of these countries there are liberal and illiberal visions of the nation. But whereas in Poland, for instance, the demythologizing exploration of the past has been a major endeavor of the intellectuals, in the Balkans the trend has been to cover up the shameful pages of national history and to fabricate new messianic, self-indulging fantasies.

The word "fantasies" is used here to refer to an ensemble of collective visions and emotions that offer explanations for the main difficulties of the transition. The truth of these fantasies is not the issue, because in the case of myths what matters is their credibility rather than their accuracy: "Myths are . . . believed to be true, not because historical evidence is compelling, but because they make sense of men's present experience."[60] And when this experience is perceived as intolerably painful, the need for myth becomes irresistible. What the nationalist myth offers is consolation, the bliss of community, a simple way to overcome feelings of humiliation and inferiority, and a response to real or imaginary threats. Furthermore, the nationalist explosion can be seen as a "perverse effect" of the revolutionary changes unleashed by the revolutions of 1989–1991. This is not to say that the revolutions failed, or that they created situations worse than those supposed to have been overthrown. "Reactionary rhetoric" ignores the fact that nationalism survived during the communist years in distorted and surreptitious ways, that it had permeated the official doctrines, and that the revolutions of 1989–1991 only created the framework for its full-fledged expression and possible transcendence.[61]

As early as 1987, Romanian dissident mathematician Mihai Botez proposed the "ethno-communist state" as a prognosis for the future of the states in the region. He insisted that in order to stay in power, the techno-bureaucratic elites would increasingly abandon the anachronistic paraphernalia of Marxism-Leninism and espouse the more appealing symbols of national interests.[62] To preserve their monopoly on power they would practice the demagogy of "the fatherland is in danger" and would indulge in any ideological travesty, including the adoption of long-denied religious and patriotic values. That this prediction did not come true immediately is not relevant here: the fact is that after the demise of the corrupt and incompetent Leninist bureaucracies, the new elites—often recruited from among the second echelons of the previous ones—did behave along the lines anticipated by Botez. Think of Ion Iliescu's or Boris Yeltsin's participation in Orthodox religious ceremonies, not to speak of Milošević's direct mobilization of the Serbian clergy to give religious benediction to the politics of ethnic cleansing. Another example is the transmogrification of Ukraine's former president Leonid Kravchuk from hard-line Leninist ideologue and sworn enemy of Ukrainian nationalism to born-again Ukrainian patriot.[63]

The illiberal trends associated with ethnocentric movements are apparent in the case of playwright István Csurka and his splinter group from the Magyar

Democratic Forum, Hungary's ruling party between 1990 and 1994. According to their views, citizenship is ethnically defined, and therefore one cannot be simultaneously Hungarian and Jewish, or Hungarian and Slovak. Furthermore, this doctrine rehabilitates the Nazi myth about the invisible but therefore more dangerous joint Jewish and communist plot to enslave the Hungarian nation.[64] After his expulsion from the MDF in 1993, Csurka established his own political movement, significantly called the "Hungarian Road Circles" and, as a political arm, the "Hungarian Justice Party."[65] Using the rhetoric of justice, retribution, and volkisch traditionalism, Csurka and his followers claim to fight for the preservation of the "Hungarian soul" against the soiling influence of Western symbols and values. That Csurka did not succeed in earning any significant electoral support in the 1994 elections is of course a promising signal. At the same time, views close to his have surfaced among politicians of the more mainstream parties, especially the Smallholders' leader Jozsef Torgyan.[66]

In Slovakia, former prime minister and anti-communist dissident Jan Carnogursky spelled out unambiguous anti-liberal and anti-Western views when he stated: "Liberalism threatens the necessary balance between different groups in society . . . , promotes a culture of artificial consumption . . . , promotes an environment which divorces the individual from values of morality and the articles of . . . [and] allows the individual to do everything, but forgets that the devil is present in human soul."[67]

These nationalist parties and movements have a tendency to indulge in self-pity: we Poles (or Slovaks, or Ukrainians, or Serbs, or Croats) have been the ultimate victims. According to this self-serving philosophy, no other nation has ever suffered as much as the one of the speaker (or writer, or historian), who cannot understand why the outer world is so insensitive to his or her nation's unique plight. When all established certainties have been shattered, nationalism appears as the balm needed to soothe the wounds of the disaffected and disgruntled. In the whole region, half a decade after the collapse of communism, there is a growing nostalgia for the pre-Communist national and cultural values, and this explains the resurrection of the messianic myth of the nation, the burning belief in its regenerative power as a spiritual remedy able to relieve the "pain of the wound to group consciousness" (Isaiah Berlin) left by the communist experience. Polish historians, for instance, frequently describe their Poland as the "Christ of nations," always victimized, attacked and persecuted by its neighbors. Serbs and Romanians speak about their national destiny to rescue civilization from Ottoman invasions. According to these mythologies, suffering under communism bestowed on the speaker's (or writer's) nation a special universal destiny. Each ethnic group indulges in its own martyrology, frequently regarded as the most atrocious, and the most conducive to moral regeneration. Inebriated with self-serving delusions, the ethnocentric militant acts like a true believer, rejecting the relativity of all national myths. Discourses are created to legitimize the organic identification with the ethnic community. Thus, Arthur Koestler's bitter diagnosis sound eeringly timely: "Wars are fought for words. They are man's most deadly weapon."[68]

Demonizing the Foreigner

Extreme nationalism and xenophobia are synonymous. Their psychological underpinning is the belief that the whole world is conspiring to ruin one's own community. For the ethnocentric prophets in Romania or Russia, Serbia or Croatia, Slovakia or Poland, the foreigners (more often than not the Jews) were the ones who imported and imposed communism, institutionalized terror, and propagated the alien ideology of Marxism-Leninism. In this Manichean scheme, communists were foreigners, the new leaders are foreigners, dissenters are foreigners, or wimps, or traitors paid by occult secret services.

Conspiracy theories abound, from Serbia to Poland and from Romania to Russia. Russian mathematician and former dissident Igor Shafarevich has written extensively about the plot of the "little nation" (meaning Jews, Masons, liberal intelligentsia), carrier of a "nihilistic ideology" that strives toward the "ultimate destruction of the religious and national foundations of life."[69] As nostalgia for communism has merged with the exaltation of militarist and fascist symbols, the myth of the universal "Judeo-Masonic" and "Wall Street" conspiracy has become the ingredient for strong anti-Western, anti-capitalist, anti-Semitic and anti-intellectual attitudes. Yuri Belov, a top ideologue of Gennady Zyuganov's neo-Bolshevik party, sees Russia as the victim of the CIA, of mistreatment by its neighbors, and of an unfortunate historical destiny: "We are a special culture and a special civilization. You can't ignore these traditions. We were always in danger of occupation. Under the present regime we have occupation not from the outside but from the inside. The government is destroying and co-opting our national way of life. . . . The state must be saved."[70]

With few Jews in the region, anybody can be described as a Jew by the nationalist zealots. For instance, a Polish eccentric politician can claim that Pope John Paul II, Lech Walesa, the majority of the Catholic bishops, all three of the Polish cardinals, and 30 percent of the Polish clergy are Jews.[71] Less eccentric and certainly more effective was the persistent innuendo during the Polish 1991 elections that Tadeusz Mazowiecki was a converted Jew and that the whole intellectual elite of the anti-Communist underground was controlled by Jews. Being identified as "Jewish" has become the symbolic equivalent of being pro-Western, pluralist-oriented, opposed to nationalist pageants, or simply decent. In the same vein, the anti-Semitic or anti-Gypsy propaganda is an expression of anti-capitalist and anti-liberal sentiment.[72] The Roma

(Gypsy) population has become a convenient target for outbursts of hatred: the largest and least protected minority in Europe, its members are frequently accused of fraudulent use of the market economy, cheating, robbing the national economy, and all the sins traditionally assigned to the Jews. The protection of the Roma is indeed a major challenge for the emerging democracies, and the mounting wave of Gypsy activism, including the formation of their own national parties and movements, offer some hope that the politics of exclusion will not prevail.[73]

Conclusion: Tribalization or Cooperation?

To different degrees, all the countries in the post-communist world are confronted with a tension between ethnocentric-authoritarian trends and pluralist-liberal directions. They are battlefields between proponents of liberal values and those who advocate the supremacy of the homogeneous and self-enclosed nation state.[74] However, by simply decrying nationalist demagogy we do not get the whole picture; the truth is that we are dealing now in both East and Central Europe and in the former Soviet Union with the triumph of political demagogy. The former dissidents have been marginalized and their successors have tried to stir responsive chords among increasingly embittered and disenchanted populations. It is therefore important, as Steven Sestanovich insists, to distinguish between illiberal and liberal demagogues. Among the latter, one can identify nationalist demagogues whose ideology is strongly influenced by anti-communism. Taking the case of Rukh movement in the Ukraine, Sestanovich concludes: "anticommunism helps to build a national identity that is not simply ethnic. If the Ukraine evolves successfully toward democracy, liberal demagogues— liberal *nationalist* demagogues, at that—are likely to deserve much of the credit."[75] In addition, the presence of intermediary institutions and associations, usually described as civil society, is an element that can diminish the risk of exaggerated nationalist fever and the transformation of fundamentalist rhetoric into an ideology of pogroms. Cities like Sarajevo, the cosmopolitan, multicultural capital of Bosnia, or Timisoara in the Western Romanian province of Banat, are examples which show that interethnic cooperation is indeed possible. An active civil society can hold in check nationalist passions and animosities, as long as the institutional framework is based on consensus and legitimacy. In post-communist societies, the objective of civic-oriented groups and parties is to create a sense of identification with the democratic process. The vision of citizenry as a cultural, rather than ethno-religious identity, still prevailing in Ukraine, is perhaps a beginning that could inspire other countries as well.

Radical nationalism operates with mythological constructs and brandishes the specter of the country's dismemberment (or of the persecution of national minorities abroad). The enemy is needed in order to create a false sentiment of solidarity—one based on fear and suspicion, rather than trust and consensus—and to avoid the transition to a true pluralism. "Who profits?" is therefore a ligitimate question when trying to discover the origins of ethnic tensions in post-Communist societies; in the case of Croatia or Serbia, it is obvious that the power elite have an interest in preserving a climate of fear and instability. Critical intellectuals are described as "Trojan horses" and a universal conspiracy against "national interests" is concocted in order to keep the authoritarian (or semi-authoritarian) regime in power.

Nationalism will not vanish in the foreseeable future. National identities are part of modernity and they will continue to inspire strong emotions, attachments, and arduous commitments. These nationalisms, however, do not need to be mutually destructive. Minorities can be encouraged to be part of the construction of a tolerant and diversified civilization. As European unification proceeds and East and Central European nations come closer to supranational institutions and structures, the traditional cult of sacred boundaries may turn out to be obsolete. It may be hoped that as a result of these integrative trends many East and Central Europeans will remember their authoritarian and populist leaders in the same way that Spaniards remember Franco, or Germans think of their country's historical catastrophes. For salvationism to function as a mobilizing belief system, there needs to be a widespread sense of danger. If economic transitions succeed, civil societies develop, and political life becomes consensual, such myths would lose their vindictive power. Hatred and envy will always be part of human existence, but their political impact is related to the ways human beings organize themselves and to their ability to transcend time-honored animosities and destructive follies.

Four

Scapegoating Fantasies: Fascism, Anti-Semitism, and Myth Making in East Central Europe

> We are here to remember what happened and sol-
> emnly say that "They" must not do it again.
> *(Umberto Eco, 1995)*

FAILED EXPECTATIONS result in anger and a loss of morale. The much-acclaimed advent of democratic societies in the post-communist world has turned out to be a more problematic and convoluted process than was initially thought. After the early stage of civic enthusiasm and cheerful pan-European slogans, these societies have discovered that they are very much on their own, and that Europe (or the West) is not necessarily eager to accept them as full-fledged members of the "club." True, the Berlin Wall perished as a palpable and disgraceful symbol of separation between two worlds, one of rights and prosperity (however imperfect they might be), the other ruled by power-ridden, corrupt oligarchs and plagued with scarcity, suspicion, and fear. But it has become increasingly clear that the differences between East and West (many of which predated communism) have outlived the demise of Leninism.

As people learned that political emancipation is not accompanied by immediate economic improvement, many developed nostalgic sentiments for the bygone days of authoritarian certainties. What followed in East-Central Europe (including Russia and other countries of the former Soviet Union) has been, in many respects, a climate of despondency, with dashed illusions and bitter recriminations. The question of "who is to blame?" has resurfaced as the main political slogan. Old mythologies of betrayal, abandonment, and victimhood have returned, often brandished by self-appointed national redeemers. When the individual feels inescapably estranged and experiences the surrounding world as a moral vacuum, there is ground for the rise of new varieties of intolerance. The politics of stigma and rage are rooted in excruciating sentiments of damaged dignity and wounded pride. Liberal individualism is accused of hypocrisy and parliamentarism is seen as a springboard for corrupt politicians. In times of social disruption and moral chaos, radical nationalist mythologies articulate the grievances of those who believe that their community is treated condescendingly by other groups (internal of external).

These myths construct sinister visions of the infiltrated enemy, which they usually associate with the "democratic mentality." Thus, even in 1904 Italian writer Giovanni Papini, a main inspirer of Mussolini's fascist doctrine, gave vent to this hatred for the democratic liberal establishment: "In order to love something deeply, you have to hate something else. No Good Christian can love God without loathing the Devil."[1] The Devil was the "internal enemy."

In a classical work on the rise of Nazism published in 1942, exiled German political philosopher Sigmund Neumann linked Hitler's success to the existence of large groups of unemployed individuals, disoriented by the reigning political chaos and unable to see a future for themselves within the liberal order. Without overplaying the analogies between the German situation of the 1930s and present-day Eastern Europe, one cannot ignore the persistence of strong chauvinist sentiments among the citizens of the post-Communist world.[2] These disaffected masses (primarily industrial workers, the losers within the privatization process, but also the growing intellectual proletariat) can be easily exhilarated and manipulated by the jargon of political warfare against infiltrated enemies, rapacious plutocrats, and foreign conspiracies: "They represent, one may say, the 'political reserve army' of our days. . . . They are political driftwood. They simply indicate the high tide that can burst the dikes. The permanently unemployed endanger the existing order; they also endanger the revolution. Their radicalism is not genuine. It does not go back to basic issues, to the roots of social and political evils. It has no roots because they themselves are not rooted in society. Their revolution is above all destructive. It is action, but not responsible activism. It is a 'revolution of nihilism.'"[3]

We should not forget that, in addition to being a terrorist ideology and a murderous dictatorship, national socialism was a mass temptation generated by unbearable angst and discontent with liberal institutions. In the words of historian Fritz Stern: "The temptation before 1933 was to believe in Hitler as a savior, to believe in a national rebirth. The path to National Socialism led through a wasteland of personal fears, collective anxiety, and resentments. The temptation was to surrender oneself to a dictator, to believe in a miracle. Hitler evoked human will and divine providence. . . . . Many people found it easy to overlook what was ominous and radically evil in National Socialism. They clutched at the pseudo-religious aspect of it, the promise of salvation held out so cleverly and on so many levels."[4] From our perspective this soteriological appeal of radical nationalism is crucially important: it promises deliverance through renunciation of one's critical faculties, it lambastes the liberal West for selfishness and lack of compassion, and mobilizes mob instincts in the name of ethnic purity.

What has happened in Serbia after the breakdown of Yugoslavia is the epitome of this politics of national hysteria: political values have been subordinated to the ultimate purpose of national grandeur, defined through the exclusion of all those who do not belong because of blood, confession, or simply cultural preferences. Nationalism has become a state creed, a primordialist myth employed as an instrument of war and of delirious propaganda engineered by history-obsessed intellectuals allied with power-thirsty apocalytical demagogues like Slobodan Milošević. In the words of Warren Zimmermann, the last American ambassador to Belgrade: "The breakup of Yugoslavia is a classic example of nationalism from the top down—a manipulated nationalism in a region where peace has historically prevailed more than war and in which a quarter of the population were in mixed marriages. The manipulators condoned and even provoked ethnic violence in order to engender animosities that could then be magnified by the press, leading to further violence."[5] Although it is true that many post-communist societies have adopted the dream of the ethnically homogenous community as an ideal, only Serbia has turned it into a bellicose, all-embracing ideology, supported by the massive material and human infrastructure of the Yugoslav army.

On the other hand, we should not be oblivious of the role of ethnocentric authoritarianism as state policy in Croatia, as well. For Croat president and self-styled historian Franjo Tudjman, deep-seated nationalist commitments are rooted in an all-embracing, infra-rational emotional matrix: "one can neither suppress or wipe out the inexplicable primeval links with one's native hearth."[6] Croatian writer Slavenka Drakulić captured grippingly the homogenizing reduction of one's identity to the bare fact of belonging to the pseudo-transcendent community of origins: "Along with millions of other Croats, I was pinned to the wall of nationhood—not only by outside pressure from Serbia and the Federal Army but by national homogenization within Croatia itself. That is what the war is doing to us, reducing us to one dimension: the Nation. The trouble with this nationhood, however, is that whereas before, I was defined by my education, my job, my ideas, my character—and, yes, my nationality too—now I feel stripped of all that. I am nobody because I am not a person any more. I am one of the 4.5 million Croats."[7]

Agrarian, pastoral, neoromantic visions of ethnic purity are used to oppose civic individualism. Westernizing liberals are considered "rootless cosmopolitans" unable to feel the mysterious appeals of ethnicity. It may be of an exaggeration to consider that a "clash of civilizations" is the overarching explanation for the bloody ethnic conflicts of this fin-de-siècle. At the same time, it is true that the Balkans have become the laggards of the transition, and that local elites in the countries once controlled by the Ottoman and Czarist empires have espoused ethnic rather than civic definitions of their nations. But again, this is not simply a matter of religious or cultural heritage, and Samuel Huntington underestimates the impact of communist legacies and the role of contemporary elites when he writes: "The Velvet Curtain of culture has replaced the Iron Curtain of ideology as the most significant dividing line in Europe."[8] The sources of these new movements of hatred and rage are political, not just cultural or civilizational. It is political elites (or their "organic" intellectuals) who manufacture the narratives of exclusion that later become ammunition for illiberal demagogues. It is also the intellectual elites who are responsible for the continuous rewriting (or cleansing) of history in terms of self-serving, present-oriented interests.[9]

The stronger the feelings of isolation, historical marginality, and social stress, the greater the temptation to scapegoat those who are perceived as different, "abnormal." In racist fantasies this presumed abnormality reaches monstrous proportions, as in spiteful cartoons attributing to Jews (or Blacks) physical deformities or disabilities. Magic and mystery blend in the exorcising processions, in the symbolic rituals of persecution bound to cement the community's organic unity: "Thanks to the mechanism of persecution, collective anguish and frustration found vicarious appeasement in the victims who easily found themselves united in opposition to them by virtue of being poorly integrated minorities."[10] At the same time, René Girard adds, scapegoating is not simply an attribution of guilt based on conscious falsification of historical evidence. The psychic mechanism is more complex, and the scapegoater is truly convinced that the victim fully deserves the punishment: "the persecutors believe in the guilt of their victim; they are imprisoned in the illusion of persecution that is no simple idea but a full system of representation. Imprisonment in this system allows us to speak of an unconscious persecutor, and the proof of his existence lies in the fact that those in our day who are the most proficient in discovering other people's scapegoats, and God knows we are past masters at this, are never able to recognize their own."[11]

The alleged threat to the survival of the community is thus identified with those individuals and groups who, because of their origins, religion, or cultural patterns, cannot be reduced to the homogenizing identity of the in-group. Dissidents, critical intellectuals, and ethnic or sexual minorities are thus stigmatized as pathogenic, infectious agents of dissolution ("vermin") and designated for exclusion, expulsion or, in the most extreme cases, extermination.[12] Radovan Karadžić spelled out this impulse when he admitted that his vision for Sarajevo, a city which for centuries existed as a symbol of interethnic tolerance and civility, "is like Berlin when the Wall was still standing."[13] The outsider, thus demonized, must be forcibly eliminated to protect the cohesion of the ethnic group as a community of origins, memory, and destiny. In his egregious way, Vladimir Zhirinovsky, the Russian extreme nationalist demagogue, has bluntly stated this rejection of the multiethnic nation state: "The notion behind internationalism is that of mixture; nationalism comprises the notion of quality. Nationalism is like a self-contained flat and not a communal boarding house. . . . If we acknowledge that we are constructing a national state, with a national ideology and without any kind of 'Eurasianism' or 'Atlantism', then our first task is to establish national frontiers. They must be clearly defined and then locked tight."[14]

Within this discriminatory logic, the Jew appears as the foreigner par excellence, the seditious force that threatens the ethnic paradise. Anti-Semitism as a political myth is used not because of its content of truth, which is irrelevant in this context, but because of its emotional impact. As Georges Sorel said, political myths "are not descriptions of things, but expressions of a determination to act."[15]

The existence of a sinister, conspiratorial Other, constructed as an omnipotent and fully unified group, is a fantasy meant to save the members of the dominant nation from figuring out their own needs and real interests. Even the Holocaust appears to the anti-Semite as a Jewish invention meant to instill a sense of guilt and shame among the gentiles. The uniqueness and very unthinkability of the Shoah is discarded in the name of the horrors perpetrated by Stalinism: the Gulag (tendentiously associated with the Jewish presence within the communist repressive apparatus) is used as an argument against those who call for an examination of the fascist past. Slovene sociologist and psychoanalytical thinker Slavoj Žižek accurately describes the anti-Semitic fantasies as expressions of the neurotic reactions to the impossibility of a fully homogeneous, corporate-like national entity. One may even say that totalitarian movements (rightist or leftist) need such a designated Other to achieve their mobilizational ends: "The 'Jew' is the means, for Fascism, of taking into account, of representing its own impossibility: in its positive presence, it is only the embodiment of the ultimate impossibility of the totalitarian project. . . . The whole Fascist ideology is structured as a struggle against the element which holds the place of the immanent impossibility of the very Fascist project: the 'Jew' is nothing but a fetishistic embodiment of a certain fundamental blockage."[16]

The reification of the "Jew" in the figure of the menacing alien goes hand in hand with the parochial fetishization of national history and the indignant denunciation of any attempt to demystify it. Calls for dispelling the pseudo-sacred aura surrounding the pro-Nazi or merely authoritarian figures of the past (Romanian Marshal Ion Antonescu, Hungarian regent Admiral Miklos Horthy, or the post-Pilsudski Polish colonels' regime) are seen by many East Europeans—politicians or simple citizens—as efforts to diminish their national dignity, to offend their sense of honor, and blacken their past. When all other sources of self-pride and collective identity have vanished, the past becomes a principle of legitimation, and myths are resurrected to justify one group's historical primordiality, cultural preeminence, and superior claims to territorial domination. German romantic philosopher Johann Gottlob Fichte's impassioned call, the foundation stone of modern nationalism, is music to the ear of Eastern Europe's ethnocentric militants: "The noble-minded man's belief in the eternal continuance of his influence even on this earth is thus founded on the hope of the eternal continuance of the people from which he has developed, and the characteristic of that people as indicated in the hidden law of which we have spoken, without admixture of, or corruption by, any alien element which does not belong to the totality of the functions of that law."[17] Ethnic or other minorities are thus treated as sources of unrest, divisive and cantankerous groups whose loyalty to national survival is seen as dubious. They must be silenced for the language of the dominant group to run supreme.

The Past That Never Fades

The denial of the past and a stubborn indulgence in a mixture of self-pity and self-idealization seems now to be contagious in Eastern Europe's protodemocracies—and not only there. Think of the endless German, French, Italian, and Austrian debates about resistance, collaboration, and complicity in the genocidal actions during World War II. In France, it took more than two decades after the end of World War II for the political establishment to admit the staunch anti-Semitism that had been at the core of the Vichy regime, and the widespread collaboration of French officials (both in the Vichy-controlled area and the Nazi-occupied part of France) with the Germans in the deportation of Jews to the extermination camps. Former socialist President François Mitterrand's stance (consistent in this respect with the time-honored Gaullist approach) was that an institutional and legal chasm separated the French state and the Vichy regime and that there was therefore no need for the Republic to apologize for the crimes committed by an illegitimate government.[18] Even now it appears scandalous to many French intellectuals to affirm, together with Isaiah Berlin or Zeev Sternhell, that France, rather than Germany was the birthplace of Fascist ideology.[19]

The trivialization of fascism has become rampant. For example, Italy's Gianfranco Fini, the leader of the neofascist National Alliance, brought into the political mainstream by the watershed March 1994 elections, bluntly praised dictator Benito Mussolini as "the greatest statesman of the century."[20] Several years ago such a statement would have provoked moral shock, but it seems that many Italians have forgotten what fascism was about: a system that denied individual rights, made a mockery of justice, annihilated civil society, subordinated the citizen to an all-controlling and all-pervasive police state, and treated entire groups as subhumans.[21] The electoral success of the Italian post- or neofascists is part of a trend toward redefining right-wing radicalism and providing it with a veneer of respectability and a rhetoric responsive to the growing anti-foreign and anti-immigrant sentiment in these countries. This post-modern fascism is not explicitly anti-Semitic, although it expresses nostalgia for regimes and leaders that made racism the cornerstone of their politics. In the words of Italian sociologist Franco Ferrarotti: "I would define them as diluted Fascists. It's a kind of respectable, presentable fascism, although that's an oxymoron. And they express the mood of this country, a very conservative country where many people have made it and made it quickly. They want to keep it, so they go to the right."[22] To achieve their revisionist goals and rewrite history in accordance to their views, the neofascists have been silent on Mussolini's post-1938 anti-Semitic policies and focused instead on his early achievements in public works, administration, and anti-corruption campaigns.

In Austria, Jörg Haider, leader of the rightist Freedom party, has spewed xenophobic slogans, appealing to those sectors of the electorate disenchanted with the established party system. Haider has often combined anti-immigrant stances and populist calls for "an Austria for the Austrians" with intense rejection of social democratic policies. The anti-establishment rhetoric serves Haider to posture as the would-be national redeemer. According to him: "In Italy the political system is collapsing because it is corrupt. In Austria it will also be the same over the next few years, and a completely new political system will be the result."[23] We recognize in this statement the combination of revolutionary, anti-establishment fervor and xenophobic passion which has always been the sign of fascism.

These neorightist movements use discourses of national self-defense to attack their liberal opponents. The evil is identified in both the weaknesses of the liberal system (decried as the "humanitarian ethos") and the foreigners who take advantage of the generous asylum and immigration policies. Tolerance is often presented as the main threat to the future of the country—an expression of liberal wimpishness—and pluralist values are caricatured to allow the new radicals to appear as champions of "law and order." In the words of Italian neofascist youth leader Giuseppe Scopelitti: "The difference between us and the left is values. The left favors abortion and euthanasia, while we are opposed. The left wants to liberalize drug use, and we are against it. We believe the family should be the center of society, and we don't like to see a Europe that authorizes homosexual marriages." [24] The same views have frequently been voiced by French rightists grouped in Jean-Marie Le Pen's National Front.

In Germany, the Nazi past remains a continuous referent that motivates contemporary political and strategic choices. Symptomatic is the soul-searching historical debate (*Historikerstreit*) on the uniqueness of the Holocaust, a discussion provoked primarily by historian Ernst Nolte's relativization of the Nazi genocidal dictatorship as part of the "European civil war"; it is part of a conservative intellectual trend committed to restoring German national pride.[25] The decision to move the capital city from Bonn to Berlin by the year 2000 has stirred heated debates and polemics between those who think that the past should not control the present, and those, like social philosopher Jürgen Habermas, who fear that the old demons of German nationalism could be awakened as a result of this restoration of a traditional symbol of imperial power. This danger should not be overestimated, however. Democratic traditions have coalesced in Germany, and no mainstream political party or movement is seriously challenging the country's constitutional consensus. The German experience shows that in democratic polities the exercise of confronting and coming to terms with the past has benefited from free access to archival resources, the existence of networks of unfettered communication, and the established traditions of free circulation of ideas and information.[26]

The nostalgia for a romanticized past and the growth of violence-prone, xenophobic movements in the advanced democracies are not a revival of fascism or Nazism in their original sense. Few of these groups have adopted Hitler's biological racism and his monomaniacal fixation on the Jews. In focusing on ethnic differences and calling for the exclusion of the non-belonging minorities, the neofascists are aggravating an unavowed racist trend existing within the liberal states. But it would be an exaggeration to go as far as French political philosopher Etienne Balibar, to say that "racism has become universalized."[27] In reality, what has become universalized is a search for roots, a yearning for identifying bonds that, because they appeal to warm emotions and cherished memories, can play the role of a secular creed. After all, the origin of the term "religion" is most likely found in the Latin *religare*: to link, to tie fast. As historian John Lukacs notes, the fact that the neofascist Italian Social Movement changed its name to National Alliance suggests more than a tactical device: "Nationalism, in one form or another, is still the most powerful political force in the world, a surrogate religion. . . . But the era of dictatorships, especially in Europe, is past. Nostalgia is often an element in politics, but never its governing force."[28]

This may well be the case in consolidated democracies, but it is doubtful that one may be so certain about the post-communist world. Citizens of the post-communist societies desperately look for sources of self-esteem, and there is little in their present that would offer rewarding psychological incentives. No one can deny that most of these societies have been long deprived of their natural and legitimate national pride. The problem is, however, that in its exclusive form, nationalism ceases to be a liberating force and becomes a coercive one. In times of social and institutional turmoil, one group's claim to dignity is seen as irreconcilable with others' similar aspirations: "full-blown nationalism has arrived at the position that, if the satisfaction of the needs of the organism to which I belong turns out to be incompatible with the fulfillment of the goals of other groups, I, or the society to which I indissolubly belong, have no choice but to force them to yield, if need be by force."[29]

For the radical nationalists in post-communist Hungary, Poland, Russia or Romania, it is again the Jew, the liberal, the critical intellectual (as embodiments of the Other) who are concocted as the source of all evils.[30] In addition, whatever the communists endorsed tends to be demonized. If the communists claimed to be Marxists, the hypernationalist argument goes, there must have been something evil at the very bottom of the socialist idea, a secret desire to enslave these nations and impose "Judaic" domination. In the West, such ideas are primarily found in the lunatic fringe. The same thing can not be said about the post-communist societies, where fantasies of persecution offer immediate mental gratification to large strata of frustrated individuals.

In Eastern Europe and the former Soviet Union, the vestiges of long-perpet-
uated and jealously guarded historical fallacies and self-serving fabrications
have become part of the new vindictive as well as redemptive mythologies.
Nationalist narratives of hatred have emerged that ascribe the guilt for all that
happened to foreigners, to those "who brought communism." This is clearly
the case in Russia, where the motley black-red coalition (Stalinists, fascists,
Black Hundreds, orthodox fundamentalists) uses the myth of Judeo-communism to offer immediate scapegoats for the popular discontent and widespread
sentiment of historical failure. Gennady Zyuganov's political writings blend
the "white" themes of heroic nationalism and imperial grandeur with the "red"
exaltation of equality and social justice: "By unifying the 'red' ideal of social
justice, which is in its own way, the early substantiation of a 'heavenly truth,'
namely that 'all are equal before God,' with the 'white' ideal of the nationally
conceived statehood, understood as the form of existence of the centuries-old
holy ideals of the people, Russia will obtain, at last, the long-awaited social
consensus of all strata and classes as well as restore supreme state power,
bequeathed to it by the tens of generations of ancestors, acquired through
their suffering and courage, and sanctified by the grief of the heroic history of
the Fatherland!"[31]

In all post-communist societies, political operators use popular prejudice
and superstitions to mobilize anger and designate certain ethno-cultural or
religious groups as collectively guilty for their country's predicament. If Slovakia is internationally isolated, the causes are not its government's hostility to
liberal values but the evil machinations of the Zionists and the Hungarians. In
the same vein, if Croatia receives criticism for the authoritarian policies of its
president, Franjo Tudjman, the blame is transferred upon the Serbs or, again,
the Jews. As for Serbia, it is not its aggression against Bosnia and the persecution of Albanians in Kosovo that explain the country's pariah status within the
international community, but rather some bizarre world conspiracy fomented
by Germany, the Vatican, and, of course, the Jewish-controlled Western
media.

There is no more persistent, enduring, and tragically effective mythology of
scapegoating and vindictiveness than anti-Semitism. Implicitly or explicitly,
anti-Semitism has accompanied the political and cultural evolutions of most
of these nations during their delayed and often distorted modernization. As a
general rule, their encounter with modernity coincided with the Jewish emancipation, the struggle for minority rights, and the decline of feudal, agrarian,
and communitarian forms of existence. Jews were seen as agents of transformation and innovation. Furthermore, their association with capitalist
practices and institutions permitted the blending of anti-industrialism, anti-
Westernism, and xenophobia into a resentful conglomerate. The anti-democratic and anti-capitalist nationalism of the interwar period had anti-Semitism
as its core ideological component. Now that the market economy has re-

emerged and individuals are faced with unexpected economic hardships, the public outbursts of old animosities and hatreds is not entirely accidental. One may even say that they have always been there, but less noticeable because of the camouflage created by Leninist jargon. In reality, collectivism and distrust of liberal principles were consistently inculcated by communist propaganda.

The paradox is that anti-Semitism functions these days in Eastern Europe (but not in the former Soviet Union) in the almost complete absence of its intended and palpable target: the Jews. A striking expression of the ultimate irony of this situation is a joke circulating in Poland: "Why do you have anti-Semitism when there are no Jews any more?" "For the same reasons we have traffic jams although we don't have cars." In other words, anti-Semitism serves primarily a symbolic function, in that it identifies the nonexisting Jews with the causes of national disasters from communism to the effects of economic liberalism during the transition stage, including skyrocketing prices, plummeting living standards, huge social gaps, and rising unemployment.

The meaning of anti-Semitism is primarily linked to the need to find an immediate figure for the enemy. Historically transmitted by cultural, often religious traditions, anti-Semitic stereotypes are thus reintegrated into the political discourse by the advocates of the ethnically pure community. In the words of István Bibo, a major Hungarian political thinker, "anti-Semites are those who have acquired a coherent image regarding various dangerous attributes of the Jews, their cupidities and cheatings, their cynicism destructive of moral and political values, and their appetite for vengeance and power. From this point of view, the anti-Semite can be honest or venal, tender or bloodthirsty, innocent or culpable, what matters is that *he carries with him a fixed and deformed image of a fragment of social reality*."[32] Indeed, it is characteristic of the anti-Semitic imagination that it operates with full-fledged, self-contained fantasies of destructiveness, plots, and betrayal.

In its post-romantic, Wagnerian anti-capitalist form, anti-Semitism opposed the myth of blood (pure, untainted by mechanical civilization) to the all-corruptive and corroding power of gold. As democratic capitalism itself was attacked as a degenerate civilization, Jews appeared as "infectious" agents of national destruction. German anti-Semitic writer August Julius Langbehn could thus write in 1891, in the thirty-seventh edition of his influential book *Rembrandt als Erzieher* (Rembrandt as Educator): "The modern, plebeian Jews are a poison for us and will have to be treated as such."[33] Jews were thus essentialized as enemies of the soul, incarnations of demonic efforts to dissolve the organic community rooted in shared bonds of ancestry, mores, and destiny. Associated with the Enlightenment and its ideals of tolerance and universal civic rights, Jews were targeted as the main enemies by all those for whom modernity, that is, capitalism and liberal democracy, appeared as a social and moral catastrophe: romantic thinkers, Catholic doctrinaires, social demagogues, and racist maniacs.[34]

One should not exaggerate: similarities do not mean full repetitions, and Eastern Europe has not returned to its interwar politics of exclusion, when the rulers considered the persecution of Jews and other minorities as a respectable means of legitimation. Whatever the popular sentiment in post-communist societies, mainstream opinion makers and political personalities have condemned such spiteful forms of xenophobia. Western influence in this rejection of traditional anti-Semitic stances is significant: for instance, under Western pressure, Romania's former president Ion Iliescu frequently distanced himself from the attempts to rehabilitate Marshal Antonescu, although members of the government and other supporters of the ruling coalition were active in the revisionist campaigns. According to them, no Holocaust ever took place in Romania, Jews enjoyed a privileged status compared to that in other countries, and Antonescu should be lionized as a "good man" during a most tragic period of Europe's history. But even these Antonescu nostalgics do not say that the politics of extermination was in any way justified. Their point is to deny, not condone it. In Russia, general Aleksandr Lebed insisted that he was not an anti-Semite after he had made some disparaging comments on Jews in June 1996. In spite of the venomous anti-Semitic and anti-Western pamphlets issued by Zyuganov and his allies, Russia's new urban middle class has little sympathy for such ethnocentric outbursts. This popular rejection of ethnic scapegoating also appeared in a poll taken in 1996: out of two thousand Russians asked which of ten groups were responsible for the country's economic crisis, the lowest number (9 percent) blamed the Jews.[35] One cannot speak of state anti-Semitism in any of these countries.

As all these countries compete to enter the European structures, their elites' rhetoric is predominantly liberal, leaving for the marginal demagogues to voice deep-seated racist and chauvinistic sentiments. This was not the case during the interwar period, when the region was a hotbed for rabid anti-Semitic, often murderous ideas and movements, from Warsaw to Zagreb, and from Budapest to Bucharest.[36] These interwar anti-Semitic ideologies were not just expressions of home-grown agrarian populism, or of aristocratic contempt for liberalism and its supporters, but also imports and adaptations of Western anti-democratic, anti-Enlightenment, and anti-capitalist theories and mythologies. In this respect, one should benefit from revisiting the major points raised by Hannah Arendt in her classic discussion of the role of nationalism in the formation of totalitarian ideology. For Arendt, nationalism in the West represented the symbolic linkage between the atomized society made up of uprooted individuals and the strongly centralized state: it offered sentiments of belonging and identity that did not entail exclusion or persecution. In the East (the Dual Monarchy, the Czarist Empire, the Balkans), Arendt argued, where continuous shifts of boundaries deprived communities of conditions for the realization of the "national trinity of people-territory-state," tribal nationalism gradually converted into mystical pan-movements, attributing to one nation a messianic role that ideologues proposed as a antidote to the despised values of liberal individualism and civic patriotism:

> "Tribal nationalism is the precise perversion of a religion which made God choose one nation, one's own nation. . . . The hatred of the racists against the Jews sprang from a superstitious apprehension that it actually might be the Jews, and not themselves, whom God had chosen, to whom success was granted by the divine providence. . . . Guided by their own ridiculous superstition, the leaders of the pan-movements found that little hidden cog in the mechanic of Jewish piety that made a complete reversion and perversion possible, so that chosenness was no longer the myth for an ultimate realization of the ideal of common humanity—but for its final destruction."[37]

Tribal nationalism suffered major blows in this century, but its deep causes have not disappeared. Tribal nationalism is a response to historical marginality or humiliation, an attempt to compensate for failure, defeat, or mere perceived contempt from other groups. This is not necessarily the case in Russia, where nationalism developed rather as an ideology of victory and historically justifiable pride. Napoleon's defeat in 1812, hardly a source of humiliation, and the myth of Borodino are essential for Russian nationalism.[38] As a general trend, however, nationalist fever and "Caesarist" expectations tend to rise whenever there is widespread sentiment of political disarray, institutional weakness, moral malaise, and legal anarchy.

No less worthy of attention is a revival of the fascist "cultural" fashion in the region: it is somewhat *de bon ton* among the ultranationalist youth in Bucharest and Zagreb to admire Corneliu Zelea Codreanu, and Ion Antonescu, Ante Pavelić, and profascist collaborationist Cardinal Alois Stepinac. Indeed, fascination with the fascist past is visible in most former Axis satellites. In Croatia, for instance, it took a lot of public pressure in 1993 to prevent the renaming of Marshal Tito Square in Zagreb into Mile Budak, after a fascist writer who authored the 1941 "Law to Protect the Popular and Aryan Culture of the Croatian people," which included lines such as: "Jews are banned by race from collaborating in, or influencing in any way, the development of popular and Aryan culture, and from participating in any way in the work, organizations, and social, youth, sporting and cultural institutions of the Croatian people generally, and especially in literature, journalism, plastic and musical arts, urbanism, drama, and film."[39] The unqualified idealization of the pre-communist past, both by Serbs and Croats, and the failure of both sides, regardless of the different degrees of responsibility, to propose liberal democratic programs led to the breakdown of the centuries-old political culture of Serbian-Croatian cooperation.[40]

Such fascination with fascism is embodied by Romanian-born French philosopher E. M. Cioran (1911–1995). As a desperate young intellectual stifled by the parochialism of his country's dominant culture, Cioran admired the Iron Guard, Europe's third largest fascist movement, and savagely attacked liberal values. In his early Romanian writings—which he later repudiated as delirious and fanatic—he tried to formulate the guidelines for a Romanian "national revolution." In a self-critical confession written in 1949 and published posthumously in 1996, Cioran addressed his early romance with the Guard:

> We were a band of desperate individuals in the heart of the Balkans. And we were doomed to fail; our failure was our only excuse. . . . [The Iron Guard] was the only sign that our country could be anything but a fiction. It was a cruel movement, a mixture of prehistory and prophecy, mystique of prayer and of revolver, and it was persecuted by all authorities, and it wanted to be persecuted. . . . It had been founded on ferocious ideas: it disappeared ferociously. . . . Whoever between twenty and thirty does not subscribe to fanaticism, to rage, to madness is an imbecile. One is a *liberal* only by fatigue, and a democrat by reason."[41]

Young Cioran was not exceptional; witness the case of "Beta, the disappointed lover," the epitome of anti-liberal Polish intellectuals discussed by Czeslaw Milosz in *The Captive Mind*: "None of these young people believed any longer in democracy. Most of the countries of Eastern Europe had been semi-dictatorships before the War; and the parliamentary system seemed to belong to a dead era. . . . This lack of any sort of vision led him to see the world as a place in which nothing existed outside of naked force. It was a world of decline and fall. And the liberals of the older generation, mouthing nineteenth-century phrases about respect for man—while all about them hundreds of thousands of people were being massacred—were fossil remains."[42]

What was unique was Cioran's passion, his immense poetic gifts, and his astounding moral indifference to the human losses provoked by this century's totalitarian millennialisms. The fact that a man as intelligent and sophisticated as Cioran could lionize in his early writings Lenin and Hitler, Codreanu and Mussolini, fosters in many of his latter-day readers their already boiling radical fever and anti-democratic ardor.[43] But this new form of "aesthetic" attraction to fascism among disoriented, angry youth is not limited to the former Nazi satellites. As reported by Western human rights groups, Polish skinheads and other extremists frequently use the term Jew as a label for their targets regardless of whether they are actually Jewish. And this is not a trend limited to the East, as the skinhead groups have created a global network of racists. In England, a skin rock band called "British Standard" sings a text that captures this fascination with power, uniforms, and violence: "The Iron Guard of Europe/ has risen from the grave./They march along as one now./A New Order they must save." The hints of Codreanu's Iron Guard and Hitler's "Neue Ordnung" are unmistakable.[44]

Post-Leninist Discourses of Rancor

Contemporary political ideas cannot be understood without reference to similar ideas of the past. Nationalism, for instance, as a discourse of political mobilization is a set of ideas and emotions inspired by the romantic critique of modernity, on the one hand, and the cultivation of a vision that identifies state, ethnicity, and linguistic community, on the other.[45] Excessive nationalism, especially during the second half of the nineteenth century, was an expression of the rise of imperialist ideas, pan movements, and the increasing fascination with Darwinian social biology and Louis Pasteur's microbiology. The disenchantment with modernity and the yearning for the pre-revolutionary order led to the coalescence (in Austria, France and later Germany) of the new visions of exclusion, based on the exaltation of the mystically defined nation. Thus, belonging to the nation becomes an inescapable fact, a primordial and inexorable definition of identity.

Western narratives of *Blut und Boden* had direct and catastrophic effects in East-Central Europe, where the nationalists imported and elaborated on the theses formulated by Louis Drumont, Charles Maurras, Maurice Barrès, Arthur de Gobineau, Richard Wagner, and so on. These narratives were reformulated by East-Central European intellectuals in quite original ways, as Eastern Europe's radical nationalists tried to offer a cataclysmic, uncompromising response to the dilemmas of modernization.[46] Thus, in the Romanian case, the mystical revolutionaries rejected democracy together with the Western ideas of rule of law, individualism, and the whole legacy of Cartesianism, in the name of a strange and eclectic mixture of *élan vital*, Orthodoxy, ultraspiritualism, theosophical superstitions, and imperial delusions about a Byzantine mission of the Romanian nation.[47] Polish anti-Semitism had a strong Catholic component; after Pilsudski's death in 1935, Polish authorities embraced ethnoreligious anti-Semitism as an official state creed, encouraging deep-seated anti-Jewish sentiments.[48] In Poland, as in Hungary and Romania, it was impossible to separate the anti-communist from the anti-Semitic obsessions of the rightist inter war movements.

Projection on the Jew of fears and phobias, and the identification of the Jew with the figure of the alien, the unassimilated foreigner, intent upon dissolving all traditional bonds and loyalties, were subdued by the appalling persecutions and the Shoah during World War II. One tragic example of enduring popular anti-Semitism was the Kielce pogrom in Poland. On July 4, 1946, forty-two Polish Jews who had survived World War II in the Soviet Union and returned home were forced out the building where they were being sheltered and beaten to death by a furious mob. The pretext for this massacre, and for the others that murdered as many as two to three thousand Jews during the following month, was that Jews had abducted and killed a Christian boy—a resurgence of the old blood libel. This atrocity took place in a city where twenty thousand Jews had been exterminated by the Nazis during the war, under the benevolent eyes of the local government and police authorities.[49]

The salience of Jewish militants in the communist parties further strengthened the stereotypes portraying Jews as perennial evil-doers and carriers of anti-national feelings and actions.[50] Ironically, the popular anti-Semitic imagery of the Stalinist period was embraced by the direct beneficiaries of the new regimes, that is, the apparatchiks who were swiftly recruited among workers and peasants to "ethnicize" the new states and party bureaucracies. The myth of Stalinism as a "Jewish colonization" totally ignored the persecution of the Zionists and the stubborn resistance of the Jewish religious communities to ideological regimentation.[51] But the anti-Semitic fantasy contributed to the moral anesthesia that allowed Poles, Romanians, Hungarians, and so on, to avoid seriously coming to terms with their history. Instead of showing compassion for the victims of the fascist persecutions, "common-sense" narratives indulged in self-congratulatory, narcissistic tales about the Poles, Hungarians, or Romanians as the most victimized group under the Nazis or under the Stalinists, or under both.

In the figure of the Jew, the anti-Semite resents assumed success and adjustment to the hardships of the bourgeois world as well as participation in and responsibility for the advent of communism. That the two can hardly be reconciled is not recognized as a problem: the anti-Semitic fantasy unifies the opposites and sees both communism and capitalism as façades for the same monopolistic ambition. The Aryan or Russophile myths are simple, reverted projections of the conspiracy myth used in the anti-Semitic tradition: Germans and Russians appear as the most martyrized nations (usually under invisible Jewish domination) whose resurrection cannot occur unless the Jews and their supporters are unmasked. Part of the anti-Semitic pastime during the last one hundred years of hatred has been to expose the real names of assimilated Jews. From Drumont's *La France Juive* to Corneliu Vadim Tudor's *România Mare*, the obsession with "enjuivement" (Jewish penetration, infiltration, and so on) has remained constant in radical populist circles. Nothing is more important for Russian radical nationalists like Vadim Kozhinov or Igor Shafarevich than to demonstrate how the October Revolution was nothing but a plot fomented by Lenin, Trotsky, Zinoviev, Radek, and their fellow "Judeo-Bolsheviks" paid by the Germans.

It must be emphasized that communism did not simply freeze nationalist and xenophobic passions, as is so often and mistakenly maintained. In Tito's Yugoslavia, Stalin's or Brezhnev's Russia, and Gomulka's Poland ethnocentrism did not disappear without a trace as a result of official denials; it remained part of a popular subculture, and resurfaced in the prejudices and superstitions of the middle level bureaucracy, beneficiary of the communist privileges and venomously hostile to "cosmopolitan" Jewish elements within the leadership, the media, and the academic world.

The alliance between nationalist intellectuals and xenophobic bureaucrats was one of the main features of the last stage of Sovietism in most East-Central European countries. Hungary was somewhat exceptional, but even there the reform communist Imre Poszgay decided to join his efforts in 1988–1989 with the nationalist Magyar Democratic Forum rather than with the allegedly Jewish-dominated, liberal Alliance of Free Democrats. Ironically, even the GDR elite, the least entitled to use nationalism as a source of belated and desperately needed legitimation, rehabilitated after 1984 the mythology of Prussian national grandeur and incorporated Martin Luther into its state pantheon. One also needs to analyze the symbolic economy of Romanian communism which adopted and refunctionalized most of the major themes of the interwar nationalist right, minus religious mysticism.[52]

As we witness the transition to civil societies from hierocratic secular despotisms, nationalist discourses of hatred, adversity, and envy are the most powerful rival ideology to the vision inspired by the ideas of the Enlightenment. In this conglomerate of resentful, but often poignantly expressed ideas, anti-Semitism is not necessarily or always the central theme.[53] But it remains a significant and potentially essential element of the politics of ressentiment to the extent that the figure of the Jew can be transmogrified into the figure of the presumed source of all calamities.[54]

The mythologization of the Jewish figure, its phanatasmagoric recreation in the imagination (since the real Jews are for all practical purposes extinct in the region), serves as a variety of agendas for different political actors: it is used to help explain the intensity of political debates and the prevailing role of the media (Jews and the media are forever associated in the anti-liberal imagination). Jews (or the "Judaified" political actors) are also directly connected in this delusional framework to the dismal conditions of the economy (International Monetary Fund, World Bank, Transnational Corporations–these are all united in the imaginary Zionist-capitalist world).[55] Jews are indicted for being simultaneously revolutionary and counterrevolutionary, radicals and conservatives, leftists and rightists. Contemporary anti-Semitic and anti-capitalist fixations within the post-communist landscape are thus resurrecting Louis Drumont's vindictive outcry: "The only one who profited from the Revolution is the Jew. Everything comes from the Jew; everything boils down to the Jew."[56]

In defining national and political identity of the new states, reference to the Jewish question often becomes central: think of the ongoing debates in Poland on the relation between secular and clerical values, Pilsudski's inclusive vision of the national community, and Dmowski's ethnocratic program. No less important, the Jewish question inevitably resurfaces in the exploration of two catastrophic experiences: World War II and the responsibility (as perpetrators or bystanders) of autochthonous populations for the Holocaust; and Stalinism and the presumed disproportionate Jewish presence in party leadership and secret police.[57] Marginally, but not completely irrelevantly, fringe groups continue to brandish pseudo-theological arguments against the "deicide" people. Traditional and modernized versions of anti-Semitic, exclusionary discourses co-exist. In Poland, for instance, anti-Semitism resurfaced as part of the anti-communist campaign to help Lech Walesa get reelected in the 1995 presidential election, but it failed to stir positive mass responses. As he lost much of the electoral support, the former Solidarity chairman had two last resources to use against the increasingly popular former Communist Youth leader Aleksander Kwasniewski: religious nationalism and visceral anti-communism. The latter, as we have seen is often colored by anti-Semitism. After Solidarity organized a meeting at which anti-Semitic slogans were chanted denouncing Kwasniewski's alleged Jewish origin, Walesa did nothing to condemn such behavior. At the same gathering, demonstrators called for sending foreign minister Wladyslaw Bartoszewski (an Auschwitz survivor) and former Solidarity advisor Jacek Kuron (another potential rival to Walesa) to "gas chambers." "Is the political memory of the Poles so short that they forgot what the gas chambers were and who built them up?" asked journalist Janina Paradowska in the weekly *Polytika*.[58] It was former communist Kwasniewski who gave proof of civic dignity in declaring: "In Poland, if someone is better educated and speaks other languages, they say you are a Jew. If that's the definition of a Jew, okay, I'll be a Jew." As to the question about confirming or denying these allegations, Kwasniewski rightly stated: "If I accept such a forum, I accept the whole discussion. The question is crazy. I'm a Pole, and I would like to be proud of being a Pole. But after such a question, that such a question is even raised, I am not proud."[59]

The rise of clerically influenced authoritarianism and the readiness to use anti-Semitism as a political weapon appeared disturbingly clear when Walesa postponed and actually avoided an unequivocal disassociation from anti-Semitic remarks made in his presence by an influential priest during Mass in June 1995. According to Father Henryk Jankowski, a long-standing figure involved in the Solidarity movement, the "Star of David is implicated in the swastika as well as the hammer and sickle." Furthermore, he called upon Poles to beware of the foreign agents in the government: "Poles, bestir yourselves. We can no longer tolerate governments made up of people who have not declared whether they come from Moscow or from Israel." And as if this had not been enough, Jankowski reiterated his views a few days thereafter in response to criticism of such statements: "The Star of David symbolizes not only the state of Israel but also the Jewish nation. Like all other people, Jews happen to do unbecoming things in public life just as they happen to do very noble things indeed. I am talking chiefly about banking and finance circles. Their actions have led to many a human tragedy."[60] As there are very few Jews among the top Polish politicians, this rhetoric was meant to enhance Walesa's credentials as the advocate of a purely Polish state based on Catholic traditions and inimical to foreign exploitation. Its thrust is obviously at loggerheads with

Pope John Paul II's strong condemnation of anti-Semitism, and indicates the existence of a deep division within the Polish Church between the xenophobic reactionaries, unhappy with the line of the Vatican II Council, and those who support an open-minded, tolerant direction. Walesa's initial silence and long-delayed distancing from Jankowski's remarks suggest his own readiness to tolerate, if not directly to encourage, anti-Semitism as an acceptable part of the official political debate. Kwasniewski's victory showed that anti-Semitism, religious fundamentalism, and fierce anti-Communism did not work well as electoral ploys.

Not so paradoxically, the theme of anti-Semitism continues to appear as a serious topic in Romania. In that country, many among the intelligentsia still take seriously interwar mystical philosopher and political adventurer Nae Ionescu's ideas on the Jewish question and Romanian self-identity as Christian Orthodox.[61] Indeed, the peculiarity of the Romanian situation is that intellectuals of both democratic and radical-populist persuasion tend to cherish the same anti-Western, deeply nationalist, and communitarian ideas so influential during the interwar period. Even distinguished liberal intellectuals have often deplored Western insensitivity to the plight of the Romanians under communism, and have insisted that an exaggerated focus on the fascist legacies could result in the exoneration of Stalinist crimes. This approach was carried to an extreme by the radical nationalists for whom the discussion of the Jewish Holocaust (which they deny) is only a device meant to prevent the indictment of the "Holocaust of the Romanian culture," presumably engineered by Jewish communists and their offspring.

In the absence of the real Jew, the anti-Semitic discourse tries to eliminate the mythical one. Ironically, in some cases, especially in Ukraine, there is a tendency to mythologize the Jew in a positive, favorable sense—exonerating Ukrainians for their role in the Czarist pogroms and mass massacres of World War II. The new mythology holds the Russians responsible for the past atrocities. Ukrainians were at the worst simple instruments of policies fomented by the now "diabolized" Russians. As a whole, however, negative rather than positive stereotypes about the Jews continue to imbue the hateful imagination of the nationalists.

In all these countries, the old anti-Semitic literature has come back with a vengeance: books by A. C. Cuza (the prophet of Romanian racism), the "Protocols," and Mein Kampf have been reprinted. Public opinion surveys indicate an inordinate concern with "Jewish power." Especially in Romania, where the December 1989 revolution continues to be shrouded by so many mysteries, there is the powerful temptation to ascribe to invisible, secret societies and groups the crucial role in those uncanny events.[62]

The more traumatic and unpredictable the changes, the more the anti-Semitic phantasms can explain all the transformation as an outcome of a plan fomented by "bankers, the Mossad, the CIA," and (repeating the old syncretic myth) the KGB. The myth of the omnipotent Jew is the counterpart to the feelings of angst and hopelessness experienced by so many denizens of the former communist world; this is primarily the case with right-wing populists in Hungary, but it also accounts for the mounting frustrations and anti-Semitic undercurrents among Serbian intellectuals who resent what they regard to be Jewish lack of solidarity in the struggle against the presumed common enemy (Croats, Germans, Catholics, Muslims). The corollary to the mythological axiom "Jews control the world" is that each time failure occurs, Jews (or their substitutes) can serve as targets for blame.

Ideas propagated by a certain part of the intelligentsia, usually the circles made up of nationalists who were associated with the decaying communist regimes, organize much of the shame, anger, and hatred that are behind anti-Semitism. For example, attempts to propose a discussion among Romania's intellectuals of Antonescu's military dictatorship, the Holocaust in Romania, and the concentration camps run by Romanian military in Transnistria provoked an interesting reply: silence, denial, and rejection of the topic as a falsification of realities, shrill rhetoric about Judeo-communism and anti-patriotism of the Jews in Bessarabia and Northern Bukovina in 1940, and the most aggressive charge, "effort to culpabilize the whole Romanian nation."[63] These are common accusations found in all of these countries. Jews are criticized for deliberately hyperbolizing their plight in order to obtain reparations and compensations. The functions of myth are thus fully used: it is all-explanatory, it offers consolation and refuge from doubt, and it fosters sentiments of self-esteem and self-confidence.

Redeeming Mythologies: Communist Anti-Fascism and Heroic National Resistance

To justify the elimination of their non- or anti-communist adversaries, the East European Stalinists used the instrument of anti-fascist propaganda. As in the case of France, there was a mystique of the resistance combined with a deep need to deny collaboration as a large, even mass phenomenon.[64] In none of these countries (with the exception of certain attempts in the Solidarity underground) was the participation of indigenous groups in the exercise of racist policies during World War II seriously examined. One could easily grow up in communist Romania, Hungary, Czechoslovakia, or Poland (not to mention the former USSR) ignoring the scope and implications of the destruction of European Jewry during World War II.[65] Currently, anti-Semitic habits of the heart are either denied or underrated. The usual response to any mention of Jewish grievances is part of what I call "competitive victimization."[66] To the Jewish claim that their fate in Eastern Europe (especially during World War II) was one of mass murder, extermination, horrible persecutions, and endless discrimination, the answer is often characterized by insensitivity and irascibility. The argument is that Romanians, Poles or Hungarians have also suffered under the communist regime, and that conditions in Stalinist concentration camps were not superior to those in Nazi ones.[67] The banalization of the Holocaust is related to the feeling that this is not a universal human issue, affecting the humanity in all of us, but rather an attempt by Jews (and their friends) to monopolize the quality and memory of suffering. Jews are accused of trying to confiscate all the benefits of universal compassion by insisting so much on the uniqueness of the Holocaust. This trivialization of the horror motivated Walesa's refusal to admit the overwhelmingly predominant Jewish martyrdom at Auschwitz and the rhetoric about the millions of Polish Jews having died as Polish citizens.

In all the Sovietized countries of the region, communist anti-fascism was based on the mythology of global class warfare and the alleged heroic role of the communists as the vanguard of the resistance movements. In Poland, the myth was used to delegitimize the supporters of the pro-Western Home Army. In Romania, the minuscule Romanian Communist party used it to assert its patriotic credentials against the historically democratic formations. The most egregious case of "anti-fascist hijacking" was the GDR, where the myth (constitutionally enshrined) claimed that the East German state was the exclusive inheritor of the democratic and revolutionary traditions of the working class. The proletarians had been paragons of internationalism, and anti-Semitism had been a form of manipulation of the masses by the bourgeoisie in order to achieve its goals of domination, and so on. As we know, no real soul searching took place in the GDR because the official line maintained the fiction of complete discontinuity with the Nazi past. In the same vein, the Romanian communists seemed to have no pangs of conscience in trying to get public support for the fiction of "national benevolence" toward Jews during World War II.

The consequence was that the new ruling parties, except in Hungary, avoided any serious analysis of the pre-communist forms of racism and exclusiveness as part of the national traditions. Moreover, in all these countries myths were manufactured to advance the thesis of "brotherhood and unity" (a theme that reached its most glaring and utopian form in Tito's Yugoslavia). In fact, socialist internationalism was nothing but a camouflage meant to conceal the realities of ethnic intolerance and animosity. The ruling elites themselves had serious problems of identity: think of the need for many Jewish communist leaders to adopt pure Romanian, Polish, or Hungarian names in order to emphasize that at least onomastically they belonged to the national communities. For people like Mátyas Rákosi, Ernö Gerö, Valter Roman, and many others it was the chance to rid themselves of their original identity and assert themselves as exponents of the working people of the country they had been born or raised in.[68] Many of these militants had absorbed cultural anti-Semitism from the early writings by Karl Marx, for whom Jews, money, and capitalism were inextricably linked with each other. With very few exceptions, therefore, the communist intelligentsia failed to comprehend the nature of Nazi anti-Semitism and its absolute centrality in Hitler's ideological universe.[69] But, for the anti-Semites, this name changing was merely an attempt by Jewish political radicals to lull their opponents and receive acceptance on the base of a fraud. Needless to add, the flight of Eastern Europe's Jewish communists from their original condition and the attempt at complete assimilation did not succeed. As Communist parties grew increasingly "national," these people lost their prominent positions and were eventually marginalized or, as in the case of Poland, forced to emigrate.[70]

Is contemporary anti-Semitism simply a continuation of the pre-1939 forms of ethnocentrism, or is it part of a broader background of uncertainties about national identity? My response is that the resurgence of anti-Semitism is part of the region's unresolved adjustment to modernity, an outburst of premodern, nativistic, and an indigenista-style set of sentiments.

Can one see it, however, as a truly major threat to democratic institutions in East-Central Europe? My response is that one has to refrain from both acute panic and overly optimistic denial. Anti-Semitism, like other forms of tribalism and racism, is part of a political culture of fear, panic, anguish, and suspicion. These emotions may erupt periodically, especially when employed by beleaguered elites in search of unifying myths of danger and betrayal. Think of Corneliu Vadim Tudor and his România Mare party using the presence of Petre Roman as premier (1990–1991) to speak about a world-wide, spiderlike Jewish conspiracy. According to this scenario, Petre Roman, born in 1946, and who is half Jewish, half Spanish, represented "genetically" the "Cominternist" (i.e., Jewish) interests in Romania.[71] The whole history of the Romanian Communist party is thus recast in such a way as to explain teleologically the Jewish rise to power. It matters little that many of the militants executed during the Great Purge in the USSR were Jewish, and the persecution of the Zionists during the Stalinist terror matters even less. The meaning of communist anti-Semitism is completely skipped within this self-serving framework: neither Rudolf Slansky nor Ana Pauker can be seen as victims of the system they helped to engineer, since it is impossible to the closed mind to accept external arguments that may shatter the fully established certitudes.

As the new industrial barons emerge, anti-Semitism reemerges in the form of anti-bourgeois feelings. Despair over lost opportunities, hostility to money and market values, and the old stories about Jewish control over world finances (after all even Pat Robertson in the United States believes in them), converge in the figure of the sinister alien forces dedicated to destroying national community and exploiting the new economies as part of the "world proletariat." The new anti-Semitism is intimately linked to anti-North Americanism, and has much in common with the mythologies manufactured by Third World elites and their Western supporters to explain failure, dependency, and crisis. It is an irony that the new discourses of ressentiment, in spite of their radical rightist intellectual origins, are in reality expressions of radical leftist hostility to multinational companies, free circulation of capital, foreign investments, and impersonal procedures in the development of liberal institutions. From state socialism, the new tribalism inherits the collectivist, egalitarian, and anti-market philosophy.[72]

Conclusion

Anti-Semitism is thus part of the syndrome of exclusiveness and chauvinism that includes race, gender, and social contempt.[73] In times of despair and confusion, shattered selves tend to favor intolerant solutions to traumatic experiences. The Other is stigmatized or penalized for all the perceived injuries and insults. Equally significant, unavowable self-hatred, particularly enhanced by feelings of uselessness, marginality, and what Max Weber called "sterile excitement" is one of the major resources of the new discourses of rancor.[74] The essentialization of the Jew as the Other is part of the mythological construction of the East European national identity: instead of a positive affirmation of what a nation is, it is often described in terms of antithesis. Radical nationalism in Eastern Europe is thus programmatically and consistently antagonistic to a different figure, the "Constitutive Other" as it were: Jews, critical intellectuals, Gypsies, liberal free thinkers, Freemasons, women, homosexuals.[75]

The background of ethnic fundamentalism is conspiratorial: born out of the secret societies of the nineteenth century, nationalism has inherited a fascination with alleged occult machinations and intrigues. The anti-Semitic imagination thrives on the ground of intrigues, the uncanny, and the opaqueness of the public sphere. As in the case of France during the events that led to the Dreyfus Affair, there is anomie in these societies, a sense of loss of identity as a mass psychological condition, and a sentiment that at least the current generation will not enjoy the advantages of a free and prosperous society. Militant nationalism brings people together, gives them the feeling of warm belonging, a sense of glory, a pride for their presumably heroic ancestry, and more than anything else the image of the enemy. Individuals under this type of stress need a figure to worship, and (even more so) one to hate. The cult of death and the pseudo-heroic sacrifice for the presumably national will (a substitute for a civic community) are used by demagogues who claim that only ethnic purity can protect the future of the group. Yet, such nationalisms are not simply East European phenomena.[76]

The repudiation of otherness as a form of "sickness," the persecution of the immigrant (who wants to take our jobs), the adversity to the foreigner, are part of a growing syndrome of fin-de-siècle universal malaise. The collapse of communism has abolished many of the established taboos, and there is more space for expressing views that a decade ago appeared as borderline. Who could have believed that we would witness the growth of an obscene body of Holocaust denial literature (conspicuously promoted and advertised by the East

European neofascists)? The fatigue with tolerance and the yearning for strong responses to what punks, Islamic fundamentalists, Orthodox theocrats, and neo-Nazis see as the "decadence" of the West generates new myths of vindictiveness and desperation. The frustration with the existing order, seen as corrupt and ignoble, makes people look for alternative solutions. One example of this trend from the West is the Northern League in Italy, where a yearning for roots is indicative of the emergence of new political styles, in many respects located beyond traditional distinctions between Left and Right. And human rights (traditionally a province of the liberal left) are often under siege in the name of the new collective identities, putatively more responsive to insecurity and angst. Whenever the mystique of blood and earth takes over the public discourse, new versions of fascism are possible. The origins of fascism are indeed situated in this tragic break with modernity in the name of modernity, in the revolt of deep strata of the political psyche against the liberal atomization and the readiness to relinquish or limit civic rights on behalf of supra-individual, communal values. This is the thrust of Robert Wistrich's wise warning:

> We are dealing here with a general European and perhaps even a planetary malaise, involving a fundamental breakdown in moral and societal values. The ghosts of Europe's past will not be exorcised by the facile search for scapegoats in the present nor by futile exercises in normalizing the collective traumas of history. The search for roots and for a secure national identity can often be liberating experiences—especially in the service of freedom from tyranny, oppression, and humiliation. But even the noblest patriotic sentiments are liable to become 'the last refuge of the scoundrel' unless they are balanced by an elementary respect for dignity, solidarity, and universal human rights.[77]

The problem with the post-Leninist societies is that there is very little in their past they can look back to a sources of inspiration for such tolerant behavior. Liberal traditions existed, to be sure, but they were anemic and consistently besieged. A latecomer to the region, and intimately associated with Jewish and German minorities, modernity was more a veneer underneath which sentimental-rural nostalgias continued to smolder. With the exception of interwar Czechoslovakia, all these societies were prone to authoritarianism: in the name of their resistance to Bolshevism, Eastern European regimes promoted emergency measures, xenophobia, and distrust of liberal institutions and values. Now, as they exit from Communism, what they would get from the past is a memory of exclusion, persecution, tribal strifes, mutual scorn, and a lot of self-glorification.[78] Instead of exorcism, most of these societies have cultivated collective narcissism. And the more they admire themselves, the happier they are with their heroic virtues, the greater becomes the temptation to execrate the neighbor, the foreigner, the Other.

Five _____

Is the Revolution Over? The Myth of Decommunization and the Quest for Political Justice

> There should be a place for forgiveness wherever
> there is confession of guilt and repentance.
> (*Václav Havel*)

> Thus are we still continuing the revolution, or do
> we say that the war is over?
> (*Adam Michnik*)

CAN COMMUNISM be brought to trial? How should the fledgling democracies deal with the former ruling elites? Is it possible to rectify the aberrations of the past by bringing to justice those who were responsible for the creation and perpetuation of the totalitarian order? How does one establish a persuasive hierarchy of guilt and, even more significantly, how does one avoid the risks of engaging in collective punishment? To put it briefly: how can the post-communist political communities reconcile legitimacy and legality? These disturbing questions indicate the moral, political, and legal challenges connected with the imperative of a revolutionary break with the ancien régime.

As the communist order fell apart, many in the region found it mandatory to engage in rituals of purification. Very few initially objected, for instance, to the execution of Romania's Nicolae and Elena Ceauşescu in December 1989, although the legality of the trial was, to put it mildly, questionable. After all, did the Italian partisans not execute Mussolini in the name of revolutionary expediency? Was tyrannicide not justified by the ultimate obligation to save the revolution? Bringing the leaders of the old regimes to trial appeared as both a form of historical retribution and a moral catharsis.

Decommunization, like post-1945 de-Nazification in Germany, is both a destructive and a constructive endeavor. On the one hand it abolishes authoritarian institutions, on the other it means the establishment and the consolidation of a political order respectful of civic rights. Despite all their differences, and there were many, communism and fascism shared the same hostility to liberalism, middle-class values, individual autonomy, and the state of law. Decommunization, like de-Nazification, is a mental (cultural, psychological) process as much as a political, economic, and legal one. The relentless zeal of flaming decommunizers to limit the civic rights of former communist activists and secret police officers and informers, as in Albania under stridently anti-communist former President Sali Berisha, covers staunch Jacobin propensities. Authoritarian methods are used in the name of the "sacred" struggle against the neocommunists and their allies.[1] In other words, the logic of decommunization does not oppose a virtuous, heroic camp of former victims and dissidents to a vicious one made up of hypocritical post-communist operators. The reality is much more confusing.

Filemakers and Filebreakers

On January 13, 1990, thousands of Romanians gathered in Victory Square in the heart of Bucharest to burn their Communist party cards. In the spring of that year, Bulgarians assaulted the headquarters of the Communist party (rebaptized Socialist) and smashed the red star that had long crowned its roof. Many of these symbolic rituals had an intoxicating power and allowed citizens to express their grievances against the misery and hardships that had been imposed in the name of the "radiant future." But from the very beginning some people, primarily critical intellectuals, saw the rhetoric of decommunization as pregnant with self-righteous forms of fundamentalism, no less intolerant than the one supposed to be eradicated. They feared that the justice of the victors could easily turn into injustice. Later, as elections took place in all Eastern Europe and ex-communists used democratic procedures to reorganize themselves and participate in the political game, many felt that political justice had failed and the revolutions had not fulfilled their anti-communist tasks.

How to treat the former communists and secret police thus became a serious moral and political issue, dividing these societies and creating schisms not only at the political level but also within families. In some countries, as files were offered to public scrutiny, dissidents discovered that their own spouses had long spied on them. More than one acclaimed civic rights activist turned out to have cooperated with the secret police. Notions like forgiveness, forgetfulness, guilt, and responsibility acquired explosive power. The memory of the dead, of the countless victims of the times of terror, as well as the remembrance of long decades of torpor, cowardice, and submission to the omnipotent party-state apparatus were used by different political actors to pursue their own agendas.

Some people in the region, usually referred to as "liberals," feared that decommunization could result in horrible vendettas, the prologue to a Night of St. Barthelmy that would forever doom these new polities to cycles of spiteful hysteria, vengeance, and bigotry. For others, often described as "radicals," decommunization is the justifiable political and legal response to the need to break with the past, cleanse the elites, and usher in a genuinely new life. Former communists have decried it in the name of their right to legal procedures but, as a general rule, they have shown little expression of atonement for the decades when the same procedures were denied to their opponents. In their view, insistence on memory would be counterproductive. Ironically, this approach is shared by some celebrated ex-dissidents, including Miklos Haraszti and George Konrád in Hungary, Adam Michnik in Poland, and Martin Palous in the Czech Republic. For these liberal intellectuals, the vindictive passion of the decommunizers is in many cases a camouflage for the absence of impressive anti-communist credentials in the past. For years, the dissidents had opposed any calls for violence and had pleaded for a negotiated transformation of the status quo. Now that such "pacts" had been achieved, they argued, it would be disastrous for the revolutionaries to renege on their commitments. This perspective values legality as the main achievement of the revolutions and grants communists the benefit of doubt.

Needless to say, the ex-dissident's motivations in opposing purges are fundamentally different from the ex-communist's, but they tend to say similar things: let bygones be bygones, a new beginning has arrived, no one should be held guilty just because of previous political affiliations. Individuals should be judged as individuals, and their value should be weighed in accordance to their personal actions.

The problem with this approach is that it tends to see the past as an amorphous morass that abolished individual responsibility and tainted almost everybody. In the case of former dissidents, it reflects a refusal to adopt the Manichean moral high ground that divides the social body into "angels" and "rascals." There is, however, an excess of generous modesty in George Konrád's vision of an almost universal complicity with the old regime: "In a satellite state all citizens, humble or proud, are servants. Find me an honest man in a totalitarian or even relatively liberal yet paternalistic society. You'll look long and hard. Find me a truthsayer in a society where the state is the father—state socialism, for instance—and where the man at the top has the power of a king. In a satellite state it is fitting to lie or, rather, it is impossible to know what is a lie and what is the truth."[2]

Even Václav Havel, who in the past insisted on the need to live in truth, thereby implying that there was a way of escaping the official lie— obliquely endorsed this approach when he said in 1990 that the divide between guilt and innocence passes through everybody's conscience, through the heart of each man and woman.

The post-communists relished this generous philosophy. Poland's martial law ruler Wojciech Jaruzelski applauded Adam Michnik's moral sense and even expressed regret for having sent him to jail. The former president of Romania's Chamber of Deputies, Adrian Năstase, himself the executive chairman of the ruling party and a close associate of the country's then president Ion Iliescu, declared in 1995 that focusing on the past (be it the fascist or the Stalinist one) would derail people from constructing their future. Why so much insistence, he asked, on what happened under profascist dictator Ion Antonescu or Stalinist tyrant Nicolae Ceauşescu?[3] Gregor Gysi, chairman of the parliamentary faction of the German Party of Democratic Socialism (PDS), the post-communist formation created from the ashes of Ulbricht's and Honecker's Socialist Unity party, insists on the need to condemn Stalinism vigorously in the name of the "betrayed ideals" of Marxism. His party issued a public apology to the victims of that system, whether they were ordinary citizens of the German Democratic Republic GDR or party members. At the same time, Gysi rejects the analogy between the East German regime and the Nazi dictatorship as an attempt to criminalize the very nature of the GDR experiment: "The PDS has good reason not to embrace equating the GDR and the Nazi regimes in the name of the theory of totalitarianism. The party has always tried to criticize and pass judgment on the GDR from a socialist standpoint. We criticize East German society not because it was socialist but because it was not nearly socialist enough."[4]

One can understand the stance of the former dissidents as a moral imperative to avoid collective punishment. The perverse techniques of the Leninist autocracies consisted of involving as many people as possible in the rituals of ideological indoctrination. Conformity and acquiescence rather than opposition and criticism were the mass behavior, and only a few people dared to engage in direct oppositional activities. Hungarian sociologist Zsuzsa Ferge argues that this has created an "undigested history," a mixture of guilt and outrage that upsets almost everyone in these societies: "To one degree or another, most people had to live a double life, and after a while they came to accept this as a natural state."[5] To be sure, most people did not collaborate with the secret police and not everybody has a skeleton in the closet. But, no less significant, most people did not do anything to subvert the system. They accepted its rules in the same way they breathed, and ate, and slept. The system entered their mental metabolism. True, the Polish independent, self-governing union Solidarity, with its almost ten million members, was an exhilarating case of social mobilization and political radicalization during 1980–1981, but it was thwarted by martial law, and its aftermath was marked by apathy, disgust, and social passivity. In short, there were very few genuine heroes during the last decades of the communist regimes, when the ruling elites resorted to inclusion and conformity rather than naked terror to ensure their domination.[6]

The vast majority of the people who lived under communism were participants in the systemic self-reproduction: some were active supporters of the status quo, others were just "cogs in the wheel," adjusting themselves to the existing constraints and trying to secure for themselves and their families minimal forms of decent survival. This is not to say that everybody was equally responsible for the system's actions. Some people were traitors, others were betrayed. Some agreed to work for and be paid by the secret police (either as active cadres or "informal" collaborators), others became ideological activists or members of the party/government nomenklatura and persecuted those who dared to think differently. Judges issued sentences that sent the dissidents to jail, allowed house searches, and gave legal cover to countless human rights abuses. Thousands worked for the gigantic censorship machines and did their utmost to obliterate any form of independent thought and discourse. After all, the revolutions of 1989 were not gratuitous, aesthetic exercises: they were directed against a social and political order that could not have functioned without certain institutions and their servants. The gray area between the marginal opposition groups and the center of power was itself polychromatic. To take just one example: Václav Klaus, the Czech prime minister so active in the decommunization campaign, had been neither a communist party member nor an active dissident. For the long period of Husák-style "normalization" that followed the suppression of the Prague Spring in August 1968, he worked as a researcher in economics and even contributed under a pseudonym to the underground media. In other words, one did not need to be a hero in order not to be a scoundrel.

As a general rule, the post-communist parties have tried simply to discard the Stalinist past as irrelevant for their current performance and to focus instead on the social achievements of the socialist regimes, as well as their own ability to provide economic and political managerial experience. For many of these politicians, one might say, the past is another country. What happened under the deposed totalitarian order is simply not their business. The moral implications of such oblivious behavior are enormous: no democracy can be established and long endure on blatant lies or shameful silence. An obvious historical example of willful obliviousness is the case of the United States. The Declaration of Independence of the United States from Britain was officially silent on the shameful issue of slavery, although those that penned and signed the document debated the issue and put it off for politically expedient reasons. The result, four score and seven years later, was that American democracy very nearly perished at the hands of its own citizens.

In the aftermath of the fall of communism, willful obliviousness becomes particularly unsettling when one notices the rise of the former communists to new positions of power and influence. As one astute American observer of the transition writes: "the balance between forgiveness and justice is difficult to establish, especially when those who are to be forgiven behave as if they deserve to be thanked rather than chastised, when they suddenly speak of tolerance and virtue, when they abruptly wrap themselves in the cloak of democratic values and an honest work ethic that they claim always to have upheld."[7] This is indeed the case with the former Polish president Wojciech Jaruzelski, responsible for the martial law and crucially involved in other moments of violent repression, who has gone out of his way in post-communist Poland to refurbish his image as a pristine patriot committed only to the good of his nation.

In all these countries the myth has risen of the well-intended, honest, hard-working communists who simply did their best within the existing order. This political myth is intended to exonerate the communist leaders from responsibility for the past repressions and economic mismanagement. It fundamentally falsifies the meaning of what really happened and blurs the distinction between those who defended the system and those who fought for change. Ironically, advocates of this myth share with the radical anti-communists a homogenous view of the communist parties. This vision (endorsed by both the extreme right and the extreme left) refuses to admit that in some countries the elite was deeply divided between reformers and hard-liners. Selective memory shies away from acknowledging the fact that many dissidents were disillusioned ex-communists.[8] This process of voluntary forgetfulness does not solve but only postpones the need to come to terms with reality.

Indeed, in the case of countries that have never thoroughly addressed their extreme right-wing authoritarian past (such as Slovakia, Serbia, Croatia, Hungary, Poland, and Romania), decommunization must involve an overall coming to terms with legacies of anti-Semitism, intolerance, and Christian fundamentalism (Orthodox and Catholic). This is often an excruciating task that even some of the most liberal intellectuals treat with embarrassed reticence.[9] This process is often convoluted, with competing actors engaging in mutual accusations of bad faith, self-hatred, selective memory, no less selective amnesia, and deliberate falsifications. The argument is often heard: after all, we have not exited from fascism, why should we bother discussing what happened during World War II or even before it? Nationalist anti-communists extol the virtues of the ethnic community from which they would eagerly exclude anybody whom they suspect of insufficient patriotic ardor. As for the post-communists, they often try to use the anti-fascist card as an alibi for their presumed good faith in having served Stalinism and imposed their dictatorships. Ideological distinctions are thus covered with self-serving masks that permit rival actors to stigmatize each other in the name of abstract notions like nation, justice, or freedom.

To ask for a serious coming to grips with the past is not simply a moral imperative: none of these societies can become truly liberal if the old mythologies of self-pity and self-idealization continue to monopolize the public discourse. In this respect, decommunization is also a vital search for identity, for the assertion of a genuine rupture with the past. The return to normalcy, or the building of liberal polities, means the courage to face the abdications, betrayals, and self-delusions that turned so many individuals into accomplices of an evil system. According to scholars who have studied the transitions to democracy in Latin America and Southern Europe, post-authoritarian societies cannot simply freeze or abandon their memories. The past must be known, confronted, grasped.[10]

But, will the "working through" of historical legacies (what the Germans call *Geschichtsaufarbeitung*) be limited to cultural awareness, or will it result in political and legal punishment for those responsible for the crimes of the old regimes? The issue is thus to combine, in a fair and balanced way, the legal and historical efforts at mastering the past. Again, the German post-Nazi lexicon is useful: *Geschichtsbewältigung* has signified precisely the attempt by the younger generations to understand the past, to face it without protective veils and rationalizations. In this sense, the "Memorial" initiative was created in the USSR in the late 1980s as a civic movement from below to recover memory, to document the mass crimes, and thereby to allow society to know what happened during the Stalinist reign of terror.[11] The principle underlying its workings is not revenge but moral recovery. This is probably the least painful and most constructive approach: enabling a society to know its past without engaging in endless and excruciatingly difficult legal actions whose ultimate effect may be simply to create new victims and new martyrs.

For Adam Michnik, an end should be put to the bellicose desire for purging the old elites lest the new order be plagued with vindictiveness and injustice. His worst fear is that the persecution of the former communists by using communist bureaucratic methods and relying on frequently dubious secret police documents would only prolong the agony of the old order and envenom the public climate: "My blackest dream is that we will take all our communists and send them to Siberia. And then what will we have? Communism without communists."[12] Václav Havel has placed himself morally on Michnik's side, but as president of his country he refused to prevent the enactment of the lustration (purification, screening) law once the parliament adopted it in October 1991. The Czech lustration law banned former high party officials, secret police agents and collaborators, and members of the People's Militia (once the party's paramilitary units) from holding jobs in the state administration, state media, and state-owned economic units for a period of five years.[13] On the other hand, Evangelical Pastor Joachim Gauck represents the most consistent pro-decommunization approach in the former GDR: for him only full disclosure of the secret police activities in the past can allow East Germans to become mature citizens.[14] In short, the choice is between two strategies: the "policy of the thick line" that judges individuals exclusively in the light of their commitment to the new democracy and covers the past with the blanket of forgiveness, on the one hand, and the logic of lustration, with its attachment to the principle of radical separation from the past. The first strategy considers the Leninist order as irrevocably defunct, a definitively ended historical cycle, and proposes a future-rather than past-oriented approach to politics, individuals, and culture. The second is, in its extreme forms, exclusive and rigoristic: it looks to communism as an unmitigated evil, and uses a Manichean moral compass to distinguish between "angels" and "devils."

The myth of lustration as political catharsis is bound to enhance the sense of true beginning. It emphasizes discontinuity, the resolute cutting off of the umbilical cord with an ambiguous past. In reality, however, it is based on an unquestioning reliance on the secret police files, which can lead to unjustified persecutions and limitations of individual civic rights. As British journalist Timothy Garton Ash, one of the most perceptive analysts of Central Europe's political culture, has put it, lustration is a good example of how *not* to go about decommunization. This is not because of its lack of legitimacy but because of the absence of serious provisions for due process, appeal, or redress, as well as for a thorough examination of the validity and trustworthiness of the files. However, the clumsy formulation of the lustration law did not make it meaningless. On the contrary, in Garton Ash's words, "it is precisely if you don't establish regular, fair, legal procedures for dealing with the problem of past collaboration and crimes that you are most likely to end up, sooner or later, with irregular, blatantly political ones."[15]

One cannot thus simply dismiss as aberrations the anger among many Poles, Romanians, or Russians who feel deprived of any moral satisfaction and denounce collusion among the elites in order to explain the failure of decommunization. The problem with the lustration law, however, is that it created a sense of legal helplessness among those who were discovered on the lists: defending themselves, going to the courts and challenging the secret police documents is a long and nerve-racking process.

Lustration is a part of the overall treatment of the communist past. These new polities have to decide whether the previous regimes were criminal in both their intentions and practices; if this was the case, the punishment of the guilty persons follows logically. In the Czech case, one can refer to the "Law Concerning the Illegitimacy of the Communist Regime" adopted in July 1993. This law, the most consistent legal indictment of a deposed Leninist regime, was passed by an large majority of the Czech parliament (129 in favor, 34 against, and 3 abstaining). The culpability of the former power holders was stipulated in no uncertain terms:

> The Communist Party of Czechoslovakia, its leaders and its members, are responsible for the ways our land was governed in the years 1948–1989 and in particular for the systematic destruction of the traditional values of European civilization, for the conscious violation of human rights and freedoms, for the moral and economic decline accompanied by judicial crimes and terror against dissenters, for substituting a command economy for a market one, for the destruction of the traditional principles of the laws of ownership, for the misuse of education, training, science and culture for political and ideological goals, for the reckless destruction of nature.

The charges against communist domination are factually correct, although the law does not take into account the strictly centralized and militaristic nature of Leninist organizations and makes little distinction between party elites and ordinary members. In all state socialist regimes, from Bulgaria to East Germany, communists exerted their power unchecked, in full contempt of law and public accountability. They despised their subjects and used the secret police as their main instrument to cultivate fear and suspicion among citizens. Civil society was continuously and systematically attacked. The stern conclusions of the Czech law, signed by Václav Havel, among others, refuses any semantic equivocation:

> The regime based on Communist ideology, which determined the direction of the state and the fate of its citizens in Czechoslovakia from February 24, 1948, to November 17, 1989, was criminal, illegitimate and deserves condemnation. The Communist Party of Czechoslovakia was a criminal organization, deserving condemnation, just like other organizations based on its ideology; its activity was aimed at suppressing human rights and the democratic system. Resistance to the regime by individuals or groups of citizens, based on a democratic political, religious or moral conviction, manifested by acts of resistance or other activities or knowingly and publicly expressed, whether on the territory of this state or abroad, even if in cooperation with a democratic foreign power, was legitimate, just, morally justified and worthy of respect.[16]

Justified in its moral thrust, the law glosses over historical nuances and political distinctions. It ignores the decisive role of the communist reformers in unleashing the Prague Spring. It treats the communist experience as a fully homogenous era and disregards the inner logic of communist disintegration. These adamant anticommunist legislators seem to forget that some of the most courageous critics of communism came from among the disenchanted party members. This is not to say that communist institutions did not have a criminal nature (in the sense of illegal), but simply that not all communists were equally responsible for their perpetuation. Some tried to humanize them, as Imre Nagy and his associates did during the Hungarian Revolution of 1956, or Alexander Dubček and the majority of the Czechoslovak communist leadership during the Prague Spring. Furthermore, revealing the atrocities of the past can provide a therapeutic effect only if decommunization is historically grounded. Condemnation should be accompanied by relentless endeavors to comprehend how it was possible to control so many people for such a long time. If decommunization is to serve as a foundation for a new beginning, it must generate a better understanding of human motivations, highlight the institutional underpinnings of the old regime, and explain the mechanics of submission manufactured under the old ideology.

Political psychology as much as historical awareness is required in the difficult enterprise of post-communist justice. Arthur Koestler knew something about this when he wrote in 1950 that focusing on the past is not a sterile waste of time: "The answer is simply that these things are neither 'past' nor 'done with.' Only those who worked inside the totalitarian machine know its true character and are in a position to convey a comprehensive picture of it."[17] Archives should thus be open to researchers, but such researchers should always keep in mind that these documents include only the information the communists wanted to be preserved. Extreme caution is necessary to avoid any tempting extrapolations. This need to grasp the past in all its complexities, to refuse simplistic classifications and distinctions between artificially designated groups of innocents and villains is emphasized by Petr Pithart, the first post-communist prime minister of the Czech Republic: "Only now, as the new democracies of Central and Eastern Europe struggle with serious troubles, is the so-called 'black box of communism' being opened. In this important sense, communism is far from being a topic for historians. Wrong illusions about what communism was and was not, what the people subjected to it were and are result in disappointment. And mass disappointments result in mass movements. Today's nationalism is one of those movements."[18]

The pace and intensity of decommunization varied from country to country and reflected the prevailing attitudes toward the legacies of the deposed regimes. Initially, during the first stage of the revolutions, the figure of the communist symbolized much of what Poles, Bulgarians, or Hungarians abhorred: ideological uniformity, doublespeak, secret police surveillance, scarcity of consumer goods, eternal lines for food, and contempt for human rights. Hence the uncompromising decommunizers had a large and vibrant constituency. But most people got tired of their rhetoric and found their own latter-day plight more important than the punishment of the former leaders. What happiness can one discover in having a decrepit Stalinist like Bulgaria's former boss Todor Zhivkov tried for ludicrous charges of embezzlement?[19] And if such political fossils are found guilty, who benefits from this verdict?

Punitive political justice has little impact on the squandered lives of the individuals who suffered under communism. Its restitutive impact is insignificant. The calls for purges have ceased to generate mass support; although in 1990 thousands of East Europeans were ready to take to the streets in the name of militant anti-communism, this is not the case any more. Other issues are more pressing nowadays—the social safety net, unemployment, hyperinflation, corruption, crime—and the same citizens who resented communism are now ready to cast their votes with the ex-communists in many of the new democracies.[20] The overall reason for this left turn in post-communist electoral behavior is to be found in the combination of nostalgia, rage, malaise, and fear so characteristic of the sudden breakdown of the old order and the painful constitution of the new one. In some cases, as for instance in Poland, Latvia, Lithuania, Georgia, or Azerbaijan, the ex-communists appear less vehement and viciously nationalist than some of their anti-communist rivals. Moreover, some of these former party bureaucrats have broken with their past and try to push for reform.[21] As a general trend, however, this "communostalgia" (a term coined by William Safire) is based on two psychological premises:

obliviousness toward about the harshness and squalor of the communist days and frustration about the costs of the transition to a free market.[22]

For the time being, the politics of remembrance advocated by former dissidents has lost its emotional appeal. Instead of identifying the major cause of the dismal state of the economy in the legacies of communist bureaucratic mismanagement, many people engage in daydreaming about the safety and stability of the "old days." Such nostalgia further embitters and radicalizes the decommunizers. But the ebb of anti-communist ire can be misleading because as a political myth decommunization still has inflammatory power. Its sources run deep, and as the transition meets unexpected challenges, as the former communists behave in ostentatiously condescending ways, new waves of indignation could flow and threaten the fragile consensual order. It would be naive to think that decommunization is over and, to use the title of a famous film by French director Alain Resnais, *la guerre est finie*. As the Hungarian political philosopher György Bence's warned:

> There is, nevertheless, a public outcry for political justice aimed against the greatest beneficiaries of the old regime. This outcry is partly spontaneous and partly instigated by demagogues. But the sentiment is truly shared by a large part of the public, and it is grounded in economics. The country is on the verge of bankruptcy. The standard of living of whole segments of the population, especially the elderly and the retired, is already at an intolerable low level. Hardships are expected to increase. In contrast, the former communist leaders are living quite comfortably, sometimes even opulently, on generous state pensions. They often enjoy illicit benefits from their former positions, for instance in the form of valuable real estate. And as they are the only social group with adequate financial means, they use the country's new economic freedoms to become capitalists. This, at least, is the perception of the least privileged strata of the society. And demagogues stand ready to stir up vindictiveness and manipulate the desperate.[23]

Indeed, in some post-communist societies (Bulgaria under Videnov, Romania under Iliescu, Serbia, Slovakia, Russia, Ukraine, and the Caucasus, more than Hungary or Poland), the resurrection of the old faces and habits under new or not-so-new masks has created a widespread feeling of powerlessness and despondency among the opposition. People witness fatalistically the restoration of nomenklatura-style privileges for the power elite. In Russia, for example, fear and favor are rampant, and the government is immune to press scrutiny.[24] Even some of the most dynamic and imaginative independent writers seem to be unable to see how the country can escape its current predicament. By contrast in Romania, the most lucid writers and journalists see the origins of the crisis in the legacy of pathological corruption, heated nationalism, embedded violence, and other components of the Balkan traditions enhanced and exacerbated by Ceauşescu's dynastic communism.[25] Popular discontent with Iliescu's efforts to preserve the old order resulted in his defeat in the November 1996 presidential elections. The new president, Emil Constantinescu, a former rector of the University of Bucharest, emphasized in his campaign the need to undertake major reforms and establish the rule of law. Furthermore, Constantinescu insisted on the importance of restoring the truth about the country's recent history.[26]

Justice, Amnesty, and Forgiveness

Václav Havel gave an excellent definition of the moral urge that motivates the proponents of decommunization and the quest for justice, while being fully aware of the risk that the whole process could degenerate into lynchings, in the name of the quest for revenge: "One must somehow manage to steer between Scylla and Charybdis. I think that both concepts, in their extreme form, are faulty. The history of our country shows that every time we took the approach of thinking that we should not be interested in whatever had happened in the past—that it was not important—the consequences were always severe. It meant that we did not remove an ulcer that was poisoning the whole system. The ulcer kept festering and producing new toxins. I think that the need to cut out this ulcer, to administer justice, is clearly justified and natural."[27]

More than anything else, Leninist regimes tried to control human minds. Unlike traditional tyrannies, these were utopian dictatorships that claimed to know what social happiness is and how it is to be accomplished. Their ideological frenzy was the rationale for aiming at full control over needs and thoughts. And if the East German dissidents are right in describing the activities of the Stasi (East Germany's secret police, probably the most ubiquitous and effective in any totalitarian state ever) as an "Auschwitz of the soul," is it moral to ask people to simply ignore what happened by invoking the need for social and political reconciliation? Can reconciliation work properly in the absence of atonement? Will there ever be de-Stasification if this institutionalized infamy is simply forgotten? Whatever the faults of the lustration laws in the Czech Republic and Germany may be, it is hard to deny that they at least tried to shed light on the past and prevent the former communist agents and activists from coming to power again within the new government structures.

No less important, if these decommunization laws are to be effective, they should not simply lead to the exposure of informers without punishing their superiors, who are truly responsible for the functioning of the police state. Moreover, the punishment of a few party and government officials does not diminish the widespread, diffuse guilt among so many who, with more or less enthusiasm, helped the system go on. In the words of Vojtec Čepl, a Czech law professor: "While secret police informers who collaborated for personal gain deserve condemnation, members of every profession committed their own characteristic sins and crimes: plumbers stole pipes, waiters diluted wine, scholars distorted the truth and told outright lies, teachers confused the minds of their students, and civil servants acted corruptly and harassed citizens who dared to oppose them."[28]

The argument that lustration would cleanse the moral atmosphere can always be countered by the no less compelling point that the lists of secret police collaborators were drawn by experts in duplicity, forgery, and disinformation. None of the secret police forces of the former Warsaw Pact countries was interested in fairness and accuracy. Furthermore, passing absolute judgment on the individual choices and presumed abdications that took place under ambiguous circumstances of the past is morally objectionable. How can one make sure that the lists are exhaustive? Can one single abject instance in one's life be more important than years of selfless dedication to dissident values?

One of the most famous controversies unleashed by lustration is the case of Czech journalist and member of parliament Jan Kavan, widely discussed in books dealing with the transition from state socialism.[29] Kavan had reason to feel wounded and humiliated when his former comrades accused him of collaboration with the secret police: after a life of uncompromising struggle for democratic values, the man who, as founder of the London-based Palach Press had been involved in the publication of Havel's and other Charter 77 activists' essays and documents, saw his reputation questioned by a parliamentary body solely on the base of information from the secret police archives. The alleged exposure and investigation of Kavan and nine other members of parliament were widely covered by the media. Very little attention was paid, however, when the courts cleared those who appealed for justice. In Kavan's own words: "Havel became critical of the procedure precisely because the lustrating commission did not bother to establish the individual guilt, they were satisfied with the fact that some of the MPs were 'registered' as agents and others had a thick file."[30]

The problem with lustration as an unyielding form of decommunization is that it has no interest in the presumption of innocence. Once mentioned on the list, people have little power to defend themselves. Others treat them as pariahs. Rumors abound and leaks from different commissions charged with decommunization reach the media. Most absurdly, even Havel's name appeared in one of the secret police files, describing him as a "candidate for recruitment" in 1965. But a "potential collaborator" is the most vague and undefinable term: it simply means that an overzealous secret police officer tried to impress his superiors by naming as many as possible potential "conquests." But, Jiři Ruml, a former dissident who, was the chairman of the parliamentary lustration commission, seemed to have confidence in the secret police documents: "Everything we have in the register is very reliable. It was impossible to falsify the register. We don't have a single case of falsification of the register."[31] In this Kafkaesque context, a simple conversation was twisted into a gesture of complicity, and the targeted person had not the slightest idea that he or she had already been put on the record in the unfathomable archives of secret police.

No one gave a better assessment of the ambivalence of lustration than Havel himself in an interview with the Czech magazine *Mlady Svet*:

> Just imagine someone who was importuned all his life by the secret police, and has learned how to take evasive action, to prevaricate and equivocate. At last, he thinks he has just escaped their clutches, that he has successfully deceived them. After the revolution, this person feels an enormous sense of relief; now he can breathe easily because they, the secret police, can no longer bother him. . . . And now, suddenly, there is a new fear: he hears how, one after another, people who were marked as secret police collaborators swore they had never been collaborators, that someone had put them on a list without their knowledge, that on the basis of a single meeting in a cafe they were entered on a list of "candidates" for secret collaboration or something worse, just so some cop could get to chalk up the credit. . . . It's exactly what would interest me in a play, the situation of someone who felt he'd made it through the system unscathed and suddenly is terrified that maybe he hasn't after all.[32]

All these cases notwithstanding, and with all its glaring anomalies, Czech lustration has at least prevented a velvet restoration. More or less revamped post-communist groups and parties have not surfaced as major political actors. The price may have been too high; many developed a distrust of the new legal system and its commitment to individual rights. The faults of lustration should not be misconstrued, however, as an argument against its validity and legitimacy. Indeed, decommunization has been charged with the most horrible intentions, its proponents having been described as McCarthyites, witchhunters, rabid right-wingers, rabble-rousers, and so on. Some of them are. Others are not. The fact that impure people are associated with this strategy does not necessarily make it politically worthless and morally repellent. Indeed, one cannot ignore those who emphasize that decommunization is not a mirror image of communism's intolerance: "No one, after all, is being put to death for his crimes. Former agents are simply unable to hold public office or public-sector jobs—hardly a harsh sentence in a part of the world where state salaries are low."[33] Indeed, one is tempted to ask: how is it possible to establish the rule of law and a procedural democracy when the citizens of these countries do not trust their political elites and remain unconvinced that the break with the totalitarian past has become irreversible?

In reality, decommunization was mainly a cultural and political issue of the first stage of Eastern Europe's anti-communist revolutions. As communist regimes in these countries were not identical, and the revolutions did not follow the same path, the separation from communism pursued different roads. In many respects, the urgency of decommunization has been directly related to the readiness (or lack of it) of the former rulers to renounce their privileges and engage in the democratic game. For this very reason, the issue remains vitally important in Bulgaria, Serbia, Slovakia, Russia, and Ukraine, where the members of the communist nomenklatura are still enjoying full power, in contrast with Poland, Hungary, the Czech Republic, and the Baltic states, where substantive changes have taken place both in politics and in the economy.[34] But even during the second stage, that of democratic consolidation, the issue remains relevant.

Delays in decommunization and the economic empowerment of the former nomenklatura may have tragic consequences for the moral and psychological sanity of the new democracies. On the other hand, there is little doubt that nationalist populism is as inimical to liberal values as the post-communist social demagogy. It is therefore legitimate to question hasty generalizations about the communist presence as the main threat to democracy. According to such views, rightist conservative, neopopulist, and nationalist parties are benign forces, whereas the ex-communists, no matter how much they endorse pluralism and the free market remain hostages to their authoritarian heredity. In other words, once a communist, forever one, and therefore an enemy of democracy. Needless to add, this perspective lumps together market-oriented and truly reformed post-communist parties (such as the Polish Alliance of the Democratic Left) with the unreconstructed descendants of the old Leninist left (such as, for instance, Serbia's Socialist party or Romania's Party of Social Democracy).[35]

Decommunization is not simply a matter of punishing certain individuals but a long-term process aimed at establishing legal institutions and law-abiding behavior among both elites and ordinary citizens. This is particularly important for Russia (and other successor states of the USSR), where legality has such a precarious heredity. In the words of Richard Pipes: "As for Lenin, he made no secret that he regarded law as an instrument of government: He defined 'dictatorship of the proletariat' as authority unconstrained by law. And he constructed on this principle a pseudo-judiciary system that Stalin inherited and perfected. In the entire history of Russia, and especially during the Communist reign, lawlessness was not simply a fact of life in the relationship between state and citizenry but an institutionalized principle, the quintessence of the system."[36] This is the reason why, if decommunization is to take place for the benefit of a democratic order, it has to observe legality more than anything else. Otherwise, it would be a prolongation of old anti-democratic, authoritarian, even Bolshevik methods.

Decommunization bears upon some of the most difficult questions of the transition: it is a political myth linked to the nature of the revolutions, the role of the dissidents, the levels of mass compliance with the old regime, and the possibility of overcoming the burdens of the past. Will the new republics be established on legality, so that people could or should not be punished for past deeds unless they were illegal according to the *then* existing laws? Or should one see the whole communist stage as an experiment based on lawlessness, as the late Leonard Shapiro argued in his masterful *History of the CPSU?*[37] This tension between the new legitimacy and legal continuity (the principle of legality) is indeed a main source of controversy and heated debates. As Jacques Rupnik has argued, what is at stake is a double political game: that of decommunization and that of constitutionalism.[38]

All of the East European revolutions were confronted with the classic question: what to do with the deposed tyrants? Should they benefit from legal procedures and be allowed to play the game of universal (in other words nobody's) responsibility for the past crimes?[39] And what to do with the servants of the old regime, including the masterminds of ideological pageants and the experts in surveillance and indoctrination? Polish constitutional expert Wiktor Osyatinski sums up this dilemma: "Every revolution faces three questions. First, what to do with the king. Second, what to do with his courtiers. And third and by far the most difficult, what to do with the people's frustrated expectations. And then it occurs to the new leaders—aha! We have a king we haven't guillotined yet!"[40]

In all the countries of the region, there has been an intense need among the public for identifying the sources of the people's fears, those responsible for economic ruin, and the engineers of the huge mechanisms of mental and political regimentation. On the other hand, there has been the risk that the decommunization could run amok and usher in a new reign of terror. The moderates (or opponents of lustration) considered the legacy of communism too wide and all-permeating to be simply eliminated by legal treatment. Radicals, in turn, disputed the very principle of legal continuity with the past. These revolutionary *enragés* claimed that for the revolution to be complete, the old legal order must be exposed as fraudulent. The deposed leaders, the former nomenklatura, should be held responsible for their actions against their own nations. Liberals, in turn, saw that this logic could result in a prolonged civil war, with unnecessary victims and the perpetuation of a climate of panic. But, as Pastor Joachim Gauck has often said, public trust cannot be built in the absence of transparence, especially regarding the activities of the secret police. Defending the legal framework created in united Germany and the record of his commission in charge of the Stasi files, Gauck—himself a former human rights activist persecuted during the communist regime—insisted that the citizens' legally guaranteed access to their secret police files is mandatory if the new order is to restore dignity and truth as public virtues:

> I believe the law is absolutely correct. Thanks to this law, we are not walking in the fog; we can eliminate the doubts and restore the faith in democracy to the segment of society that had come to think this country could not be democratically ruled. Those who, like Lothar de Maziere [post-communist GDR prime minister] claimed that opening the files would result in public unrest, the settling of old scores, and even murders have been proven wrong. Of course some conflicts have arisen, but

they were to be expected. Just imagine what would have happened if the files had been kept secret: not only would it have been impossible to create a climate of trust, but the files could have been used to threaten and blackmail people. The road we have taken is difficult and painful, but in my opinion is the only road open to us."[41]

Not to reveal the truth about the past is conducive to public discontent, frustrations, and a general feeling that the old guard is still running the show. This sentiment is palpably present in Russia, Romania, Serbia, and even Poland, where the second echelon of the former ruling class exploited nationalist and anticommunist passions, only to strengthen its power and eventually preempt any serious coming to terms with the past.[42] Economically, this group uses its political hegemony to engage in the shabby operations often described as "nomenklatura privatization." In the words of French political scientist Françoise Thom: "The second echelon claims to prize competence above all else in recruiting officials. The nomenklatura has thus maintained its hold on positions of authority, as only its members can claim the necessary managerial experience. The second echelon portrays itself as a centrist force, opposed to extremism of all varieties and committed to social peace and consensus. It poses as the champion of human rights, which it says are threatened by radical anticommunists. The second echelon is also systematically attempting to reinforce executive power at the expense of the legislative bodies at every political level."[43]

The rise of this second echelon has been an all-pervasive phenomenon in most of the post-communist societies. No less significant is the fact that these individuals are nonideological ex-communists. The adversaries of decommunization, especially former Polish, Czech, and Hungarian dissidents, have maintained that these people will necessarily play the new game of pluralism and tolerance. Others have been more skeptical and wonder whether the end result will be liberal democracy or rule by the mafia, and in the worst tradition of Latin American corrupt authoritarianisms.

From my perspective, the decommunization debate was significant at least for three reasons: first, because the consolidation of democracy, East or West, is unthinkable without a thoroughgoing break with the previous legacies of authoritarianism; second, because any new order needs credibility, and this is impossible in the absence of an identification of those directly involved in the repressive actions of the previous regimes; and third, as real crimes took place, justice has to be done if the new democracies are to become and remain genuine states of law and develop a high level of social capital. Decommunization has been a complex and manifold process; it has attempted a moral regeneration of societies long permeated by duplicity, hypocrisy, and systematic lies; sought historical truth and the understanding of the political and human instruments that made communist autocracy possible; and finally, served as a legal endeavor to identify individual guilt and respond to it in accordance to the laws as they functioned at the moment of the incriminated actions. Collective punishments are by definition counterproductive and morally reprehensible. To punish individuals for having worked for an institution regardless of the concrete circumstances of their personal behavior is fundamentally wrong: based on this fallacious logic, Oskar Schindler would have been found guilty of exploitation of slave labor during World War II.

Guilt must be individually assigned, and every individual has the right to explain the reasons for his or her actions. Otherwise, the new political order shares with the old one the same contempt for individual rights, the same obsession with "class justice." In fact, no liberal order can be instituted on such a vindictive principle. Not vengeance but truth ought to inspire the search for historical reparations—and such reparations are fully legitimate.

The myth of decommunization has tended to acquire aggressive, often violent tones. A case in point is that of Jaroslaw Kaczynski, once a close associate of Lech Walesa, who has been called a latter-day Saint Just for his adamant demand for the execution of those who ordered martial law: "The authors of the martial law," Kaczynski wrote in Michnik's *Gazeta Wyborcza* (of all places), "should probably be hanged. If this is true . . . that there was no threat and that Polish authorities knew it, they should be convicted and executed"[44]

This approach is a firm and unequivocal denial of the logic of the Roundtable agreements which led to the end of communist dictatorships in Poland and Hungary. In contrast to the Spanish, post-Franco "Madrid syndrome," based on reconciliation and mutual guarantees of impunity between the two partners in the negotiation, this approach is based on retroactive punishment. This is the ultimate expression of the myth of "them" versus "us." As a vindictive and scapegoating myth, it offers a clear-cut view according to which the world had been divided in two distinct categories: the perpetrators and the victims. The old party is designated as criminal as a whole, while in reality millions had been members and participated in different rituals (party meetings, May Day parades, party educative sessions, party schools) without either sharing the professed values or condoning the persecution of the dissidents. For many, in reality, the sin was one of omission rather than commission. With its aggressive overtones and salvationist energy, decommunization is a myth these societies need in order to justify and consolidate their own newly acquired political identity: post-communist, therefore noncommunist. It generates feelings of pride and self-esteem among individuals who normally have very little to be proud of in terms of resistance to the old order, except their "clean hands."[45]

This phenomenon has been captured by Zhelyu Zhelev, Bulgaria's president between 1990 and 1996 and a former dissident himself. Because of his reluctance to endorse the purges, Zhelev became the target in 1993 of strong criticism from frantic decommunizers. In an interview with Adam Michnik, Zhelev described his detractors:

"They are, in fact, mirror images of the communists. They possess the same nature as the communists. The only thing that distinguishes them from the communists is their opposition to communism. They possess the same kind of hatred as the communists. Their ideology is an ideology of hatred of the enemy, therefore they keep dreaming up new ememies. I tell you, these people have not changed one little bit."[46]

The picture should not be oversimplified: some of those who insist on decommunization have impeccable credentials as former human rights activists and should not be condescendingly dismissed as hot-headed fanatics. Jan Olszewski, briefly Polish prime minister in 1992, and since 1995 chairman of the rightist Movement for the Reconstruction of Poland, was one of the most active lawyers on behalf of Solidarity—through journalist Tina Rosenberg refers to him simply as "a radical called Jan Olszewski." Antoni Macierewicz, minister of the interior Olszewski government, was not simply a former "Maoist sympathizer"—actually Guevarist, to set the record straight—as the same author describes him, but also one of the driving forces of the Committee for Workers' Defense created in 1976.[47] In that capacity, he worked closely with Kuron and Michnik on behalf of the persecuted workers and played an important role in creating the premises for the alliance between workers and intellectuals that was to lead to the rise of Solidarity. When Olszewski voiced in 1992 the need to begin "the end of communism," he based his strategy on a rigid dichotomy between those guilty for "betrayals, lies, crimes, and cruelty" on the one hand, and those having "clear consciences and clean hands." In his view, to give up decommunization was a risky proposal, since it would only confirm the "cynicism of the guilty and discourage everyone else."[48] Thus one cannot simply discard the radicals as loonies of the right. Some of them may be unreconstructed nationalists, others are not. Even Leszek Moczulski, the leader of Confederation for an Independent Poland, although ready in 1995 to ally himself with the leftovers of the Communist party's anti-Semitic faction, served years in prison because of his calls for a break with the USSR and the establishment of a democratic regime. We may dislike some of these people's views, they may strike us as not exactly liberal in a Western sense, but not all of them are motivated by envy, jealousy, or rationalized shame.

To understand the divisions between former friends or at least allies in the anti-commmunist struggle one has to look into the composite nature of dissent and understand that it never was monolithic. Within the anti-communist movement there were socialists and Trotskyites, liberal democrats, and conservatives. Each one has responded to the issue of decommunization in the light of his or her moral belief system. In other words, although we may disagree with the revengeful drive of the decommunizers, we should not treat all of them as bloodthirsty Jacobins.

When in 1992 a conference was organized in Warsaw on the topic of decommunization, Adam Michnik, editor of the country's most circulated newspaper, *Gazeta Wyborcza*, refused to attend, arguing that he was not ready to engage in a practice leading to the erection of guillotines. Influenced, I suspect, by his readings about the fate of previous revolutions, Adam Michnik has tended to exaggerate the prospects for the repetition of the past; to prevent the repetition, he proposed the strategy of compassion, forgiveness, and reconciliation: "Every revolution, bloody or not, has two phases. The first phase is dominated by the struggle for freedom, the second by the struggle for power and revenge on the votaries of the old regime. . . . [The] logic [of revenge is] implacable. First there is a purge of yesterday's adversaries, the partisans of the old regime. Then comes the purge of yesterday's fellow oppositionists who now oppose the idea of revenge. Finally there is a purge of those who defend them. A psychology of vengeance and hatred develops."[49]

Although Michnik's reluctance to endorse political justice can be understood, his position left a burning question unanswered: how can the new polities be constructed on the principles of law and truth if the former tormentors continue to enjoy their privileges, while the victims are denied any legal satisfaction? What is to be done with Ceauşescu's Securitate thugs, Enver Hoxha *sigurimi*, or Husák's secret police officers who persecuted for two decades any initiative from below and sent Havel and other Charter 77 activists to prison more than once? Michnik himself offered a poignant synthesis of this moral conundrum: "When I was still in prison, I promised myself two things: first, that I will never belong to any violent organization that would give me orders for struggling against communism; and second, that I would never take revenge on anyone. On the other hand, I kept repeating to myself a certain stanza from a poem by Zbigniew Herbert, who wrote: 'And do not forgive, because it is not within your power to forgive in the name of those who were betrayed at dawn.' I think that we are condemned to such dialectic. . . . We can try to convince people to forgive, but if they want justice, they have the right to demand it."[50]

In reality, instead of savage punishments of the old potentates, what has happened has been their retrenchment and even return, the vilification of the dissidents, and the emergence of new coalitions based on common guilt, shame, and contempt for those who had indeed opposed communism.

Decommunization: De-Nazification or Witch-hunt?

Decommunization has often been compared to de-Nazification, and for good reasons. The two totalitarian regimes pretended to incarnate the sense of history and have imposed, in the name of their mythological ambitions, unspeakable hardships and persecutions upon their subjects and hostages. They differed of course in many respects, but in terms of their contempt for "bourgeois law," they were strikingly alike: legality was just a simulacrum of justice, with judges, lawyers, and prosecutors completely controlled by the state apparatus.

Debates have not been so much about the rationale for decommunization, which any seriously thinking person cannot deny. The discussion instead has focused on the methodology of decommunization and, intimately related to it, its consequences for the moral constitution of the new order. Whereas decommunizers have seemed to favor a cathartic and vindictive political myth, the anti-decommunizers (often former dissidents of leftist persuasion) have operated with the myth of consensus and reconciliation.[51]

Invoking the technical difficulties of handling the secret police files properly, Bruce Ackerman proposes a most uncompromising solution, namely the destruction of the secret police files: "Once the security apparatus is dismantled, millions of files remain, containing reports, both true and false, about countless inhabitants. What to do with these stinking carcasses? Burn them, I say. . . . The point is *not* whether many were guilty of this or that wrongdoing. To the contrary, there were too many collaborators, and it is beyond the capacity of law and bureaucracy to assess the shades of gray accurately."[52]

But is the fact that we deal with a daunting task sufficient reason to give up any investigative effort and close the record? What kind of societies will these be once their memory has been artificially amputated? Burning the files, in my view, is a form of pretending that the horror never existed. The fundamental philosophical question is the nature of the Leninist regimes and our view of them from a liberal perspective: if we agree that they were systematic forms of controlling and coercing human will, then there is no moral imperative that compels treating their history differently from the treatment of Hitler's horrendous legacy.

Although it would be absurd to deny the evolution and even in some cases liberalization of these regimes (especially in Hungary and Poland), their nature at the intentional level did not essentially differ from one another. True, the age of unmitigated terror passed once Stalin died (except in Albania and to some extent Romania). But the criminal foundations of these regimes remained unaltered: none of them was based on popular consent, and none of them accepted minimal accountability for their actions. All continued to function as secret police empires based on universal suspicion, infringements on basic human rights, and contempt for individual dignity.

The danger, in Ackerman's view, is that the new, liberal governments would legitimize, by mere reference to them, the most infamous practices of the old regime. Michnik, too, is afraid that insistence on the files allows "secret police colonels to give out morality certificates." The bottom line in this approach is that the distinction between perpetrators and victims would be too vague to be considered a valid signpost. Moreover, this scenario alleges that the secret police files are blatantly dishonest, created for purposes of blackmail and intimidation. This is a questionable point: secret police files, we know from the

Czech and German cases, were subject to continuous verification, as the authorities wanted to make sure that the officers were not exaggerating their "accomplishments."

The risks implied by Ackerman's proposal are no less costly than the evil it tries to neutralize: once the files disappear, a whole segment of society's historical memory vanishes. In the former GDR, the Gauck Commission has managed to keep the Stasi documents under control, and researchers as well as citizens have had the possibility of consulting them. Understanding the importance of this issue, the German state has allocated a budget of over 200 million DM per year for the three thousand employees working in these archives. It is a costly operation, but it has worked. The unmanageability of the secret police files is itself a political myth to prevent further investigation of the modus operandi of the deposed institutions and their human carriers. By the same logic, what should have been done with the archives of the Nazi regime, or with the documents regarding collaboration under the Vichy government in France? The archives, after all, speak about felony and scurrilous behavior, and also about those who rejected them. No doubt there were many collaborators and informers, but it has been a gross exaggeration to deny the existence of diverse forms of resistance and mechanisms of refusal within the late Leninist regimes.

The issue is not to legalize vindictive punishment but to rescue collective memory. This point was luminously raised by Hungarian president Arpad Göncz, himself a former political prisoner and dissident, when he proposed an alternative approach to the calls for corrective justice. In 1992 Göncz endorsed the Constitutional Court's decision to oppose the extension of the statute of limitations in order to administer justice to those responsible for the mass repression that followed the crushing of the 1956 revolution. He urged the parliament to establish instead a Commission for Historical Investigation to examine the processes, events, and details of the period between 1944 and 1989. Indeed, Göncz's proposal seems to be a logical way to avoid the pitfalls of retroactive criminal justice. In his message to Parliament, Goncz stressed that "a complete disclosure of events and naming of persons responsible for the violation of law might help familiarize us with the nation's tragic recent past, and might help, without infringing the constitution and existing legal principles, to ease the tensions prevailing in our society because of lack of clarity about the past."[53]

For the people who live under post-communism, decommunization has not been an abstract philosophical notion. They know who terrorized them, who opened their correspondence, tapped their phone conversations, forced many of them to become informers, and established a labyrinth of suspicion, betrayal, and fear in the name of the "radiant future." This point was strongly defended by former Charter 77 activist Petruska Sustrova, who served in the early 1990s as deputy minister of internal affairs in the Czech Republic. To those who have decried the lustration laws as "McCarthyite" and denounced them as "humanly insensitive," she responded that lustration was precisely a legal way of not letting the past spill over the present in an anarchic way. Questioning the validity of the witch-hunt analogy, Sustrova wrote:

> The analogy is misleading. The women burned at the stake centuries ago as witches were innocent; witches never existed. But the secret police and their collaborators existed in a real and proven way. The women accused of witchcraft paid with their lives. What has happened to the members of parliament who have been exposed as agents of the security police? If they haven't left office on their own, they still hold their seats, taking part in deciding the laws that will govern the nation. They continue to enjoy parliamentary immunity and to receive parliamentary salaries. . . . It is not a question of revenge or of passing judgment—it is simply a question of being certain about one's associates, about those who write our newspapers, and about the men and women who govern our country."[54]

In spite of many dire predictions, the impact of the lustration laws on the Czech polity has not been collective hysteria or mass panic. Instead, as Josef Darski, a Polish journalist who has written extensively on the issue of decommunization, noticed: "The Czech republic is the only post-communist country where the purges of ex-agents and decommunization have been actually carried out. . . . The Czech Republic has the best economic performance of the former Soviet bloc, the broadest privatization (a process widely accepted throughout Czech society), the largest participation of people in political life and in democratization generally, the highest public approval rating for any government in the region, and the least alienation towards the transition process."[55] In my view, other factors have played a very important role in the Czech success story, including the self-destruction of Czechoslovakia's Communist party after the Soviet invasion of August 1968. Over half a million party members were expelled in 1969 because of their refusal to endorse the Husak leadership document that justified the Soviet invasion as a correct class-inspired gesture of solidarity with the country's beleaguered socialist forces.

Darski's point is nevertheless significant: it was precisely because they created a legal structure that the Czechs could pursue decommuization within procedural limits, even though these procedures were seriously flawed.

In some cases, as for instance the Baltic Republics, decommunization cannot be fully disassociated from de-Sovietization. In Lithuania, a number of spectacular revelations occurred 1991–1992, including proof that former prime minister Kazimiera Prunskiene had cooperated with the KGB since 1980. No less important, proof was produced that Algis Klimaitis, a top foreign policy advisor to Prunskiene, was himself a KGB agent. He was arrested, so Lithuania has dared to bring KGB agents to justice.[56] Compare this to Iliescu's Romania, where countless media reports on the penetration by the

KGB (or its current reincarnation) of the top echelons of the post-Ceauşescu leadership did not lead to any ousters, let alone trial.[57]

Requiring the former top nomenklatura members and secret police cadres to refrain from running for public office for a period of five years was not exactly a form of human debasement. Actually, the existence of a legal code for dealing with former party and police officials prevented continuous corruption of the public discussion by leaks from uncheckable secret files. Whereas in the Czech Republic a full list of former secret police collaborators was published, in Bulgaria a law was passed penalizing any disclosure of secret collaborators of the ex-security police. In Romania, where the files have been theoretically sealed for another thirty years, periodic leaks happen, usually in the pages of the pro-Iliescu media, whenever they are needed to incriminate political adversaries. Many of the former secret police officers (especially those involved in foreign trade and technological espionage) have resurfaced as omnipotent economic movers and shakers, so it is reasonable to suspect that they are among the most interested in not having these files and lists brought to public knowledge. The myth of privatization, which for all practical purposes serves the goals of the same invisible mafia-style network, is the symbol needed to justify the transfer of national wealth into their hands.

The Danger in Derailing Decommunization

Decommunization is a myth that failed. Instead of political trials and purges, most of these countries have experienced the return of the communists and even "recommunization." Far from suffering the persecution that the anti-decommunizers brandished as a danger for the new legality, the former communists reorganized themselves. As cynicism has always been the "ethos" of the nomenklatura, the former party bureaucrats and plan barons reemerged as business operators and even successful political managers. For instance in Poland, Aleksander Kwasniewski, the last boss of the Communist Youth and leader of the Alliance of the Democratic Left, became Walesa's successor as the country's president. How did the former dissidents react to this? Bronislaw Geremek, in Bucharest, when asked in May 1995 about this restorative trend, said that he prefers to take the post-communists parties' prodemocratic statements (at least in Hungary and Poland) at face value: "The former communists are now interested in only one thing: power. And they can get it through democratic procedures, understanding that it is better this way than being imposed by the Central Committee. My problem, now, is for us to be able to take the power by using the same democratic procedures. I do not know whether they have indeed changed, but I notice that they accept the rules of the democratic game."[58]

Still, these are not innocent individuals with pristine political records; while they were making their careers in the Communist party, Poland or Hungary had other political choices available. Young Aleksander Kwasniewski, for instance, could have joined Solidarity during its first legal stage, between August 1980 and December 1981. He preferred to remain a disciplined communist, not for ideological reasons but because of opportunism and sheer conformity. Many of the neo-communists actively participated in the anti-worker and anti-dissident activities of the 1970s and 1980s. Some of them, like Hungary's Gyula Horn, climbed the career ladder during the repressive campaigns after 1956. Romania's former president Ion Iliescu is perhaps the most obvious case, since he served as the head of the National Students' Association between 1956–1958, when hundreds of students were arrested and imprisoned for their solidarity with the Hungarian revolution.

It is not simply that such people should receive absolution. In reality very few of them has ever expressed remorse for his or her communist past.[59] Think of former East German defense minister Heinz Kessler, for whom the defunct GDR was not a huge prison but a legitimate state committed to social justice and peace. A reincarnation of the officer guide in Franz Kafka's *Penal Colony*, Kessler refuses to express the slightest regret or recantation, and looks forward with great hopes for the revival of his old dreams: "I don't think the collapse of socialism in Eastern Europe means that there will be no other attempts to do what we did. The systems that are now in place are not solving people's economic, social and environmental problems. Other ways have to be found. New social structures will emerge, including some that will embrace the social principles I believe in. After all, what good are moral privileges if you are poor and starving?"[60]

Unlike Kessler, Jerzy Urban, the former spokesman for the communist junta on Poland, was never driven by ideological passion. He supported Jaruzelski because he deeply resented dissident intellectuals, the Church, and Solidarity. Blending cynicism, arrogance, pornography, and brazen self-promotion, Urban founded in early 1990s a highly successful weekly tabloid called *Nie* (No) in which he has equally castigated liberalism, nationalism, clericalism, and free-market profiteers (never mind that he happens to be one of them).[61]

Forgiveness in the absence of recantation is just a hollow offer.[62] In many cases, the former communists even take pride in their past and look at their ex-dissident opponents with undisguised arrogance. That of course has fueled further resentment among the former victims (or simply passive noncommunists) who complain that the revolution has been abducted. As economic reforms totter and the benefits of the market are slow to reach large social strata, as the former communists get increasingly rich and powerful, the myth of decommunization serves the social longing for retribution: the nation is seen as pure, innocent, and victimized by these aliens who have always known how to take advantage of every opportunity—yesterday as communists, today as reformists and capitalists. And, needless to say, like all political myths, decommunization has a basis in social and economic realities.[63] In dealing with the problem of decommunization one should adopt an historically comparative perspective: its meanings have been different in the former GDR and in Poland, or in Hungary as against Czechoslovakia, in Russia as against Lithuania, or in Romania as against the former GDR. The charismatic intensity, institutional solidity, and ideological consistency of the communist regimes differed from country to country, but the moral imperative of retribution for past crimes cannot be dismissed in the name of a philanthropic ethos of universal forgiveness. Whatever one may think of the post-1956 dynamics of Leninist regimes, it remains true that their first stage was marked by unspeakable cruelty and fanaticism. From the viewpoint of this book—the role of myth in the shaping of the new societies—this is an essential point: how can one ask the Albanians, the Romanians, the Poles, the Czechs, or the citizens of the Baltic States, for example, to forget the mass deportations, the destruction of their countries' elites and the methodic persecution of any source of independent action or thought? After all, even the liberal communists were ready to initiate political rehabilitation of the main victims among their own comrades (Lászlo Rajk, Lucrețiu Patrașcanu, Nikolai Bukharin) and legally (albeit often perfunctorily) punish some of the sadistic secret police officers. In the Soviet Union, Lavrenti Beria and some of the most ruthless interrogators were shot in the aftermath of Stalin's death.

Adam Michnik is right in saying that the logic of vendettas is counterproductive and intrinsically inimical to a state of law. But the issue is precisely to avoid populist explosions of hatred. Once taken over by political elites, clearly formulated and assigned a precise direction within an legal framework, as in the case of lustration in the Czech Republic, such a purification need not lead to arbitrariness, mob justice, or bloody confrontations. This approach was endorsed in June 1996 by the Parliamentary Assembly of the Council of Europe, which adopted the report on decommunization prepared by a commission headed by former Romanian deputy premier (in the Petre Roman government) Adrian Severin.[64] The main objectives for the liquidation of the totalitarian communist structures identified by the Severin Report are: the demilitarization of civilian institutions; decentralization of local, regional, and national (state) institutions; demonopolization and debureaucratization of society; prosecution of abuses committed during the totalitarian period; opening personal files held by the secret services; and the return to the legitimate owners of properties illegally confiscated or nationalized by the communist governments. Purging laws applied to former communist officials should not punish presumed culprits, but rather protect the new democracies.[65]

Discarding the problem of political justice as a resentful fantasy manipulated by irresponsible rabble-rousers is a dangerous view. Whatever one's feelings about it, decommunization as a political myth has expressed deep social frustrations, the sentiment among many that "our revolution was hijacked," that no change has taken place (and if it has than it has been for the worse), as well as the widespread belief that past misdeeds should find due punishment. And this is a major point: crimes did take place which were not just diffuse forms of illegality, minor exercises in surveillance, but direct and extremely obtrusive violations of human rights and dignity. Can a rereading of the Amnesty International reports on the region published in the late 1980s be called revisionism? Former secret police officers are to be prosecuted not because they abided by the laws of the ancien régime, but because they infringed upon them, or because they applied them with excessive, criminal zeal. No law allowed for the imprisonment and physical intimidation of the Czech Chartists and the members of Public Against Violence group in Slovakia; what these civic activists did was in full accordance with Czechoslovakia's then Constitution and the Helsinki Agreements.[66] The assassination in London of Georgi Markov, the Bulgarian critic of the Zhivkov regime, was not covered by any law. The bombs sent to Radio Free Europe journalists were unmistakable cases of terrorism.

The application of justice, of course, is extremely complicated. The case of Markus Wolf, the East German super-spy was still provoking debate in 1995. Wolf, who was involved in countless shabby operations intended to destabilize the West German constitutional order, was brought to trial and sentenced in 1993 to a six-year prison term. In May 1995, Germany's Constitutional Court reversed the sentence and decided that Wolf had not been tried properly. The charge of treason, it ruled, did not apply to somebody who had done the traditional job of a chief of an intelligence agency in a country that, until 1990, was internationally recognized as a sovereign state. The objection to the legal validity of the case against Wolf is persuasive. The Constitutional Court did the right thing, even if many feel morally outraged, considering that Wolf never expressed repentance for his deeds. But repellent as his previous political behavior might have been, it was not treacherous with respect to the interests of the GDR, and this was the point.[67]

To extrapolate from the case of Wolf to a theory that decommunization is not feasible is risky. Comparing the Eastern European regimes to the Latin American cases, Tina Rosenberg writes: "Germany faces the great legal conundrum of the post-Communist Europe: Where is the crime? Latin America's dictatorships were marked by murders, torture and kidnappings—criminal acts by any definition. But while these were carried out by regimes of criminals, Eastern Europe was ruled by criminal regimes. Officials who murdered and tortured must be prosecuted, but, at least after the 1950s, Europe's communist dictatorships were less given to violence than to invasive surveillance and restricting basic freedoms."[68] Were they? Can one so leniently generalize about decades of coercive regimentation, persecutions and indeed terror? Can the disappearance of miners in Jiu Valley in Romania, after the aborted strike against Ceauşescu in the summer of 1977, be simply ignored? Or the fate of the opposition in Albania or Bulgaria? Or the mass arrests during the Martial Law in Poland? Even more disquieting are statements such as: "Tapping telephones and inducing children to spy on their parents fell within the law."[69]

What law? On the contrary, the official constitutions guaranteed the privacy of correspondence and telephone conversations.

Neither the rise of the new elites nor the marginalization of the former dissidents can be understood without reference to the debate on decommunization. During the first post-1989 stage this was the main political bone of contention, creating strong animosities and turning old friends into bitter enemies. Let us look into a specific case, a historical detail as it were, but an utterly tragic one. In this respect, as in many others, the devil is in the details. Gheorghe Ursu was an engineer working for a Bucharest technical institute whose main guilt was that he did not keep secret his strong anti-Ceauşescu views. On the contrary, he deliberately left his satirical poems on his desk and told his colleagues that he was keeping a diary in which he was chronicling the infamies of the Ceauşescu dictatorship. The Securitate was on his track, hoping to demonstrate that Ursu was the center of a plot meant to overthrow the government. Arrested on September 21, 1985, he was savagely beaten in the Securitate jail and died two months later, on November 17. At the request of his family and of a number of former dissidents, an investigation was initiated at the beginning of 1990. As the investigation indicated clearly that the culprits were among the top brass of the pre- and post-1989 police, the general prosecutor replaced the magistrate in charge of this potentially explosive case (the former prosecutor in the Ceauşescu trial) with an obedient clerk who did his utmost to procrastinate. In June 1996, Ursu's son, Andrei, sent an open letter to Ion Iliescu asking him to intervene on behalf of legality, appoint an objective investigator who would have the courage to apply the law, and initiate the only logical procedure: bringing Ursu's assassins to trial under the charge of murder with premeditation. More than a decade after the killing in cold blood of a man whose only crime had been to keep a diary in which he unmasked the horrors of the Ceauşescu regime, the Romanian authorities are still dragging their feet, and permit Ursu's torturers to enjoy freedom, a good life, and even further their careers within the police.[70] What is at stake in this case is the very notion of a state of law and the trustworthiness of post-communist justice.

Conclusions

There have been in all post-communist societies two parties strongly opposed on the issue of decommunization. On the one hand, the decommunizers, actively committed to eliminating from public life the former supporters of the Stalinist regimes. On the other hand, there have been those who considered the whole approach mistaken, able to lead only to the fragmentation of the body politic, to endless settlings of scores and the poisoning of the new republics. Clearly, the debate on the need to confront the past rages on. On the other hand, the attempts to generate mass enthusiasm for legal prosecution of the former potentates have failed. This explains the drift of former radical decommunizers like Jan Olszewski and his Movement for the Reconstruction of Poland toward nationalist populism that blames the current ailments on the enduring influence of the corrupt post-communist nomenklatura over business and politics.[71]

The argument for de-communization relies on the need to build up a new society based on truth. Nobody can, after all, offer forgiveness in the name of those who suffered the effects of totalitarian criminal operations. As both Václav Havel and Arpad Göncz have pointed out, one can offer absolution on one's own behalf but not as a general measure of pardon. The paradox of decommunization was formulated in a strikingly clear way by Miklos Haraszti: "Who will decommunize the decommunizers?" "Who will screen the screeners?" "Who will purge the purgers?"[72] In the German case, the judges who tried Erich Honecker and his closest associates were imported from the West. The question is, how can one find "pure" judges in the other countries, when one knows much too well that, of all in Leninist societies, the legal profession was the most penetrated by the secret police?

If the issue is to identify the persons guilty for certain decisions and their application, there is serious argument between the decomunizers and their critics. The major conflict starts when one proposes measures bound to castigate certain categories collectively for having belonged to the political nomenklatura of the old regime. The most virulent call in this direction occurred in Bulgaria, under former prime minister Filip Dimitrov; Romania, in the "Proclamation of Timişoara" issued in March 1990; and Poland, under the Olszewski government.[73] The Mazowiecki government opposed decommunization from the very outset on the basis of the argument that the whole logic of the Roundtable agreements in Poland was based on an historic compromise between the former powerholders and the Solidarity counter-elite.[74] To engage in decommunization would have meant to breach a contract and to cancel an agreement under mob pressure. The trial of Erich Honecker and his associates in the former GDR justified some of the apprehensions of opponents of decommunization; instead of demonstrating the illegal nature of the previous regime, the trial simply created a judicial mess, allowing the former Politburo members to complain about being political victims of the Western "victors."[75]

As it has turned out, rather than being a popular demand decommunization has been an issue for elite confrontations. Decades of complicity with the existing order have made people skeptical of the very possibility of distinguishing between various shades of guilt. Add to this the widespread feeling that any attempt to apply legal mechanism is futile—communism instilled in its subjects a strong distrust of law. In fact, however, decommunization is a process that transcends the legal system. Communism created its own model of "civilization" and decommunization is a matter of decades. Although it is outrageous to see many of the former leaders enjoying the benefits of transition, the very nature of the state of law is to be universal and impersonal: former communists should be as entitled to due process as any other person.

In the economy of this book, the issue of decommunization is seen as a political myth used by certain members of the elite to enhance their image as national avengers, or pure crusaders for justice. It is based on the fallacy that society had not participated in the reproduction of the old order, and denies the logic of anti-politics (which emphasizes the values of tolerance and non-violence). Based on collective fears and longings, the strategy of decommunization, functioning as a political myth, conveys strong images of the foe and offers galvanizing reasons for emotional engagements in the struggle for his elimination. As liberal institutions and values have developed in the region, the myth has collided with the imperative of individual rights, including the right to bring to justice, pass judgment and, if found guilty, convict the persons (not the institutions) responsible for past misdemeanor.

Six_____

A Velvet Counterrevolution? Dissidents, Dreamers, and Realpolitik

> It is no accident that here, in this milieu of unre-
> lenting danger, with the constant need to defend
> our own identity, the idea that a price must be paid
> for truth, the idea of truth as a moral value, has
> such a long tradition."
> (*Václav Havel,* Summer Meditations)

WHATEVER HAPPENED to the former dissidents of East-Central Europe? Was their philosophy just a figment of utopian imagination, an indulgence in self-decep-tion about the nature of politics? Was their resistance and the ethical wager it implied an ephemeral moment of intellectual self-aggrandizement? These ques-tions bear not only on the realities of post-communism, but also on the rela-tionship between Western intellectuals and their peers in the East.

Were we wrong to assume that post-communist politics would abide by the universalistic principles professed by the dissidents of the 1970s and 1980s? Did we, in the West, exaggerate the role of these communities of free thinkers and tend to ignore (because we knew very little about them) the true emotions prevailing in the "other Europe"? Were the "sophisticated rebels" isolated figures not only because of the secret police harassments but also because of lack of communication with their fellow citizens?[1] Formulated this way, the questions beg for a positive answer: yes, there was a lot of moral idealism in the dissidents' creed, in the call by Václav Havel and Andrei Sakharov for a "politics of truth," in George Konrád's exaltation of anti-politics, and in Adam Michnik's vision of civil society. But the real issue is to what extent these ideas mattered in the breakdown of communism and, even more important, to what extent their carriers catalyzed the emergence of a political-intellectual class, a civic intelligentsia as it were, that formulated both the program of resistance and the main lines of the future governing order. That they did it in a sketchy, elusive way is no surprise: the future appeared stagnant in these societies, the questioning of the existing order was itself a gesture that many regarded skep-tically—a heroic, almost suicidal behavior with no chance to lead anywhere but to prison or the mental hospital.

During those days of fear and hopelessness, the Western intelligentsia's recognition of the dissidents' refusal of the Leninist status quo was essential.[2] The pages of *The New York Review of Books*, as well as *Dissent*, *The New Republic*, *Les Temps Modernes*, and *Times Literary Supplement* and so on. showcased essays signed by Adam Michnik, Bronislaw Geremek, Jacek Kuron, János Kis, and Miklos Haraszti. The "misjudgment of Paris"—Tony Judt's sarcastic reference to the overinflated role attributed to these critics of bureaucratic socialism by the French intellectuals—was indeed the solidarity of Western anti-communist liberals with the anti-communist liberals of the East. The new vision of politics put forward and experienced by Eastern-bloc dissidents was contagious. The resurrection of such topics as direct democracy, social capital, and civic trust in Western debates on the preconditions for democracy and democratization cannot be separated from the tribulations of the East European attempts to rehabilitate the ethos of civil society.[3]

Now things have changed. The Western intellectuals—epitomized by *The New York Review of Books*—seem tired of their old protégés, whose current performance has not lived up to a speculative belief in the great promise of the velvet (or kind, or gentle) revolution. There is a sense of exasperation, the equivalent of a too quickly requited love, evident in the harsh criticism heaped onto the once lionized resistance. If there is disillusion with the breakup of Czechoslovakia, if there is despair because Poland is ruled by a coalition of leftist parties headed by reformed communists, the blame lies with the West's early enthusiasm for the dissidents. As for Romania, it was seen until very recently, as in Ceauşescu's days, as "the odd man out," another confirmation that liberalism has no future in the Balkans. The "return to Europe" was an important political myth of the revolutions of 1989. Dissidents were applauded because they embodied this hope for a fast integration into the West. What happened in fact was a slow and often frustrating process in which the European Community showed little hurry to admit the poor Eastern relations into its midst. As Tony Judt pointed out, "the idea of Europe is looking more than a little tattered in Prague, Budapest, and Warsaw. As a result, those same intellectual dissidents who were most outspokenly 'European' in their pronouncements and ideals are now multiply discredited with the local electorate; seemingly naive and out-of-touch with local sentiment, they are accused of being spokesmen for a cosmopolitan interest which is antagonistic to the needs of the nation."[4]

But, even if momentarily in decline, the philosophical and political approach of the dissidents, the call for a politics of openness and transparency, and the effort to bring morality into politics cannot be simply dismissed as another illustration of intellectual propensity for delusions. This fact is not fundamentally altered even if we hear, from time to time, strong voices from among the former dissidents who tell us that all their moral endeavors had been nothing but a short-lived mirage.

East Meets (and Disappoints) West

In a provocative essay, Hungarian philosopher and former dissident G. M. Tamás recalled the anomaly of the dissident condition as such: isolated from the majority of the body politic in their own societies, the dissidents were seen as being in continuous defiance of the everyday, opportunistic conformity: "This was because the dissidents challenged the notion that political reform was the only way forward. With their emphasis on 'rights' and 'liberties,' they also challenged the dominant political discourse of interest and naked power."[5] A number of influential Western writers, among them Tony Judt and Theodore Draper, now muse that the West should have known better than to believe the East capable of creating political communities based on trust and morality, and recognizing the sovereignty of the individual. There was little liberal tradition in the region, and besides, Central Europe was simply a myth with few prospects of emerging as a reality. Articles appear in which the former dissidents are depicted as incorrigible naïfs, Quixotic figures eternally out of touch with the barbarous reality of their countries' history and unsavory political habits. The legacy of dissent is seen as an exercise in futility, a preposterously sublime attempt to ignore political culture and its coercive power. Yes, they were nice liberals, these Michniks and Havels, but there was no real constituency for their civic utopias. To the extent that they had an historical mission, it was by necessity short-lived, because once the revolutionary fever subsided, people looked for politicians and ideas they could feel akin to. Dissidents, in this perspective, had to fail because their values did not belong in the post-communist order. Equally opposed to technocratic pragmatism and to populist demagogy, dissidents cultivated democratic individualism, a political choice dramatically unpopular in the region.[6]

The problem with this approach is that it tends to construct a myth no less problematic than the one it tries to rectify. It remains to be demonstrated that there was no liberal tradition in East and Central Europe: after all, the main struggle in this century, as John Lukacs says, was the conflict between collectivist, ethnocentric visions and liberal, civic trends.[7] East-Central Europe is no exception to this conflict. In all these countries, liberalism emerged as a means of modernization, for the development of parliamentary democracy and free-market pluralism, in a continuous struggle with the populist direction that often supported authoritarian solutions. In Hungary, for instance, the interwar period was dominated by the conflict between the Western-oriented urbanites and the populist, often xenophobic, intellectuals; the former were supporters of liberalism, the latter adopted a strategy based on the idea of Hungary's special, "third" road to modernity, neither socialist, nor capitalist. The former endorsed bourgeois, society-oriented values, the latter saw the city as corruptive and inimical to the mythological "national soul," and emphasized community-oriented values such as roots, belonging, and tradition as fundamental for one's identity.

The current outburst of populism, carried to extremes by István Csurka and his partisans within the "Hungarian Justice Party" but present in Poland as well, among Solidarity's enragés, is a prolongation of this legacy: anti-Western, anti-bourgeois, anti-liberal, anti-intellectual and, to be sure, anti-Semitic. Only in rhetorical terms anti-communist, this trend shares with communism the sense that the individual's identity is defined by his or her belonging to a transcendent entity: it used to be the Communist party, it is now the nation. As in the past, this entity is defined through exclusion. And critical intellectuals are by definition excluded. They have to be presented as enemies of the public order, duplicitous preachers of an absurd ("puritanic") morality, cosmopolitan agents of dissolution.[8]

The breakdown of the political myth of the dissident as national redeemer is rampant in the East. The reasons for this situation are manifold: the dissolution of the once united anti-communist movements, psychological fatigue among the former dissidents, the organizational skills of the ex-communists and their tactical ability to adjust to the new conditions, and the difficulty of articulating and maintaining a moral stance within environments plagued with corruption, cynicism, and greed. On the other hand, it is surprising that during the years since the "glorious revolutions," many among the Western intelligentsia have tended increasingly to distance themselves from their beleaguered colleagues; instead of analyzing the resources of resentment, focusing on the ambivalence of the political situation in those still traumatized societies, we have received long sermons showing how misleading the dissidents' philosophy of "rights and truth" was. With few exceptions, the general tone has been one of either benign neglect or condemnation.[9] In this, the Western intellectuals have echoed a phenomenon widespread in Eastern Europe. Listen to the endless complaints in Poland against Michnik and Mazowiecki, accused of "softness" on communism and often regarded as culpable for the electoral victories of the post-communist Alliance of the Democratic Left. In the Czech Republic, former dissidents close to Havel lost power to the programatically "down-to-earth," neo-liberal Václav Klaus, in whose view the very term "civil society" has become superfluous.[10]

The anti-dissident rhetoric that has emerged everywhere goes from the supercilious treatment of the critical intellectuals as incurable moralists to vicious attacks against them as wreckers of national cohesion.[11] Nationalist and populist demagogues have often singled out civic activists like Michnik, Konrád, or Havel as responsible for their countries' prolonged difficulties. Their ascribed fault was that they refused to call for revenge and thereby endorse the vindictive mythologies of post-communism.[12] It is true that nobody has been physically molested, and no dissident has been subjected to measures similar to those used by the defunct communist regimes.[13] But they have been humiliated, slandered, reduced to irrelevance. To some extent, this may be their own fault: accustomed to lofty intellectual polemics, they did not know how to make themselves popularly accepted and endorsed. On the other hand, it would be wrong to see this as simply the dissidents' error: it is also an expression of the lack of political maturity and civic awareness within these societies.

Meanwhile, those who were the troublemakers within the late Leninist regimes continue to harass the new elites in the post-communist order. They do it because they refuse to do now what they objected to doing in the past: they refuse to lie about their views and feelings. They rejected the ugly politics of resentment under communism, and they continue to reject it under the new conditions. Former dissidents like Bronislaw Geremek, Jacek Kuron, and Adam Michnik in Poland; Miklos Haraszti, János Kis, George Konrád, and G. M. Tamás in Hungary; Jiři Dienstibier, Václav Havel, Martin Palous, and Petr Pithart in the Czech Republic; Miroslav Kusy and Martin Simečka in Slovakia; and Gabriel Andreescu and Mircea Dinescu in Romania are opponents of the new radicalisms, be they civic or ethnic. Of course, dissidents did not all evolve in the same direction: some adjusted to the new dominant dogmas and gloated at the pleasure of initiating purges.[14] Others realized that a new social contract was needed, one that would permit a rapid healing of the national wounds. In Michnik's terms: "On the one hand there were those who followed the path of a 'velvet revolution,' one that would take place through democratic change, without violence, hatred, or revenge; and on the other, there were those who wanted 'cleansing,' and who campaigned for rigid decommunization—using the quintessential Bolshevik technique of destroying people by using information from the police archives."[15]

For Michnik a main problem of post-communism is to avoid the Manichean perspective: angels versus rascals.[16] He rejects the simplistic view according to which communism was nothing but a foreign graft on Polish reality, that only non-patriotic people could be attracted to it. The whole saga of the anti-totalitarian awakening in the former Soviet bloc would thus be denied any relevance. The 1956 revolution in Hungary with its libertarian search for direct council democracy, the Warsaw University student rebellion in March 1968, the Prague Spring, and even Solidarity are "de-historicized" in this schematic picture. The meanings of 1989 are still open for debate. In the West, much of the debate has been carried on in *The New York Review of Books*, a journal known for its commitment to an open and uninhibited coverage of Eastern Europe. Its pages carried not only Michnik's pieces opposed to the logic of retaliation but also historian Theodore Draper's series of articles extremely critical of Havel's presumed tactical blunders. Draper's main argument was that Havel and his civic liberals refused to cope with the revolutionary imperatives that would have required a complete break with the past. In other words, he argued that the velvetness of the revolution, its inconsistency, its tolerance of the other side doomed the Czechoslovak experiment to failure.[17]

For Draper, the main error of the Civic Forum in November 1989 was that it allowed former communists to remain in government positions. The first question that comes to mind is: was there a choice? What would have been the Soviet reaction to the complete purge of the communists from the power structure? A new intervention? We know now that Eduard Shevardnadze had to fight rabid opposition within the Politburo to the politics of "benign support" for change in Eastern Europe. A radical break with the communists would have played directly in the hands of Ligachev and those of his ilk.[18] No one foresaw the collapse of the USSR, and the initial strategic expectation was that Eastern Europe would remain for a long period, between East and West—not free to join the European Union, NATO, and radically move away from a "special relationship" with Moscow. The logic of the 1989 revolutions therefore followed from the principles of the new evolutionism as spelled out primarily by Michnik, Geremek, Kis, and Havel: the whole strategy of dissent was based on the premise that an "historical compromise" could and should be reached between those in power and the exponents of the powerless.

I deliberately exaggerate these points, because they represent key elements in understanding the logic of revolutionary change in East-Central Europe. Criticizing the dissidents for lack of political acumen and presenting them as pathetic amateurs whose current plight is well deserved indicates a general sentiment of disillusionment with another imaginary paradigm that failed. In fact, the struggle continues, the politics of post-communism still needs these people if civil society in its real sense, as an area of autonomy that allows the individual to control rather than to escape the state bureaucracy, is to be constructed. This civil society already exists, even if only in embryo. There is a genuine fourth estate in all these countries, and political parties have emerged that articulate competitive visions of the public good. Such evolutionary civic and societal developments would have been impossible had the efforts of people like Michnik and Havel been absent. Think of Albania, Bulgaria, Croatia, Romania, or Serbia: it is precisely because civil society was less mature and Leninist authoritarian practices less challenged by social initiatives from below that the democratic transition there has taken a much more convoluted and uncertain path than in Central Europe.[19]

Now that the political rather than the ethnic nation is to be constructed, voices like Michnik's and Konrád's are vitally needed. "The truth is the vital thing," Max Weber said before his death, and truth is what these societies need. Sick with legends, they need to achieve self-knowledge. As Michnik put it:

> Maybe intellectuals represent today some dinosaurs, belonging to a bygone time. I hope, however, that we are still representatives of the intelligentsia in our region. In my view, truth is the fatherland of the intellectuals. We have to tell the truth. No form of government has the right to liquidate civic rights. Human rights are founded on natural rights. In the same vein, we have to resolutely oppose any form of hatred. . . .

I do believe in the existence of a republic of letters, a homeland for those who want to remain faithful to a certain tradition valuing the autonomy of mind. In this respect, the intelligentsia is not a matter of status, but an ethical profession. I know this may sound like a utopia, but I prefer it to the utopia of the ethnically pure state.[20]

That Michnik's position does not ingratiate him with the mob is perfectly normal. What is troubling is that distinguished Western scholars see his and like-minded intellectuals' struggle for liberal values in East and Central Europe as a desperate, impossible undertaking.

If we were to believe Theodore Draper, the main problem with Havel and his Charter 77 supporters was that they had very little of a "constructive project." In the same vein, many former communists accuse the ex-dissidents of being prepared only to fight against communism, while holding a lamentably nebulous image of the future polis. But under Gustav Husák's regime of institutionalized oblivion, for example, with hundreds of thousands of Soviet soldiers on Czechoslovak territory, to have imagined a post-communist order would have been nonsensical. If the self-limited, Marxist revisionist Prague Spring was dashed, how could one even discuss a post-communist system? It was precisely the strategy of civil society to approach the change in a gradual way, to nurture a slow, almost invisible growth of independent, alternative spaces of freedom within the overall unfree system. This was the meaning of the new evolutionism, and nobody could anticipate both the speed and the scope of the breakthrough that was to happen in 1989.

But here we deal with a general revision of the assumptions that for many years inspired the Western liberal approach to the region: first the dissidents were celebrated as symbols of freedom, and the revolutions of 1989 were seen as a reenactment of the other intellectual rebellion, the 1848 "revolution of the intellectuals" (to use L. B. Namier's famous term). As disenchantment set in, ethnic passions intensified and the dissidents were repudiated or marginalized, blame became the new line. Timothy Garton Ash was the spokesman of the first stage, Theodore Draper and Tony Judt are spokesmen of the second. This is important because the change in the *New York Review* line is indicative of a change in the estimate of the role of ideas (primarily moral ideas) in transforming and shaping political reality. Initially, Garton Ash saw the meaning of 1989 as a clash between visions of reality, one based on social engineering and cynical "dictatorship over needs" (a term coined by the critical Marxist Budapest School), the other acknowledging human spontaneity and responsibility. In an essay written in early 1990, Garton Ash stated unequivocally: "As in 1848, the common denominator of these revolutions was ideological. The inner history of these revolutions is that of a set of ideas whose time had come, and a set of ideas whose time had gone." As if this statement was not emphatic enough, he added: "There is a real sense in which these regimes lived by the word and perished by the word."[21]

What is at stake in Garton Ash's assessment of the role of intellectuals in unleashing the anti-totalitarian revolutions is the power of ideas at the end of the twentieth century. Moreover, what is at stake is the international significance of the principles of a political life embedded in the values of truth-telling, and openness and civility. Is this a utopia? Is it time to renounce the ideal of civil society in favor of a pragmatic recognition that politics is a cob-web of sordid complicities, betrayals, manipulations, and intrigues? But if the value of ideas is thus curtailed (or even denied), if anti-politics is seen as a chimera of the dissidents and of their former Western supporters, how can one make sense of what happened in 1989? The bureaucratic machines of state socialism were utterly real, and the police were well armed with tanks and truncheons and tear gas. With the exception of Romania, the former elites ingloriously left power, and their first successors were precisely the dissidents. The fact that Mazowiecki, Havel, and Göncz refused to organize political trials against their enemies indicates the solidity of their moral commitment; they had not lied when they pledged that they would not turn from oppressed into oppressors. They may have exaggerated in their exaltation of civil society (and so did Garton Ash and this author), but the idea had genuine galvanizing power.[22]

In Poland and Hungary, the presence of civil society prevented the slide into new forms of authoritarianism and permitted the rise of a political na-tion.[23] To be sure, civil society under communism meant not participation in public life but flight from the ubiquitous state into private forms of self-organi-zation. The solidarity of the outcasts held enclaves together; it showed the less daring that fraternity could exist and civility could reassert itself. To quote Garton Ash: "A concept that was central in opposition thinking during the 1980's was that of 'civil society.' . . . It contained at least three basic demands. First, there should be forms of association, national, regional, local, profes-sional, that would be voluntary, authentic, democratic, and not controlled and manipulated by the Party or Party-state. Second, people should be 'civil': that is polite, tolerant; and, above all, nonviolent. Civil and civilian. Third, the idea of citizenship had to be taken seriously.[24] Item three is the main contribu-tion of these events: 1989 renewed the idea of citizenship, and allowed indi-viduals to redefine and express themselves as political beings.

We should not forget that the revolutionary promise of 1848 was smashed by external reaction, whereas no threatening force exists nowadays outside these countries to oppose the democratic development. That Solidarity and dissident forums could make mistakes goes without saying; but not to realize that these groups represented an unprecedented form of politics that went against traditional and conventional distributions in terms of Left and Right is to ignore what the annus mirabilis was about. The revolutions did not take place only because of economic deprivation (which was and is real), but pri-marily because people were tired of mendacity and fear.

Still Dissenting, Still Living in Truth

It has often been argued that the revolutions of 1989 were not strictly speaking revolutions because they lacked an ideological program, or a myth about the better order to come. In reality, their uniqueness, and also their major contribution to the revolutionary tradition was the repudiation of institutional utopia. Daniel Chirot correctly pointed out that the main lesson of the collapse of Leninist regimes in Eastern Europe for the next century is that "more than ever, the fundamental causes of revolutionary instability will be moral."[25] Long infantilized, reduced to political muteness, forced to worship empty symbols, the millions who took to the streets in 1989 were in fact espousing the moral calls of the dissidents. Lest we forget some essential verities, we should keep in mind that the revolutionary upsurge in Eastern Europe was less about the quality of bread than about the value and dignity of the individual. In Havel's words, the issue was to construct moral politics: "Let us teach both ourselves and others that politics ought to be a reflection of the aspiration to contribute to the happiness of the community and not of the need to deceive and pillage the community. Let us teach both ourselves and others that politics does not have to be the art of the possible, especially if this means the art of speculating, calculating, intrigues, secret agreements, and pragmatic maneuvering, but it can also be the art of the impossible, that is the art of making ourselves and the world better."[26] This sounds idealistic, almost romantic, but revolutions are explosions of a totally different principle of reality. They are indeed "moments of madness," when all old icons collapse, long-held fears vanish as if by miracle, and "human beings living in societies believe that 'all is possible.'"[27] Lack of enthusiasm for the 1989 revolutions strikes me as a failure to grasp their wider impact: they changed, though it is not clear for how long, the nature of the political game. And unless we engage in an embarrassing revision of these events, we cannot overestimate the meaning of the ideas that inspired the revolutionary actors—who were, primarily, the critical intelligentsia.

The makers of these revolutions, their original spokesmen may have left the limelight. Other actors have emerged, and that is perfectly normal. Still, it is much too early to conclude that the revolutions are over and that the critical intelligentsia of East-Central Europe has exhausted its historical mandate. Although it is true that Michnik is now the target of slanderous campaigns and that Tadeusz Mazowiecki was forced out of his prime ministership, it is also true that they continue to be major figures of the political and cultural debates in Poland. Is it so insignificant that Michnik is the editor of *Gazeta Wyborcza*, Poland's most popular and influential daily, that his columns do play a crucial role in orienting the public discussion on the nation's current problems? Is it so trivial a fact that Jacek Kuron is still one of the most popular politicians in

Poland, while the coalitions of resentment can barely achieve the minimal percentages required to enter parliament? Can we really say, together with Tony Judt, that 'János Kis and George Konrád in Hungary, Adam Michnik in Poland are already in political terms 'yesterday's men,' consigned once again to the margins of their own political culture"?[28] Konrád never aspired to become a politician, and his political views continue to inspire crucial debates in Hungary. János Kis left the chairmanship of the Alliance of Free Democrats in favor of an academic career in political philosophy, but his party became in 1994 a partner in Hungary's government coalition. Gábor Demszky, long involved in the samizdat culture and prominent Free Democrat, is the highly popular mayor of Budapest. Not all dissidents have left the scene, not all of them are losers. And the need for public moralists is more pressing than ever, East and West. Their role is essential, especially now, when angry populist, anti-liberal movements have emerged that attack the very principles cherished by the men and women of the revolutions of 1989.[29]

After all, why did so many Westerners get excited at the moment of the anti-authoritarian revolutions of 1989? Simply because a cohort of senile bureaucrats were kicked out of power? The answer is surely more profound, and it is linked to the fact that the revolutions of Eastern Europe have rehabilitated the notion of citizen as the true political subject. Their main liberal component consisted in the emphasis on the right of the individual to be free from state intrusion into his or her life.[30] This celebration of negative liberty was accompanied by an equally important focus on the revival of civic initiative and the restoration of substantive freedoms, especially the freedom of association and expression.[31] The uprisings were the palpable expression of a need to reinvent politics, to insert values that transcend immediate pragmatic and ideological considerations into real life. Václav Havel's presence in the Prague Castle is a symbol greater than his physical person enjoying (or abhorring) the presidential prerogatives. It is indeed miraculous that, out of the lowest levels of human destitution, out of the murky world of decaying Leninism, an experience of solidarity and civic fraternity could be restored. This is the deeper meaning of Havel's famous pledge in his presidential address on January 1, 1990: "I do not think you appointed me to this office for me, of all people, to lie to you."[32]

The struggle for this new politics is far from over. Because the stakes of the game played in Eastern Europe and the former Soviet Union are so high, the withdrawal of intellectuals from politics would be disastrous. The values formulated during the odyssey of dissent remain as urgent as ever. Eastern Europe's critical intellectuals (unlike their Western counterparts) know the full meaning of being unfree. They are not political greenhorns, as the former communists often like to deride them. They may be reluctant to take jobs, but this is not because of lack of expertise. Their modesty should not be taken for incompetence, in the same way the former communists' arrogance should not be seen as professionalism.

It is difficult to deny that dissent has by now created its own political tradition in the societies of East-Central Europe. Moreover, as Michnik has noted, the European tradition (including the universalistic and tolerant strands of Catholicism) is the spiritual patrimony with which the former dissidents identify themselves.[33] To see Eastern Europe as hostage to invincible traditions of ethnic strife does little justice to the true diversity of political cultures in the region. For this reason one should be skeptical of gloomy generalizations such as Tony Judt's: "Only Czechoslovakia had something resembling parliamentary party politics before 1938. Elsewhere, there wasn't even anything to be destroyed."[34] So much for the Polish non-Leninist, socialist tradition, or the Romanian constitutional monarchy and the imperfect but real parliamentary experience between the wars, of the Hungarian urban intelligensia, or the memory of 1956 and the workers' councils, or the Prague Spring, or KOR and the intellectual-workers alliance in Poland. So much for the struggles of the last twenty years, or the dissidents' saga of resistance and the patient construction of the parallel polis.

According to this utterly pessimistic view, the only thing the non-Czech nations can refer to is an atavistic past, marked by feuds, chauvinism, hatred, and profoundly anti-European sentiments. Let us, for the sake of argument, grant the shallowness of liberal tradition in this region. These countries have by now had enough of the authoritarian forms of collectivism and regimentation. There may be nostalgia for individual security and paternalistic protection, but there is little yearning for new dictatorships. István Csurka and his crusaders for the "Hungarian road"—one stripped of any Jewish cosmopolitan influences—were rejected even by the deeply conservative Magyar Democratic Forum.

The conflict in East-Central Europe opposes not the former dissidents to the nation, but the emerging liberal democracy to the forces inimical to it. What should the dissidents be doing at this historical moment? Should they limit themselves to writing memoirs, or should they rather work for the consolidation of precarious but real liberal institutions and values? If "life is elsewhere," one wonders where: in the wild competition of naked selfish interests? A former colleague who turned down Havel's invitation to fill an important government position did so on the basis of the well-worn argument of "someone has to remain independent." But this is the opposite of what responsibility is about. In speaking about this incident, Havel correctly pointed out that if all democratic intellectuals followed this escapist example, "nobody will be able to remain independent because there would be nobody in power who would make possible and guarantee your independence."[35]

To devalue Eastern Europe's critical intellectuals, to see only their failure in the years since 1989 to move the new world in a civil direction, ignoring their role in breaking the old one apart, is to abandon them midway. Given time and support, they may yet develop a new type of politics, one that allows the individual to act as a dignified and responsible human being.[36] Above all, we should avoid panic-ridden judgments about the darkness at the end of the tunnel. Whatever ethnocentric prophets may think, and whatever Western pessimists predict, liberal democracy and its advocates have a future in East and Central Europe, including Russia and some other former Soviet republics.

The need to identify presumed culprits for the failure to generate both prosperity and pluralism immediately is felt both East and West. The former dissidents have been continuously targeted for all kind of sarcastic comments. To the critiques formulated by Judt, Draper, and Tamás, new voices and new themes have been added: for instance that of the distinguished social philosopher Ernest Gellner. In an otherwise splendid critique of the normative political vision of the Frankfurt School, he presented Václav Havel as a kind of proponent of the Marcusian theory of universal alienation both under socialism and capitalism. In spite of the well-known and obvious fact that whatever Havel's philosophical sources were they did not include any form of Marxism (but rather phenomenology), Gellner wrote: "there is one Central European head of state, Václav Havel, who combines a record of a fine stand against Communism with undisguised disquiet concerning the system which replaced it, and who articulates his sincere, well-based but less than lucid criticism with the help of Frankfurt ideas."[37]

What criteria should we use to define political lucidity? After all, as Gellner himself acknowledged, it was the dissident project formulated by thinkers and activists like Havel, Kis, Kuron, Haraszti, and even Tamás that delegitimized the ruling order and ensured the non-violent transition to the post-communist societies.[38] That this project did not ensure the establishment of intellectuals in power could have been anticipated.

Indeed, Havel's ideas remind one of the anti-authoritarian tradition of the European libertarian left.[39] Many of his ideas about reflexivity, historicity, transcendence, need for human solidarity, and the role of the critical faculty in dealing with the existing world are akin to the ideas of Cornelius Castoriadis or Claude Lefort. What Havel, Michnik, and other thinkers of this orientation share with the Frankfurt School is an Hegelian celebration of the unhappy consciousness, the refusal to abdicate in front of the arrogant facticity of a presumed *terminus ad quem* of history. The displeasure with the status quo remains fundamental for the intellectual condition, and there is little reason to see how these thinkers and activists would simply bow to the dictates of the new majorities. Moreover, the dissidents have continued to call for civic behavior and participation as opposed to the mounting collectivist and egalitarian temptations.

Conclusion _____

The Mythological Construction of Reality:
Political Complexity in a Post-Communist World

> For what we need, if are to have the least prospect
> of learning how to live more decently with one an-
> other, either within individual national societies or
> within the globe as a whole, simply is *not* further
> practice in learning how to hate one another, more
> intense and fiercer doctrines of the duty and ratio-
> nality of mutual odium, yet more grandiose and
> eloquent (and still equally ill-founded) theologies
> with which to back our hatreds.
>   (*John Dunn,* Western Political Theory in the Face
>   of the Future *[1979]*)

As a result of the collapse of communism, a situation of epistemological anarchy has emerged. Traditional boundaries, embedded memories, and predictable outcomes have been challenged and overturned. The idols of yesteryear are dead, but do we know anything about the new ones? What has
remained of what, during the years of upheaval from 1989 through 1991,
appeared to be an anti-communist but also a pro-democratic consensus? How
many of the once ostensibly powerful and promising parties still matter in the
political game? What has remained of the once exhilarating calls for European
integration, civil society, and a post-Machiavellian political life? How can one
explain the fact that, even after the appalling revelations about the Stalinist
atrocities, there is a growing trend in Russia toward the rehabilitation not only
of an idealized pre-Bolshevik communal past but also of Stalin's time of terrorist ideological autocracy?[1] In the same vein, many Serbs are now worshiping
the memory of Aleksandar Ranković, the dreaded chief of Yugoslavia's secret
police purged by Marshal Tito in 1966, as a martyr to Serbian national interest.[2] The rewriting of history in accordance with self-serving fantasies of persecution and victimization is as contagious as the refusal of empathy for other
nations' similar plights.

We still do not know how stable the new democracies are, or what ideological cement keeps them together. Fragile democratic polities, with little expe-

rience of procedures, contracts, and consensus are particularly vulnerable to anti-liberal onslaughts. The rise of new mythologies of collective identity is a major trend that can lead to mass mobilization in favor of nationalist dictatorships. More in the Balkans and the former USSR than in Central Europe, democratic breakdown is as much a possibility as democratic consolidation. As fascism used the poisonous elixirs of nationalism, racism, and xenophobia to create a false consensus based on shared hatreds, the new mythologies have the potential to undermine and eventually destroy the nascent democracies of Eastern Europe. In this book, I have tried to diagnose the post-communist political mythologies, and identify both their advocates and opponents.

The Post-Communist Moral Crisis

The end of communism was followed by collective anxiety, disorientation and, more recently, disenchantment. This post-communist situation is propitious ground for exercises in myth making: from vindictive fantasies of punishment of the former oppressors to scapegoating visions about a Judeo-Masonic conspiracy.[3] The source of failure is always externalized. In short, the breakdown of the homogenizing social vision of Leninism left an open space for compensatory mythologies.

Ethnic nationalism is only the most ostentatious, visible, and all-embracing of these fantasies. Modernity itself is under attack for its supposed failure to respond to the human need for fraternity and solidarity. The national past (selectively revisited) is sanctified as the only possible reservoir of hope, pride, and dignity. Modern capitalism and industrial civilization as such are questioned in the name of romanticized pastoral values. In the words of Ferenc Kulin, a literary historian and ideologue of the conservative-populist Magyar Democratic Forum (Hungary's ruling party between 1990 and 1994): "The past forty years have basically heaped failures on us, and brought ruin on top of that; but this ruin and these failures are not only our ruin and our failures . . . but also the ruin of a two-hundred-year-old experiment . . . which we may call the period of modernization. . . . Thus, we must confront the general failure—here and now. We are in a vacuum, where the advanced Western civilizations offer no workable patterns—we must deal with it day by day, as we try to extricate ourselves from our crisis."[4] The return to soil and community are thus offered as counter-Enlightenment postulates: the individual is supposed to attain deliverance by giving up autonomy.

Still, it is extremely risky to play the prophet in such times of convulsive "great transformation." It is dangerous because of the extraordinary velocity of changes, the short political life expectancy of most new personalities in the post-communist states, the transience of ideological commitments, the fragility and vulnerability of the democratic contracts, and the vagueness of the competing rhetorics, not to mention the obscurity surrounding the making of new economic and political oligarchies.

Populist nationalism has emerged as the strongest ideological alternative to liberalism. Nationalism in Central Europe started as a romantic discovery of ethnic identity. Later, at the end of the nineteenth and during the early twentieth centuries, it incorporated the mystique of race and blood, and minorities were targeted for forced assimilation, exclusion, or extermination.[5] In this process, the role of nationalist intellectuals as bards of ressentiment can hardly be exaggerated. In fact, the Central and East European intelligentsia has never been a homogeneous, unified group. A divide has opposed those who advocate individualism, rationalism, and modernity from those who favor organic community, national symbols, and the cult of blood, soil, and ancestry. In all these countries, the 1930s were marked by heated debates between modernizers and traditionalists, Westernizers and populists, urban-oriented and village-oriented elites. Their echoes tainted the ideological conflicts of the communist period as well.

Some intellectuals are myth breakers, others are hate builders. It is true that the critical intelligentsia played an outstanding role in the subversion of the Leninist pyramids of lies. But it is also true that poets and historians have decisively contributed in this century to the production of spiteful symbols, slogans, and myths: "the intellectual as a hate-monger is an invention of European origin which is well on the way to becoming a universal phenomenon. In any case, nationalism in our part of the world is unthinkable without the literary contribution of some of the best and the worst minds of the last two hundred years. To draw the line between the two is not an easy task."[6] In all these countries, therefore, the role of intellectuals remains tremendously important in articulating either the civic visions of public good or the atavistic narratives of exclusion. Intellectuals are those who can remind their fellow citizens of the truth about communism's abysmal record as well as the dangers associated with unbound nationalism. But they can also inflame passions and instigate the elimination of presumed aliens. In short, even if they have lost much of their traditional oracular power, intellectuals do still have an excessively influential status, especially because of the weakness of professional politicians and parties.

In exploring the post-communist moral crisis, one should not forget that Marxism, in its original incarnation, was an all-embracing, chiliastic creed.[7] Generations of Marxists believed in the internationalist dream of the proletarian revolution. This myth had long since lost its credibility, but the Leninist world continued to be organized until its final hours in accordance to the utopian blueprints of the founding fathers. Until its very end, communism opposed individual initiative, the free market, and the principle of property. Civil society and multiparty democracy continued to be decried as bourgeois political fictions. Now, the millennial expectation has come to an end even for the last of its zealots. With it a whole civilization based on a collectivistic belief system fell apart. But although in the different countries the starting point of the transition seemed structurally alike, its methods, speed, and outcomes have been quite different. In Central Europe, the post-communist recon-structed Left has little patience for those who are nostalgic for the old creed. The same, however, is not true among Romania's, Russia's, Slovakia's, or Ser-bia's social populists (often mixed with nationalists); they still explicitly or implicitly stick to the leftovers of the Leninist mentality, resent the liberal capitalist West, and refuse to admit—together with the former dissident thinkers—that "the [communist] dream of final redemption is despair in the cloak of hope, the greed for power in the gown of justice."[8]

The final destination of the transition is uncertain; the temptation of a "third way" arises—a political myth that promises escape from communism without entering "the Western pseudo-paradise." This anti-capitalist utopia of a third way between a pluralistic, open society and a Leninist-style tyranny is linked to a neo-romantic rejection of modernity, demonization of private property, and the dream of classless organic community.[9] It is often associated with Peronista-style paternalistic and corporatist nostalgias and yearnings for the advent of a strongman, a national savior who would restore a sense of clarity and discipline in social affairs.[10] In the republics of Central Asia, with their lack of democratic traditions and civil society, one sees this trend in the making. Instead of open societies, most of them have created new autocracies, often run by the former Soviet-era potentates.

The demise of Leninism has changed all the established political paradigms. The transition from state socialism takes place against the background of a universal disparagement of conventional political dichotomies, including a widespread crisis of self-confidence on the part of Western liberalism. For the Western political forms are less stable and inspiring than they appeared dur-ing the Cold War era.The return of ethnocentric politics, the agonizing search for roots, and the obsession with identity are major trends of this fin-de-siécle, all over the world, often colliding with the liberal, inclusive, civic traditions. One can thus see a growing tension between nation states increasingly jealous of each other, and an emphasis on supranational, "post-conventional identi-ties" (Habermas), which are a continuation of the project of universalization of rights as unleashed in the eithteenth century.[11]

What is at stake is the future of the Enlightenment as a mobilizing cultural archetype and as a basis for both modernity and post-modernity. This gives a new meaning to the old vision of the democratic Left as repository of the Enlightenment's embattled legacy, and invites a reassessment of the moral and intellectual status of the Left in the post-ideological and post-utopian age. In the words of German sociologist Wolf Lepenies: "Precisely because politics throughout Europe is leaning more and more to the right, intellectuals must again define themselves as left. . . . Against populist politicians and intellectuals drifting towards the right, it is important to support the tedium of the Enlightenment and democracy."[12] The problem with this perspective is that it attributes to the right the historical association with populism and its visceral hostility to "rotten" parliamentary governments. In reality, both Marxist ideologues and conservative critics of the Enlightenment have found liberal constitutionalism and civil society morally and politically unsatisfactory, and have striven to propose alternative visions of the good social order.

The revolutions of 1989–1991 have thus been a catalyst for the revival of the old conflict between two rival political archetypes: liberal individualism and national collectivism. To be sure, this dichotomy is an oversimplification, but it is clear that modernity would tragically come to an end if the project of individual (natural) rights as the foundation of the liberal polity were to be fundamentally and irretrievably ruined. What we see in post-communist societies is only the magnified reflection of universal psychological and sociological perplexities (in the old Hegelian parlance we would have used the term "contradictions"), the takeover of the legitimate sentiments of belonging to a country, community, and nation by forces that pretend to give this affiliation a cosmic, inescapable value. This is indeed the resurgence of the conflict between Gemeinschaft (community) and Gesellschaft (society) as forms of inter-subjectivity.

As I argue in this book, there is nothing intrinsically wrong with national pride. The tragedy occurs when this natural sentiment ceases to mean just "love for the little platoon we belong to in society" (Edmund Burke), and is exacerbated into an ideology of hostility, hatred, and envy. At the same time, it is still to be seen whether nations and nation states can incorporate and constitutionally protect the right to multiple, trans-national identities. It took Western Europe generations to reach the point when nationalism could internalize and tolerate supranational allegiances: "Human beings have multiple collective identifications, whose scope and intensity will vary with time and place. There is nothing to prevent individuals from identifying with Flanders, Belgium and Europe simultaneously, and displaying each allegiance in the appropriate context."[13] In many post-communist societies, however, the primordialist perspective prevails. It perceives the fact of national belonging as a genetic determination and culture is simply reduced to a dispensable appendage.

It appears, as I have said, as a rationalization of political and social impotence. In the words of Adam Michnik, "The hateful chauvinism is a degenerate reaction to the human need for national identity and national sovereignty, a need that was beaten down by communism. The envious populism is a degenerate reaction to the human longing for the just social order. Into the place left empty by communist ideology, these two fiends steal. Like a cancer attacking the fragile human organism, they attack the tender emerging organism of our pluralist European democracy and our normal market economy."[14]

Landscape after the Battle: From Civic Mobilization to Political Deradicalization

Among all the uncertainties that have marked the transition from bureaucratic collectivism, at least one thing is beyond any doubt: the Leninist monolith of ideological zeal and political coercion is dead.[15] We are dealing with one of the most fascinating cycles of revolutionary change in history, which has led to the dissolution of the seemingly stable communist regimes and the initiation of democratic experiments in these countries. The open end of this process is bound to generate fears, illusions, and bitter disappointments; as things often get worse before they get better, many individuals lose patience and are ready to espouse anti-liberal creeds and movements.

The revolutions of 1989 had their own prehistory, and this included not only the dissident groups and movements but also the reformist actions of individuals like Imre Nagy or Alexander Dubček. These endeavors now appear as naive and purely quixotic, but they were nevertheless the first breaches in the Leninist walls. Now we know that reforming Sovietism was a contradiction in terms, but this was not self-evident in the 1960s and 1970s, when many intelligent and honest people were still trying to work for intrasystemic improvement. Their efforts were not completely futile. I would thus venture a hypothesis: the more developed the reformist wing of the ruling elite during the post-totalitarian stage, the more articulate and coherent its economic and political propositions, the better the chances for a consensual transition toward liberal democracy after the end of the authoritarian domination.

In Poland and Hungary, the party reformers could find partners for dialogue and negotiation among the leaders of the civic opposition. In Serbia, on the other hand, the reform-oriented wing of the Communist party was interested primarily in constitutional-territorial changes, which it believed would prompt economic growth. The political and economic failure of Titoism was blamed on territorial-administrative difficulties. Party reformists and intellectuals shared this fixation on territory and resources. The latter turned it into a political myth by building the image of a besieged Serbia, surrounded by hostile, ungrateful neighbors. In Romania, the situation was even worse: as there was no reformist group within the party elite, and the opposition was limited to individual cases of moral denunciation of Ceauşescu's vagaries, the collapse of the old order occurred as an anarchic rebellion, with no legitimate leaders of either the former regime or the opposition to negotiate the transition. As the government, army, and secret police bureaucracies were the best organized forces in the country, no wonder they could easily get rid of their critics and partially restore their domination. With the growth of civil society and the maturing of political opposition, Romania reached in the mid-1990s the level of Poland and Hungary five years earlier, as demonstrated by the victory of the democratic forces in the November 1996 presidential and parliamentary elections.[16]

It was precisely the existence of the "enlightened" faction within the bureaucratic apparatus that guaranteed the peaceful nature (smoothness, velvetness) of the transition. This faction also accounted for the absence of major social conflict and neocommunist riots during the period after the transfer of power, and the possibility of a mutual pact of nonaggression and even limited trust between the moderate forces of the counterelite and this particular segment of the ex-ruling class. I refer primarily to Poland and Hungary, where the reformists within the Communist party had not been eliminated and persecuted as they had been in Czechoslovakia after 1968. The transitions in Central Europe were significantly conditioned by this compromise between the political elite of the ancien régime and the emerging political class of the new one. They were both suspicious of the politics of radical goals: instead of despair, the pact was based on the possibility of gradualism, concessions, and reconciliation. Needless to say, for the enragés on both sides, this has meant capitulation, treason, and other similar offenses.

No development was more speedy, more striking, or more surprising in this century than the sudden collapse of the Leninist regimes during 1989.[17] With the exception of very few scholars and a number of East European dissident intellectuals, the general consensus had been that a long process of decomposition would eventually result in the end of Sovietism.[18] Precisely because Leninist regimes put so inordinate a price on the fiction of "ideological purity," many scholars counterreacted and described the role of ideology as secondary, epiphenomenal. In underrating the function of ideological mobilization they were wrong; because of too much attention to structural dynamics and party elites, they missed the real story of the evaporation of the "party line," the dissolution of elite self-confidence and even esprit de corps, and the rise of the alternative visions and movements.[19] In this respect, authors like Václav Havel, Leszek Kolakowski, and Adam Michnik were right in their emphasis on the moral and ideological decline of the old regimes. Once society began to acquire autonomy, even if initially in isolated enclaves of civic initiative, the party/state lost its aura of infallibility.

After the rise of Solidarity, was there anybody who still believed in the official Leninist tenets? To quote Leszek Kolakowski's apt diagnosis of Gorbachev's impossible task: "Once it is recognized that the leaders of an empire doubt its legitimacy, one may safely assume that the end is in sight."[20] Now, if we admit that for decades these societies did live under the spell of the communist myth, with its all-embracing pretense, if we agree that even its adversaries had to formulate their views, values, and opinions in relation to this myth, then it might be plausible to conclude that the post-communist world would be one emancipated from myth. If François Furet is right that the most powerful idées-forces unleashed by the French Revolution as foundations of the democratic political culture (*l'universel* and *le national*) have been finally domesticated by the defeat of the Bolshevik hubris, then it is intriguing why, instead of a radical repudiation of mythologies, post-communist societies seem to offer an overabundance of irrational creeds and neoromantic visions.[21] One explanation is that these creeds are not the continuation of the civic nationalism inaugurated by the French Revolution but rather belong to the tradition of counter-Enlightenment. Their emphasis is not on the universality and unity of human experience but on its ethnic particularity. With its commitment to modernity and economic progress, Bolshevism could only freeze, not tame them.

No society can survive in a state of moral prostration. Individuals do need ideas, values, and norms to inspire their actions. The post-communist world is thus experiencing the search for new (or not so new) vitally significant paradigms. Not surprisingly, these often syncretic mythologies borrow from the previously dominant creed's strong egalitarian illusions, communal passion, and distrust of the Western institutions as "formal," "abstract," or "non-substantive." As events tend to appear uncontrollable and intolerably chaotic, as this whole universe appears to have gotten out of joint, individuals look for ideological (mythological) responses to their predicament. The situation is thus strangely reminiscent of Europe after the great changes inaugurated by the French Revolution: no single loyalty has remained solidly rooted, everything is fluid, evanescent, and the most incredible metamorphoses have occurred to the astonishment, outrage, and even disgust of those who had expected the revolutions to result in the foundation of a new politics of morality.[22]

Can former communists restore their political hegemony? In examining this issue, one should take into account the role of ideology: instead of the universalistic vision of the classless, unified mankind, post-communist parties in Hungary and Poland advocate the values of private property and political pluralism and are often portrayed as the capitalist nomenklatura.[23] Thus it is not at all sure that the main enemies of liberal democracy are to be found in the reconstructed Leftist circles, rather than among the proponents of the ethnically or clerically defined versions of democracy.

The issue, therefore, is linked not only to the challenges of democratic consolidation in the region but to the prospects of crisis and breakdown of the new regimes, primarily because of lack of moral and ideological glue to keep them together. Here, the lessons from southern Europe are extremely important and Nancy Bermeo correctly pointed to an erroneous reading (dominant in the scholarship) of the problem of democratic vulnerabilities: "The primary reason the likelihood of democratic breakdown was overstated was that no one considered the other half of the regime-change dilemma. New democracies are indeed very difficult to create and maintain but successfully *assaulting* a democracy is very difficult as well." But are these new regimes sufficiently consolidated and legitimized to consider them liberal democracies? I agree with Nancy Bermeo that in order to have a reenactment of the fascist scenarios of the interwar period (Italy and Germany), three elements would be necessary: armed extremism, bipolar extremism, and judicial dysfunctionality.[24] Obviously, there is no armed extremism in countries like the Czech Republic or Hungary. This is, however, less true in Eastern Europe (including Russia and Ukraine), where criminality, corruption, and militarism have created the atmosphere of political and moral despair propitious for charismatic adventurism and explosions of self-righteous indignation. The main challenge for all these societies is thus the de-polarization of the public space, the development of countermajoritarian forms of civic activism, and primarily the development and maturing of the civil society at the level of civic, religious, and labor movements and groups.[25]

Universalist Illusions, Popular Fears

Initially, especially during late 1989 and early 1990, there was widespread sentiment that Central Europe had re-emerged as a special place with a special historical mission: to revitalize the project of Enlightenment, to test the possibility of anti-politics, to go beyond the Jacobin-Leninist world of selfishness and political greed, to reconcile the values of justice with those of freedom.[26] It seemed that intellectuals had finally come to class power.[27] For the first time perhaps since Plato's dream of a noocratic republic, the Central European setting was allowing for such a triumph of the Spirit.

But, as I have emphasized in this book, this was a myth: a positive, noble, endearing one, but nevertheless impossible. The generative myth of those days was the new political paradigm of radical cleavage with the communist past. Too few were those who expected this break to include a resurrection of the nationalist passions long held in check by the communist internationalist myth.[28] Claiming to have surmounted utopia, the revolutions themselves included strong utopian elements: the belief that time could be divided, the idealization of the European space, the expectations about imminent and generous support from the West, and the overall refusal of the former dissidents to engage in retroactive political justice.

During their first stage, the revolutions had an unmistakably liberal orientation. In rejecting the idea of collective guilt and punishment and insisting on the need for historical truth, former dissidents strengthened the public awareness of legality and accountability as foundations of a liberal civic culture.[29] This is not to say that crimes should not be punished, but rather that legal procedures should be focused on individual cases and avoid vindictive generalizations.

The naive belief in the possibility of rapidly transcending the psycho-cultural legacy of Leninism was soon to be shattered, however, by the realities of the post-communist rancor, envy, and mutual hatreds. From a society in which everything was "scientifically planned," people found themselves thrown into a universe of multiple conflicting choices. There is a joke about the former East German plant manager who was demoted to the kitchen and put in charge of sorting good from rotten potatoes. At the end of the first day he is taken by ambulance to the hospital while unconsciously mumbling: "Too many choices, too many choices."

Sociologically, the competition is between those who know how to take advantage of this situation and those who lose because of a lack of self-esteem or incapacity to accept risk as a way of living. This division runs through every social group and makes the spectrum of post-communist societies much more complex than simple income differentiation would suggest.[30] Western scholarship thus has a brand new area of examination: the disappearance of one-party, ideologically driven regimes and the emergence of new political cultures dominated by uncertainties.[31] Five years after the historic climax of the German "kind revolution"—the breach in the Berlin Wall—Peter Jakob, a spokesman for the Berlin city government, confessed: "The concrete Wall is gone, but the Wall in our minds is certainly still there. Even if the city is physically and financially whole, even if the streets and train lines have been reconnected, there is still a deep trench separating Eastern and Western emotions, feelings and understanding for each others' interests."[32]

Rather than genuine nostalgia for the old times, what we are dealing with is a culture of disaffection that idealizes the disappeared social stability. The search for legitimacy has taken different paths: in Central Europe and the Baltic states the new political class has espoused pluralism and succeeded in marginalizing ethnocentric movements. In the Balkans, on the other hand, most societies have become ethnocracies. Democratic procedures, including elections, are used to camouflage the reality of illiberal, authoritarian practices. New narratives of hatred and exclusion (East and West) are disguised in the rhetoric of historical justifications. To quote Eric Hobsbawm: "If there is no suitable past, it can always be invented."[33]

The past as inescapable destiny is thus invoked to alleviate feelings of inferiority generated by delays in modernization, and perceived or imagined subordinate status. The mystique of blood, the cult of the ancestors and of the soil, the politically manufactured contempt for Western values, culture, and institutions, the resurrection of authoritarian figures of the past are elite responses to mass anxiety in times of uncertainty.

Hostages to the Past?

A major illusion about East-Central Europe was that the pre-1989 states had no popular support, that their legitimacy was entirely fictitious. It turned out, however, that more than a tiny elite had been integrated in the structure of vested interests and mutual protection of the increasingly corrupt Leninist regimes. After the revolution there were many accomplices looking for alibis to justify their previous silence, cowardice, and even ignominy. Post-communist corruption is thus a continuation of the communist clientelism, double thinking, hypocrisy, and second economy.[34] This has reached truly catastrophic levels in Russia, where the symbiosis between political elite and the economic underworld may amount to the establishment of political domination by organized crime.[35] The initial euphoria was thus bound to be followed by periods of discontent, deprivation, and even rage. In the words of Jürgen Kocka: "The postcommunist situation is characterized by elements of breakdown, destruction, and vacuum, in which older traditions regain some weight and new structures emerge quite slowly."[36]

This struggle with legacies of the past is the hallmark of the post-communist condition. And the past is both communist and pre-communist, with strange blends of old and new mythologies. It is not only "progressive," pro-Western, "democratic," but also viscerally illiberal, reactionary, exclusive, intolerant. The collapse of communism has resulted in a desperate search for usable traditions: liberal and anti-liberal, civic and ethnocentric, democratic and populist, individualist and corporatist—all the old notions and ideas have been revisited and refunctionalized.

So powerful was the euphoria of the first stage of post-communism that it made people oblivious of the fact that genuine civil societies cannot exist in the absence of market economies and thorough-going guarantees for individual rights. Where civil society exists, even nationalism acquires positive connotations, and can thus become a liberal nationalism. The main thrust of civil society is to diminish the role of the state apparatus on the life of the individual. The anti-statist implication of civil society, however, should not be misconstrued to the point of seeing it as denying the right to *any* authority. Civil society was indeed an explosive concept under the conditions of terminally sick Leninist regimes, but the target was not *any* authority. Trying to curb the voracious appetite for power of entrenched bureaucracies does not have anything to do with an irrational "peasant uprising." Conversely, the rise of a political society does not make civil society irrelevant.

The ethos of civil society allowed forgiveness to become an important ingredient for the nonviolent transitions in Central Europe. We thus see a myth in its founding role, constructing the social cosmos around a paramount idea of justice and solidarity. Because the West was democratic and had its civil society, the dissidents were looking for similar achievements in their own region. They appealed to the reassuring function of myth: "Myth assures man that what he is about to do has already been done, in other words, it helps him to overcome doubts as to the result of his undertaking. . . . The existence of an exemplary model does not fetter creative innovation. The possibilities for applying the mythical model are endless."[37] The legitimacy of the political institutions—the public identification with the pluralist order—justifies and strengthens the project of a civil society. This is not possible when there is still conflict or open discord about the ultimate goals of political life.

The rejection of the coercive Leninist worldview with its all-explanatory pretense, amounted to a general skepticism about any "grand narrative." These revolutions (even the Polish and Hungarian "contractual" ones) were searches for the reinsertion of these societies into a modern, secularized, post-industrial and post-ideological world. Their post-modern component was linked to their relativization of the absolutist dogmas in the sarcastic, self-mocking mini-discourses of the dissidents, their cultivation of minority rights, and suspicion about any grandiose teleologies. One of the main reasons of the communism's breakdown, more important perhaps than Western pressures, was the infinite tediousness of life within the system—the omnipresence of kitsch, pseudo ethics, imperatives of production, ecocide. But in opposing the official monistic postulates and cultivating diversity, East European critical intellectuals also avoided total moral relativism, one of the options of post-modernity, which turns the assessment of mass deportations and genocide into a matter of taste.[38]

The overarching presence of two myths—Europe and civil society—in the first years after 1989 indicated the power of the democratic magnetism exerted by the West. The insistence on the European dimension was an overall trend in the region and played the role of a de-Russifying symbol. Also, of course, these countries have been competing with each other for the West's favor and assistance. What is at stake is not only economic recovery but external recognition of the intrinsic value, that is, Europeanness of one's culture. By implication, those who are not front-runners are somewhat backward, primitive, barbarian. But are they? Can one see whole cultures as being forever prisoners of their history?

Part of the reason for the ex-communists' comeback is no doubt linked to the inner tensions and fights among dissidents. There is currently a debate among the revolutionaries: did they renounce power too fast, too easily? Or, as Miklos Haraszti and Adam Michnik argue, is this defeat also the success of their commitment to a society based on free elections, rule of law, and market economy? The most important element in their philosophy was the refusal to engage in the politics of retribution and revenge. As Czech writer Ivan Klima put it: "Who can establish a borderline between guilt and innocence when that borderline runs somewhere right down the middle of each person?"[39]

The amazing thing about the 1989 upheaval was the totally non-Leninist readiness of the ruling class to give up political power. What was Leninism? A technique of seizing power by a charismatically impersonal elite called the Bolshevik party.[40] Logically, such an elite does not renounce power voluntarily. To do so, it must have lost self-confidence. The Gorbachev phenomenon was the consequence, rather than the cause of this loss of ideological ardor. Indeed, once the Soviet bureaucracy engaged in policies similar to the Prague

Spring, and gave up the Brezhnev doctrine of limited sovereignty, the collapse of Eastern Europe's Leninist regimes was inevitable. Their demise was thus the result of an acute legitimation crisis combined with the rise of independent movements and actions from below, largely described as civil society.[41] Many communists saw the old-fashioned patterns of authority and domination as blatantly ineffective and anachronistic. In countries like Hungary and Poland, the communists left power because they had realized that the Leninist game was over. In Romania, former prime minister Petre Roman, once President Iliescu's closest associate, broke with the ruling national-populist coalition and transformed his Democratic party into a dynamic formation committed to the values of European social democracy.

While in opposition, trying to reinvent themselves as part of a modernized left, some post-communists have learned how to practice the language of compromise and inclusion. Their credibility is, however, questioned by those who refuse to consider the possibility of genuine conversions. For example, when Adam Michnik once described post-communist leader Aleksander Kwasniewski as one of the most intelligent politicians in Poland, furious reactions followed: an ex-communist has to be simultaneously a moron and a scoundrel. It is hard for the firebrand anti-communist militant to accept that there are some who are neither. One should always ask, who are the post-communists? Exactly like the post-fascists in the West (Italy's Gianfranco Fini is the most obvious example), who are not just carbon-copy replicas of the interwar madmen, the post-communists share many things with their forerunners, but without the ideological fanaticism and the belief that they are the only ones to know the sense of history.

No less unexpected than the breakdown of communism has been the return of the ex-communists. No coup d'état or putsch brought them back to power, but the velvet route of electoral competition. Their return in Central Europe is part of the normally functioning democracy. Hence, Aleksander Kwasniewski's victory in the 1995 presidential elections does not amount to a return to a police state. In fact, it means the incorporation of many achievements of the revolutionary stage into the nascent consensual culture. Here, the logical and historical fallacy would be to see these people as unreconstructed Marxist crusaders. The leveling out of ideological passions noticed by François Furet applies to them no less than to the Western leftist movements and parties.[42]

The real enemies of democracy are clericalist, fundamentalist, nationalist, anti-liberal fanatics. Walesa's defeat was linked to his dubious exploitation of a Red Scare rhetoric and unqualified endorsement of the Catholic hierarchy's efforts to control public and private realms. Although Poles are overwhelmingly Catholic, public opinion polls indicate that 74 percent are against church activism in politics.[43] In addition to this mass exasperation with the clergy's inordinate influence on Walesa, the reasons for Kwasniewski's success included fatigue, especially among the younger voters, with the obsessional warnings about "Bolsheviks," "nomenklatura," and the "Red Cobweb."

A new pattern of politics, based on post-ideological arrangements, is emerging in these societies. It is intimately linked to the failure of decommunization as a new foundation myth. Instead of a politics of emotion and vengeance, both Hungarian and Polish post-communists have pursued further privatization, integration into Euro-Atlantic structures, and dialogue with the other political forces. Disappointing and even distasteful for many, the electoral victories of Poland's post-communists indicate that the age of radical confrontation is over. Trying to revive it, as certain leaders of Solidarity have done, would only imperil the democratic gains and perpetuate a state of mutual suspicion and civic disorder. Indeed, it would be much healthier to admit, together with Timothy Garton Ash, that "Poland's transition from normal abnormality to abnormal normality is already a fantastic achievement."[44]

The post-communist socialists are not the seasoned apparatchiks of yesteryear. In the meantime, many of them have gone private, and their "parties" should be discussed as heterogeneous constellations of various groups and trends ranging from a kind of egalitarian unionism (*ouvriérisme*) to the cult of business and entrepreneurship. Actually, most of them had long since broken with any proletarian idealism.[45] Especially after the crushing of the Prague Spring by Warsaw Pact tanks in August 1968, no hope was nourished regarding the inner reformability of the established order. Communist apparatchiks were performing what the anonymous, profoundly corrupt "System" was demanding. They were (and remained) primarily interested in their careers and in getting rich. This is the key to their resilience in coming back to power. What remains to be explained is why people voted for them in countries so different as Hungary and Poland, Lithuania and Bulgaria. A minimal conclusion is that not all post-communists are alike. In Bulgaria, Romania and Serbia there was no repentance; on the contrary, ruling post-communist parties embraced nationalism as the latter-day creed, postponed reforms, and denounced their critics as "enemies of the Fatherland."[46] In the countries with genuine reform communist traditions, the post-communists became in many cases genuine ex-communists (neosocialists).

But overall, anti-communism turned out to be less of a universal feeling than imagined by the tribunes of the 1989–1991 transformations. As a result, decommunization rhetoric merely alienated a large part of the electorate from the radicals: the fate of hard-core Western-style liberals like FIDESZ in Hungary (who attracted only 5 percent of the vote in the June 1994 elections) is telltale. Another example of the same phenomenon was the failure of the Olszewski government in Poland in 1993 in spite (or because) its shrill propaganda. The vindictive and scapegoating mythologies of decommunization actually helped ex-communists to appear less alien and guilty than they really were.[47]

Conclusion

The revolutions of 1989 are frequently presented as a kind of collective mirage, leading to the reentrenchment of the old bureaucracies in new forms. Because many of the former elite members remained in or returned to power, the argument goes, the revolutions failed.

It is, however, much too early to put forward any definitive conclusions on these earth-shattering events. Indeed, for about seventy years, the world was divided in two competing blocs: on the one hand, the liberal West (often decried as exhausted, too rational, mercantile, deprived of intense emotional foundations); on the other, the totalitarian ideocratic systems, united by the shared hostility to liberal values. Once communism collapsed, successor ideologies and formations strove to replace it: some favor democratic individualism, some abhor it.

The ex-communists' political metamorphoses is thus part of the invention of normality: steeped in the new procedures and arrangements, they are not the nostalgics of the old order but rather the profiteers of the new one. Whatever one may think of their candor, the fact remains that they are ready (at least in Poland and Hungary) to advocate the acceleration of political and economic reforms. Aleksandr Kwasniewski's statement is thus emblematic for this trend: "We and the post-dissidents agree on the issue of democracy, on the problems of privatization, the reduction of the deficit, the market economy, the need to reform the system of social protection; finally, we agree on the entrance to NATO and the European Union."[48] The search for new alliances is part of the post-modern experience in which traditional ideologies have lost their universalist meanings and pragmatism is more significant than perpetual settling of scores. The transformation of the Spanish Socialist party into an adamantly pro–free market actor, like the end of Mitterrandism in France, bears witness to the fact that this is more than an East European development.

It is perhaps worthwhile to remember, together with Hannah Arendt, Churchill's words written decades before radical evil became institutionalized in the horrors of the 1930s: "Scarcely anything, material or established, which I was brought up to believe was permanent and vital, has lasted. Everything I was sure was impossible, or was taught to be sure was impossible happened."[49] And, especially in these times of moral frustration, when much of the liberating effect of 1989 seems to have been forgotten, it is worth remembering that the moments of fever and ecstasy are short-lived, and what remains, after the revolutionary tempest passes, are the new institutions and the new ways people relate to each other and to the world. No triumph could be more deserved for the revolutionaries of 1989 than the enduring power of the new institutions to weather wave after wave of illiberal passions, anti-Western emotions, and populist wrath.

Notes

Introduction
After Marx

1. For the political-cultural connotations of Europe's time zones, see Ernest Gellner, *Conditions of Liberty: Civil Society and Its Rivals* (New York: Allen Lane/Penguin Press, 1994), pp. 113–18.

2. The rise of political and ethnic extremism in post-communist Eastern Europe is thoroughly examined by Sabrina P. Ramet in "Defining the Radical Right: Values and Behaviors of Organized Intolerance in Post-Communist Central and Eastern Europe," in *The Radical Right in Central and Eastern Europe*, edited by Sabrina P. Ramet (book manuscript, under review). See also the special issue on extremism in Eastern Europe and the former Soviet Union, *Transition*, vol. 3, no. 16 (22 April 1994), with an introduction by J. F. Brown.

3. For the vying conceptions of citizenry (civic and ethnic) and their impact on the new polities, see Ulrich Preuss, "Constitutional Powermaking for the New Polity: Some Deliberations on the Relations between Constituent Power and the Constitution," *Cardozo Law Review*, vol. 14 (January 1993), pp. 646–51.

4. Jane Perlez, "Abduction Casts New Doubts on Slovakia Chief," *New York Times*, 17 December 1996.

5. Ernst Cassirer, *The Myth of the State* (New Haven: Yale University Press, 1946), pp. 47–48.

6. Ken Jowitt, "Moscow Centre," in *New World Disorder: The Leninist Extinction* (Berkeley and Los Angeles: University of California Press, 1992), pp. 159–219.

7. For instance, during the presidential and parliamentary elections in November 1996, Ion Iliescu attacked his adversaries for lack of patriotism and collusion with Hungarian irredentism. The hackneyed card of aggressive nationalism backfired and he lost to the Democratic Convention leader, Emil Constantinescu, who was elected president with 54.4 percent of the vote. See Gail Kligman and Vladimir Tismaneanu, "Romania Belatedly Savors Real Democracy," *Philadelphia Inquirer*, 4 December 1996. In the same vein, supporters of Serbian president Milošević have accused the democratic opposition of national treason. See Chris Hedges, "Rally to Support Serb Chief Draws Only a Few of the Faithful, *New York Times*, 19 December 1996.

8. The literature on the Yugoslav disaster and the role of nationalism in the destruction is extremely rich. Among the most insightful sources, I recommend Mark Thompson, *A Paper House: The Ending of Yugoslavia* (New York: Pantheon, 1992); Misha Glenny, *The Fall of Yugoslavia: The Third Balkan War* (Harmondsworth: Penguin, 1992); Lenard J. Cohen, *Broken Bonds: The Disintegration of Yugoslavia* (Boulder: Westview Press, 1993), and Susan Woodward, *The Yugoslav Tragedy* (Washington, DC: Brookings Institution, 1995). For the role of the Serbian intelligentsia and party bureaucracy in the dismemberment of the federation, see Branka Magas, *The Destruction of Yugoslavia: Tracking the Break-up 1980–92* (London: Verso, 1993).

9. For a lucid analysis of the role of nationalism in communist and post-communist societies, see Katherine Verdery, *What Was Socialism and What Comes Next?* (Princeton: Princeton University Press, 1996).

10. Eric Hobsbawm, *Nations and Nationalisms since 1780* (Cambridge: Cambridge University Press, 1991), p. 91. For Hobsbawm's overall interpretation of the twentieth-century experience, see his masterful (and quite idiosyncratic) *The Age of Extremes: A History of the World, 1914–1991* (New York: Pantheon, 1994). Hobsbawm is often reproached with a certain lack of empathy with national sentiment and therefore an inability to make sense of the magnetism exerted by this ideology. In my view, he captures very convincingly the resources of nationalist messages, their encouraging and exhilarating power. Indeed, what irritates nationalist writers in Hobsbawm's approach is his rejection of the primordialist vision and his insistence on the historical novelty, and accordingly the surpassability, of the national entities. No nationalist thinker can come to terms with a vision which claims that traditions are "invented" and that individuals can be defined by more than one identity. The nationalist discourse is "mono-identitary": it forces the individual into an assigned belonging, usually defined by "imponderable," atavistic linkages to a mystical communitarian body.

11. Stjepan G. Mestrovic, with Slaven Letica and Miroslav Goreta, *Habits of the Balkan Heart: Social Character and the Fall of Communism* (College Station: Texas A&M University Press, 1993).

12. Gilbert Durand, *Les structures anthropologiques de l'imaginaire: Introduction à l'archétypologie générale* (Paris: Bordas, 1969).

13. Raoul Girardet, *Mythes et mythologies politiques* (Paris: Éditions du Seuil, 1986), p. 12.

14. Pieter Viereck, *Metapolitics: The Roots of the Nazi Mind* (New York: Capricorn Books, 1965).

15. Jacob L. Talmon, *Myth of the Nation and Vision of the Revolution: Ideological Polarization in the Twentieth Century* (New Brunswick: Transaction Publishers, 1991), with a new introduction by Irving Louis Horowitz.

16. For the significant distinction between traditional tyrannies and the ideocratic constructs ("tyrannies of certitude") of the twentieth century, see Daniel Chirot, *Modern Tyrants: The Power and the Prevalence of Evil in Our Times* (New York: Free Press, 1994).

17. Isaiah Berlin, *The Crooked Timber of Humanity: Chapters in the History of Ideas* (New York: Knopf, 1991), pp. 15–16.

18. For communism and national socialism as political pathologies, see François Furet, *Le passé d'une illusion* (Paris: Fayard, 1995).

19. Daniel Jonah Goldhagen, *Hitler's Willing Executioners: Ordinary Germans and the Holocaust* (New York: Knopf, 1996); see also the interview with Goldhagen by Maurice Wohlgelernter in *Society*, vol. 34, no. 2 (January-February 1997), pp. 33–37.

20. This is a point made by literary historian Adrian Marino, one of the few genuine liberal intellectuals in post-Ceaușescu Romania. In spite of the fact that almost everybody declares him/herself to nourish liberal views, there are not too many opinion makers ready to engage, as Marino has done, in the deconstruction of the self-serving national utopias of the pre-Roman and pre-Christian, Dacian Golden Age. See his book *Pentru Europa* (Iași: Editura Polirom, 1995), p. 36. This phenomenon of fetishization and idealization of the past is not uniquely East European, nor is the repudiation of

those who engage in a critical scrutiny of national legends. Peruvian writer Mario Vargas Llosa, Venezuelan journalist Carlos Rangel, and Mexican poet and essayist Octavio Paz have been stigmatized by the Latin American left for having dared to claim that the sources of the continent's backwardness are endogenous, and not the result of vicious exploitation by the United States. One can also mention the role of political myth in the making of post-World War II West German political culture: from the exaltation of the aristocratic anti-Nazi resistance to the praise for the German physicists who allegedly refused to produce the A-bomb for Hitler. We know now that this myth was consciously fabricated by Werner Heisenberg and other German nuclear physicists to counter possible charges of participation in criminal warfare. This myth was fundamental for the anti-deployment movement in the 1980s and for the new varieties of eco-pacifism, including radical environmentalism, in contemporary Germany.

21. See Norman Cohn, *The Pursuit of the Millennium: Revolutionary Messianism in Medieval and Reformation Europe and Its Bearings on Modern Totalitarian Movements* (New York: Harper Torchbooks, 1961); Benjamin Barber, *Jihad vs. McWorld* (New York: Times Books/Random House, 1995).

22. See Norman Cohn, *Warrant for Genocide: The Myth of the Jewish World-Conspiracy and the "Protocols of the Elders of Zion"* (New York: Torchbooks, 1969); Leon Poliakoff, *Bréviaire de la haine* (Paris: Éditions Complexe, 1986).

23. Again, Eastern Europe is not alone in breeding such myths. (The Iranian and Algerian fundamentalisms are among the most visible of these movements). Add to this the temptation to attribute all failures to external forces, to the demonized figure of the Other (the Jews, the Jesuits, the Gypsies, the Masons, the Bavarian Illuminati, the gays, or even the Council on Foreign Relations). For the mythological sources of the American Christian Right and their blending into a sui generis conspiratorial fantasy, see Michael Lind, "Rev. Robertson's Grand International Conspiracy Theory," *New York Review of Books*, 2 February 1995, pp. 21–25.

24. For the myth of Russia as the Third Rome, see Leon Poliakoff, *Moscou, Troisième Rome: Les intermittences de la memoire historique* (Paris: Hachette, 1989).

25. Adam Michnik, "The Velvet Restoration," *Transition*, vol. 2, no. 6 (22 March 1996), pp. 13–16.

26. For the revolutions of 1989 and the "end of modernity," see Zygmunt Bauman, *Intimations of Postmodernity* (London: Routledge, 1992), p. 222. Unlike Bauman or G. M. Tamás, I see the revolutions of 1989 not as revolts against modernity but rather as efforts to transcend one (and not necessarily the most legitimate) of its historical possibilities. Indeed, if the separation of powers, the supremacy of law, the distinction between private and public spheres, civic rights, the free market, and political and religious tolerance are attributes of modernity, communism itself, in its Marxist-Leninist incarnation, symbolized the very opposite of the Enlightenment's ideals.

27. Personal interview with Adam Michnik, Rutgers University, Newark, March 1992.

28. For Sorel and the search for a revolutionary alternative to both classical Marxism and liberalism, see Zeev Sternhell, with Mario Sznajder and Maia Asheri, *The Birth of Fascist Ideology: From Cultural Rebellion to Political Revolution* (Princeton: Princeton University Press, 1994), especially pp. 36–91.

29. Georges Sorel, *Reflections on Violence* (New York: Collier Books, 1961), p. 50.

30. Ibid. pp. 285–86.

31. Isaiah Berlin, *Against the Current: Essays in the History of Ideas* (New York: Penguin Books, 1982), pp. 318, 319.

32. See for instance James F. Brown, *Hopes and Shadows* (Durham: Duke University Press, 1994); Eva Hoffman, *Exit into History* (New York: Viking, 1993); and Gale Stokes, *When the Walls Came Tumbling Down* (New York: Oxford University Press, 1993). For an excellent analysis of political, cultural, military, and economic variables of the democratic transition in the countries of the former USSR, see Karen Dawisha and Bruce Parrott, *Russia and the New States of Eurasia: The Politics of Upheaval* (Cambridge and New York: Cambridge University Press, 1994).

33. See for instance Daniel Langenkamp, "Shedding Tears for János Kádár, *Budapest Week*, 11–17 July 1996, p. 3.

34. Responding to the often-heard invitations for public intellectuals to leave the scene, or to refrain from criticizing the post-communist order, Václav Havel highlighted precisely the imperative for social imagination to transcend the limitations of conventional party politics: "I do not approve of political parties behaving as if they possess a monopoly on knowledge, truth, and the solutions to problems. . . . Parties should listen to the multifaceted opinions of a pluralistic civil society, as expressed by all individuals, groups, and organizations, including educated people, experts, academics, and intellectuals. . . . Self-indulgent parties that do not become aware of this life-giving environment will weaken and wither, becoming mere elevators to authority." See Václav Havel, Václav Klaus, and Petr Pithart, "Civil Society after Communism: Rival Visions," *Journal of Democracy*, vol. 7, no. 1 (January 1996), p. 15. For Klaus's critique of "moral universalism," ibid. pp. 15–16.

35. A political myth represents "a device men adopt in order to come to grips with reality; and we can tell that a given account is a myth, not by the amount of truth it contains, but by the fact that it is believed to be true, and above all, by the dramatic form into which it is cast." Henry Tudor, *Political Myth* (London: Pall Mall, 1972), p. 17.

36. See Polish political philosopher Marcin Krol, "Where East Meets West" *Journal of Democracy*, vol. 6, no. 1 (January 1995), p. 38 for an assessment of liberal democracy: and for a thoroughgoing analysis of prospects for liberalism in post-communist societies, see Jerzy Szacki, *Liberalism after Communism* (Budapest and London: Central European University Press, 1995).

37. See Michael M. Fischer, "Working through the Other: The Jewish, Spanish, Turkish, Ukrainian, Lithuanian, and German Unconscious of Polish Culture or One Hand Clapping: Dialogue, Silences, and the Mourning of Polish Romanticism," in *Perilous States: Conversations on Culture, Politics, and Nation*, edited by George E. Marcus (Chicago: University of Chicago Press, 1993), p. 209.

38. Quoted by Girardet, *Mythes et mythologies*, p. 54.

39. Zhelyu Zhelev, "Is Communism Returning?" *Journal of Democracy*, vol. 7, no. 3 (July 1996), p. 5.

40. See for instance the interview with Adam Michnik, "Sînt absolut impotriva decomunizării" (I am totally against decommunization), 22 (Bucharest), 5–11 October 1994, p. 13. For Michnik's mordant discussion of the "prudent people with clean hands," see his article "An Embarrassing Anniversary," *New York Review of Books*, 10 June 1993, pp. 19–21.

41. Jeffrey C. Isaac, "The Meanings of 1989," *Social Research*, vol. 63, no. 2 (Summer 1996), p. 326.

42. The defeat of the dissidents is not a universal trend, as confirmed by a public opinion poll taken in Hungary in August 1996. Seventy-five percent of the respondents indicated president Arpad Göncz, a former political prisoner and dissident, as their favorite politician. *Open Media Research Institute (OMRI) Daily Report*, 19 August 1996. In the same vein, Petr Pithart, a former Charter 77 activist, was elected chairman of the Senate of the Czech parliament in December 1996, in spite of prime minister Václav Klaus's opposition.

43. For Marxism as a political mythology, and even as the consummate, most comprehensive one, see Robert C. Tucker, *Philosophy and Myth in Karl Marx* (Cambridge: Cambridge University Press, 1964) and Andrzej Walicki, *Marxism and the Leap into the Kingdom of Freedom: The Rise and Fall of the Communist Utopia* (Stanford: Stanford University Press, 1995).

44. A. J. Polan, *Lenin and the End of Politics* (Berkeley and Los Angeles: University of California Press, 1984), p. 16.

45. Gellner, *Conditions of Liberty*, p. 41.

46. See Valerie Bunce, "Comparing East and South," *Journal of Democracy*, vol. 6, no. 3 (July 1995), pp. 87–100.

47. See Ken Jowitt, "Dizzy with Democracy," *Problems of Post-Communism*, January-February 1996, esp. p. 6.

48. G. M. Tamás, "Socialism, Capitalism, Modernity," *Journal of Democracy*, vol. 3, no. 3 (July 1992), pp. 61–74.

49. See Abraham Brumberg, "Poland's Progress: The Declining Role of Anti-Semitism—and an Overbearing Church," *Washington Post* (Outlook Section), 24 January 1994.

50. See Agnes Heller and Ferenc Fehér, *The Post-Modern Political Condition* (Cambridge, UK: Polity Press, 1988), pp. 1–43.

51. Walter Benjamin, "Theses on the Philosophy of History," in Stephen Eric Bronner and Douglas MacKay Kellner, *Critical Theory and Society* (New York and London: Routledge, 1989), p. 257.

52. I share Ernest Gellner's view that, at the end of this millennium, "Civil Society is justified at least in part by the fact that it seems linked to our historical destiny. A return to stagnant traditional agrarian society is not possible; so, industrialism being our manifest destiny, we are thereby also committed to its social corollaries." See *Conditions of Liberty*, p. 213.

53. This is also reflected in the intolerance toward other Christian denominations, and primarily the Catholics (or Greek Catholics). The Orthodox Church benefited from the Stalinist persecution of the Uniates and is now irritated by the risk of having to return the usurped properties to their legal owners. This situation is still unresolved in Romania, with the exception of Banat, where Orthodox metropolitan Nicolae Corneanu, a distinguished theologian with an ecumenical perspective, decided to return the properties to the Greek Catholic Church. Personal interview with Nicolae Corneanu, Timişoara, Romania, May 1995.

54. For this ideological desire, see especially Slavoj Žižek, *The Sublime Object of Ideology* (London: Verso, 1989).

55. Aleksandr Solzhenitsyn, *Chestiunea rusă la sfîrsit de secol XX* (Bucharest: Editura Anastasia, 1995).

56. Jacek Kuron, "Manifesto: Part Two of a Program for Poland," *Common Knowledge*, vol. 4, no. 1 (Spring 1995), pp. 19–48.

One
Resurrecting Utopia

1. See John Girling, *Myths and Politics in Western Societies: Evaluating the Crisis of Modernity in the United States, Germany, and Great Britain* (New Brunswick: Transaction Publishers, 1993), p. 12.

2. Northrop Frye, *Spiritus Mundi: Essays on Literature, Myth and Society* (Bloomington: Indiana University Press, 1976), pp. 88–89. I owe to Michael Marrus the suggestion to use the literary approach suggested by Frye to interpret political confrontations and cleavages within modernity. In a truly illuminating study, he used this paradigm for rereading and reinterpreting one of the most important sources of mythological debates in French politics: the Dreyfus Affair. See Michael Marrus, " 'En Famille': The Dreyfus Affair and Its Myths," *French Politics and Society*, vol. 12, no. 4 (Fall 1994), pp. 76–90. My references to Frye and Malinowski owe a lot to Marrus's use of these sources.

3. Frye, *Spiritus Mundi*, p. 89.

4. Ibid.

5. See for instance Stephen Kinzer, "In 'East Germany,' Bad Ol' Days Now Look Good," *New York Times*, 27 August 1994. This restorative theme was the gist of Russian neocommunist leader Gennady Zyuganov's 1996 presidential campaign. He challenged Boris Yeltsin in the name of an idealized vision of the historical past, heroic values, ethnic solidarity, and opposition to the corruptive Western influences. For a perceptive analysis of Zyuganov's mind-set, see David Remnick, "Hammer, Sickle, and Book," *New York Review of Books*, 23 May 1996, pp. 44–51.

6. Bronislaw Malinowski, *Magic, Science and Religion and Other Essays* (Garden City, NY: Doubleday, 1954), pp. 96–101, as quoted by Marrus, "En Famille," p. 80.

7. The political culture of Bolshevism was a blend of Russian revolutionary radicalism and Lenin's Jacobin development of major themes in the thinking of Karl Marx. See Richard Pipes, *Russia under the Bolshevik Regime* (New York: Knopf, 1993), pp. 490–512; Martin Malia, *The Soviet Tragedy: A History of Socialism in Russia* (New York: Free Press, 1994).

8. I examined this theme in *The Crisis of Marxist Ideology in Eastern Europe: The Poverty of Utopia* (London and New York: Routledge, 1988). For thoughtful analyses of the relationship between Marxism, Leninism, and Stalinism, see Leszek Kolakowski, *Main Currents of Marxism*, vol. 3, *The Breakdown* (Oxford and New York: Oxford University Press, 1978).

9. Benito Mussolini, *Opera Omnia*, Vol. 21, p. 1,090, quoted by Jacob L. Talmon, *The Myth of the Nation and the Vision of the Revolution: Ideological Polarizations in the Twentieth Century* (New Brunswick, NJ: Transaction Publishers, 1991), p. 460.

10. Ibid. p. 549.

11. Immanuel Kant, *Religion within the Limits of Pure Reason* (1793), quoted by Elie Kedourie, *Nationalism*, fourth, expanded edition (Oxford: Basil Blackwell, 1993), pp. 20–21.

12. Girling, *Myths and Politics in Western Societies*, p. 19.

13. For the meaning and limits of East European Marxist revisionism, see Adam Michnik's pathbreaking 1976 essay "A New Evolutionism," in his *Letters from Prison and Other Essays* (Berkeley and Los Angeles: University of California Press, 1985), pp. 135–59.

14. Marrus,"En Famille," p. 81.

15. Frye, *Spiritus Mundi*, p. ix.

16. In the words of political theorist Judith Shklar: "Anyone who thinks that fascism in one guise or another is dead and gone ought to think again." See "The Liberalism of Fear," in *Liberalism and the Moral Life*, edited by Nancy L. Rosenblum (Cambridge: Harvard University Press, 1989), p. 22.

17. Eugen Weber, *Varieties of Fascism: Doctrines of Revolution in the Twentieth Century* (Malabar, FL: Krieger, 1982), and Roger Griffin, *The Nature of Fascism* (New York: St. Martin's Press, 1991).

18. For Schmitt, an original critic of Germany's liberalism during the pre-Nazi period from an authoritarian perspective and himself a theorist of political myth, see George Schwab, *The Challenge of the Exception: An Introduction to the Political Ideas of Carl Schmitt between 1921 and 1936*, second edition with a new introduction (Westport, CT.: Greenwood Press, 1989); see also the special issue of *Telos*, no. 72 (Summer 1987), consecrated to Schmitt.

19. See Stephen Holmes, *Anatomy of Antiliberalism* (Cambridge: Harvard University Press, 1993).

20. The discovery in the American mass media of the militia movement shows that this fascination with distorted history and myth is not limited to those who grew up under communism. Militia members do not realize their own anarchist ideology but have no trouble repeating stories (myths) of the tyranny of the United States government and the World Zionist Conspiracy.

21. Norman Cohn, *The Pursuit of the Millennium: Revolutionary Messianism in Medieval and Reformation Europe and Its Bearings on the Modern Totalitarian Movements* (New York: Harper Torchbooks, 1961), p. 4.

22. Eric Hofer captured this commitment to one self-explanatory, narcissistic worldview in his analysis of political fanaticism; see *The True Believer: Thoughts on the Nature of Mass Movements* (New York: Time, 1963). It is interesting that Hannah Arendt was particularly impressed with Hofer's original, totally unorthodox thinking and recommended his work to Karl Jaspers.

23. Daniel Bell, *The End of Ideology: On the Exhaustion of Political Ideas in the Fifties*, with a new afterword (Cambridge: Harvard University Press, 1988).

24. Norberto Bobbio, "The Upturned Utopia," in *After the Fall: The Failure of Communism and the Future of Socialism*, edited by Robin Blackburn (London and New York: Verso, 1991), pp. 3–4.

25. In the GDR, the myth of the Aryan nation was simply replaced with the myth of the "first German state of the workers and peasants," according to which the German proletariat did not cooperate in Hitler's murderous policies and national socialism was simply the most extreme form of the bourgeois counterrevolution. During the first years of the GDR, Ulbricht and his associates deported to Buchenwald not only former Nazis but also Social Democrats, liberals of all sorts, and other opponents of any political despotism. Not much different were Bulgaria, Hungary, and even Poland, where democratic and pluralist moments were interludes rather than durable political stages.

26. Umberto Eco, "Ur-Fascism," *New York Review of Books*, 22 June 1995, p. 12.

27. This is true not only in Russia but also in the former GDR. See Jennifer Yoder, "Democratic Consolidation and Elite Building in the Former GDR," Ph.D. dissertation, University of Maryland, College Park, May 1996. For the impact of German unification on Eastern European democratic transitions, see Stephen E. Hanson and Willfried Spohn, eds., *Can Europe Work? Germany and the Reconstruction of Postcommunist Societies* (Seattle: University of Washington Press, 1995).

28. Veljko Vujacic, "Gennady Zyuganov and the 'Third Road,'" *Post-Soviet Affairs*, vol. 12, no. 2 (April-June 1996), pp. 118–54; Stephen F. Cohen, "If Not Yeltsin: Four Voices of the Russian Opposition," *Washington Post*, 3 December 1995; Michael Specter, "The Catch Phrase Is 'Civil War,'" *New York Times*, 12 May 1996; David Hoffmann, "Nostalgic for Lenin," *Washington Post*, 8 April 1996; Peter Reddaway, "Red Alert," *New Republic*, 29 January 1996, pp. 15–18. For Zhirinovsky's neofascist calls for a "third choice" beyond "rotten liberalism" and "bankrupt communism," see "Weimar on the Volga," *Economist*, 18 December 1993, pp. 45–46 and Celestine Bohlen, "Zhirinovsky Cult Grows: All Power to the Leader," *New York Times*, 5 April 1994.

29. Personal interviews with Slavenka Drakulić, Vienna, November 1993, and Vesna Pusić, Washington, D.C., November 1996. For Drakulić's views on the conflict in the former Yugoslavia, see her book *The Balkan Express: Fragments from the Other Side of the War* (New York: Norton, 1993). In a similar vein, Romania's ultranationalists have attacked political writer H.-R. Patapievici for having dared to speak about the deeply engrained conformism and xenophobia in the country's political culture. A series of vicious articles came out in 1996 in *România Mare*, charging Patapievici of crimes of *lèse-nation* (anti-Romanianism). Even more disturbing, attacks on Patapievici came out in some of the officially pro-Western and democratic publications. For Patapievici's rebuttal of these attacks, see his article "Criticilor mei," *22*, 7–13 August 1996, p. 13.

30. Editor-in-chief of the weekly *Zavtra*, Prokhanov is Zyuganov's main ideological guru. Self-described as the "organ of the spiritual opposition," *Zavtra* unabashedly promotes a militant, integral form of nationalism, combining czarist, Stalinist, Slavophile, and staunchly anti-Semitic and anti-Western clichés. Among its contributors, one notices mathematician and former dissident Igor Shafarevich, who has made peace with his former communist tormentors and even celebrates them as "true Russian patriots."

31. For an illuminating analysis of nationalism as the dominant ideology in post-Leninist Russia, see Vladimir Brovkin, "The Emperor's New Clothes: Continuity of Soviet Political Culture in Contemporary Russia," *Problems of Post-Communism*, March-April 1996, pp. 21–28.

32. Paul Hockenos, *Free to Hate: The Rise of the Right in Post-Communist Eastern Europe* (London and New York: Routledge, 1993; revised edition, 1994).

33. Eugen Ionescu, *Război cu toata lumea* (Bucharest: Humanitas, 1992), vol. 2, pp. 269–70, as quoted in Matei Calinescu, "Ionesco and 'Rhinoceros': Personal and Political Backgrounds," *East European Politics and Societies*, vol. 9, no. 3 (Fall 1995), pp. 393–433.

34. Ionescu, *Război cu toata lumea*, pp. 273–74, quoted by Calinescu, "Ionesco and 'Rhinoceros.'"

35. A term coined by Norman Cohn, *The Pursuit of the Millennium*, p. 11.

36. Raoul Girardet, *Mythes et mythologies politiques* (Paris: Éditions du Seuil, 1986); pp. 118–19.

37. G. M. Tamás, "Socialism, Capitalism, Modernity," *Journal of Democracy*, vol. 3, no. 3 (July 1993), p. 64.

38. Stanley Payne, *A History of Fascism, 1914–1945* (Madison: University of Wisconsin Press, 1995), pp. 277–89.

39. Tamás, "Socialism, Capitalism, Modernity," p. 71.

40. See Vassily Aksyonov, "My Search for Russia's Revolution," *New York Times*, 22 November 1994 on the need for Russia to realize itself "as a true part of Western civilization."

41. See Juan Linz, "The Perils of Presidentialism," *Journal of Democracy*, vol. 1, no. 1 (Winter 1990), pp. 51–69. Juan Linz and Alfred Stepan give us a sobering perspective for assessing democratic transitions when they write: "when we talk about the consolidation of democracy, we are not dealing with liberalized nondemocratic regimes, or with pseudo-democracies, or with hybrid democracies where some democratic institutions coexist with nondemocratic institutions outside the control of the democratic state." See Juan J. Linz and Alfred Stepan, "Toward Consolidated Democracies," *Journal of Democracy*, vol. 7, no. 2 (April 1996), p. 15.

42. See Stephen Eric Bronner, "The Enlightenment and Its Critics," *New Politics*, vol. 5, no. 3 (new series) (Summer 1995), pp. 65–86.

43. See Solzhenitsyn's prescient contribution to the volume he edited, *From under the Rubble*; but also David Remnick, *Lenin's Tomb*, probably the most perceptive analysis of the psychological costs of the dismantling of Lenin's empire.

44. Richard Pipes quoted in "A Silent Revolution," *Economist*, 8 April 1995, special survey on Russia's emerging market, p. 4.

45. For the rise of organized crime in Russia, its growing grip on nuclear facilities, and the risks for international security, see Seymour M. Hersh, "The Wild East," *The Atlantic Monthly*, June 1994, pp. 61–86.

46. Václav Havel, *Summer Meditations* (New York: Vintage Books, 1993).

Two
The Leninist Debris

1. For the significance of the post-communists' political comeback in Poland and Hungary, see Tad Szulc, "They Used to Call Them Communists," *Parade Magazine*, 4 September 1995, pp. 4–5; Jane Perlez, "Walesa's Nemesis: Aleksander Kwasniewski," *New York Times*, 21 November 1995; "Poland's Communist Makeover," *Economist*, 25 November 1995, pp. 47–48. For an excellent interpretation of the November 1995 Polish presidential elections, see Viktor Osiatynski, "After Walesa," *East European Constitutional Review*, vol. 4, no. 4 (Fall 1995), pp. 35–44. Kwasniewski visited the United States in July 1996 and emphasized his bona fide credentials as a committed social democrat and supporter of pluralism. In the words of a State Department official: "Kwasniewski's emphasis is the future, the future, the future." See Jane Perlez, "Poland's Leader Leaves a Marxist Past Behind," *New York Times*, 14 July 1996.

2. Adam Michnik, "The Velvet Restoration," *Transition*, vol. 2, no. 6 (22 March 1996), p. 16.

3. Sociologist and philosopher Zygmunt Bauman gave an accurate definition of the "post-communist condition" when he said in an interview with the magazine *Odra* in January 1995 that "for the first time we find ourselves in a situation in which we know

that diversity will be with us from now on and we have to come to some sort of modus vivendi with it." Bauman's views, as well as many other significant Polish contributions to the understanding of the post-communist dilemmas are examined in Michal Cichy's illuminating article "Requiem for the Moderate Revolutionist," *East European Politics and Societies*, vol. 10, no. 1 (Winter 1996), pp. 133–56.

4. Václav Havel, "The Post-Communist Nightmare," *New York Review of Books*, 27 May 1993, p. 8.

5. Katherine Verdery coined the term "entrepratchiks" to describe this new social group made up of former communist bureaucrats (apparatchiks) turned entrepreneurs (the new propertied class) in the post-socialist societies (especially in the Baltic states, the Czech Republic, Poland and Hungary). See Katherine Verdery, *What Was Socialism and What Comes Next?* (Princeton: Princeton University Press, 1996), p. 91.

6. In Popper's view, marked by a healthy skepticism regarding any historical messianism, "we have as individuals a moral responsibility to shape the future and not regard ourselves as mere flotsam or jetsam in some irresistible current of history." See "'The Best World We Have Yet Had': A Conversation with Sir Karl Popper," in G. R. Urban, *End of Empire: The Demise of the Soviet Union* (Washington, DC: American University Press, 1993), p. 208.

7. For the relation between protest, populist, and extremist parties, see Sabrina Ramet, "Defining the Radical Right: Values and Behaviors of Organized Intolerance in Post-Communist Central and Eastern Europe" (manuscript); and Rudolf M. Rizman, "The Radical Right Politics in Slovenia" (manuscript).

8. Thomas Ort, "The Far Right in the Czech Republic," *Uncaptive Minds*, vol. 6, no. 1 (22)(Winter-Spring 1993), pp. 67–72. Rightist nationalist groups are stronger in Slovakia than in the Czech Republic. I insist on the Czech case precisely because the extremist trends in that country have received less media and scholarly attention.

9. The România Mare party left the government in the fall of 1995, and Vadim Tudor further intensified his vituperations against the political establishment, including vicious attacks against the president and the chief of the secret police (the Romanian Service of Information). To quote one of these attacks, presented as an open letter to Iliescu: "As we already established back in 1992: It was the Jews who helped you seize power, therefore you now stick to the Jews, you have no idea about the sufferings of Jesus Christ or the tragedy of the Romanian nation!" See "PRM Newspaper Accuses, Threatens Iliescu," *FBIS-EEU*, 16 October 1995, p. 63 (English translation of article published in *România Mare*, 6 October 1995, pp. 1–2).

10. Verdery, *What Was Socialism?* p. 99.

11. See the editorial "Slovakia Slips Backward," *New York Times*, 14 August 1995.

12. For an outstanding interpretation of the revolutions of 1989 as nonideological, anti-utopian, indeed "post-modern" experiments, see S. N. Eisenstadt, "The Breakdown of Communist Regimes and the Vicissitudes of Modernity," *Daedalus* (special issue on "The Exit from Communism"), vol. 121, no. 2 (Spring 1992), pp. 21–41.

13. Fritz Stern, *The Politics of Cultural Despair* (New York: Anchor Books, 1965).

14. For Karadžić's career, see Roger Cohen, "Karadžić's Bosnian War: Myth Becomes Madness," *New York Times*, 4 June 1995.

15. Many of my points on the Yugoslav catastrophe owe a great deal to my discussions with historian Nicholas J. Miller (Boise State University). For an excellent survey of the Western literature dealing with Yugoslavia's violent disintegration, see Gale

Stokes, John Lampe, and Dennison Rusinow, with Julie Mostov, "Instant History: Understanding the Wars of Yugoslav Secession," *Slavic Review*, vol. 555, no. 1 (Spring 1996), pp. 137–60.

16. See Georges Mink's distinctions between "consensualist, tribune-dominated, and confrontational" political parties (*partis consensuelists, tribunitiens et querelleurs*) in Georges Mink, "Les partis politiques de l'Europe centrale post-communiste: État des lieux et essai de typologie," *L'Europe centrale et orientale en 1992* (Paris: Documentation française, 1993), pp. 21–23.

17. After 1995, nationalist themes have become increasingly salient in the discourse of the Bulgarian Socialist party, thus continuing Todor Zhivkov's xenophobic, anti-Turkish minority policies of the 1980s. For the 1994 parliamentary elections, the Socialists signed a pre-election cooperation agreement with the Patriotic Union, a coaltion of six militant nationalist parties. During the campaign, these groups scapegoated the large Turkish and Roma minorities for the country's economic and social troubles. See Janusz Bugajski, "The Many Faces of Nationalism," *Uncaptive Minds*, vol. 8, no. 3–4 (Fall-Winter 1995–1996), pp. 24–25.

18. As Torgyan asked of an American reporter: "The Hungarians were protecting the West for centuries against the barbarians, and what did we get for that?" He continued: "When the Hungarians went against the Communists in 1956, the Americans just said our children should go against the tanks with empty hands." Jane Perlez, "Hungarians Rally to Cry of Old Party," *New York Times*, 29 July 1995.

19. "Hungary: FKGB (Independent Smallholders Party) Leader Addresses Budapest Rally," *FBIS-EEU*, 15 March 1996, p. 10.

20. Wolf Lepenies, "The Future of the Intellectuals," *Partisan Review*, no. 1 (Winter 1994), pp. 117–18. Lepenies spells out this defeat of the critical intelligentsia after the short-lived moment of euphoria generated by the revolutions of 1989: "The illusion that intellectuals can participate in European politics has faded" (p. 113). But this is still a topic to be debated.

21. Francis Fukuyama, *Trust: The Social Virtues and the Creation of Prosperity* (New York: Free Press, 1995).

22. De Michelis quoted in Nathan Gardels, "From Machiavelli to Zeffirelli," *Washington Post* (Outlook Section), 10 April 1994.

23. Jacques Rupnik, "L'invention démocratique en Europe du Centre-Est," in *Cet étrange post-communisme: Rupture et transitions en Europe centrale et orientale*, edited by Georges Mink and Jean-Charles Szurek (Paris: Presses du CNRS/La Découverte, 1992), p. 65.

24. This "synchronization" was the thrust of interwar Romanian liberal theorist Eugen Lovinescu's approach to the country's modernization.

25. For the persistence of the fascist syndrome, see Umberto Eco, "Ur-Fascism," *New York Review of Books*, 22 June 1995, pp. 12–15.

26. Fritz Stern has emphasized the psychological appeals of nationalism and socialism as combined in the Nazi ideology. See *Dreams and Delusions: The Drama of German History* (New York: Knopf, 1987), p. 157. For an interpretation of post-Leninist Russia in the light of the Weimar experience, see Alexander Yanov, *Weimar Russia and What Can We Do about It* (New York: Slovo Publishing House, 1995).

27. Viktor Kulerski, "The Post-Totalitarian Syndrome," *Uncaptive Minds*, vol. 5, no. 2 (20)(Summer 1992), p. 111.

28. There are, of course, many other dangers, including external ones, that I have chosen to ignore.

29. Julia Kristeva, *Nations without Nationalism* (New York: Columbia University Press, 1993), pp. 68–69.

30. For the concept of uncertainty, see Valerie Bunce and Maria Csanadi, "Uncertainty in the Transition: Post-Communism in Hungary," *East European Politics and Societies*, vol. 7, no. 2 (Spring 1993), pp. 240–75. Of all the authors who acclaimed the breakdown of communism in Eastern Europe, Ralf Dahrendorf was the most prescient, signaling the many perils marking the road to an open society. See *Reflections on the Revolution in Europe* (New York: Random House, 1991).

31. For the myth of the "New Man," see André Reszler, *Mythes politiques modernes* (Paris: Presses Universitaires de France, 1981), pp. 141–70.

32. See for instance Michael R. Gordon, "President of Belarus Pushes Referendum to Expand Power," *New York Times*, 25 November 1996.

33. Karol Modzelewski, *Quelle voie après le communisme?* (Paris: Éditions de l'Aube, 1995), p. 169. A brilliant historian and civic activist, Modzelewski served nine years altogether in communist jails. After 1989, he was among the vocal critics of Solidarity's unqualified support for the neoliberal "shock therapy" strategy associated with the name of the vicepremier in the Mazowiecki government, Leszek Balcerowicz. Together with other former Solidarity luminaries, including Zbigniew Bujak, he formed the Union of Labor, a left-wing political party championing an economic reform less insensitive to the grievances of Poland's industrial working class. In 1995, Modzelewski resigned his position as honorary chairman of the Union of Labor to become president of the committee in support of Jacek Kuron's presidential candidacy. The two men, Kuron and Modzelewski, represent legendary figures of Poland's (and Eastern Europe's) anti-authoritarian struggle. In 1964, they co-authored the "Open Letter to the United Workers' Polish Party," in which they subjected the bureaucratic socialist system to an uncompromising critique.

34. For interesting glimpses into Milošević's personal life, including the possible tensions between him and his wife, Belgrade University sociologist Mirjiana Marković, see Stephen Kinzer, "Serb First Lady Plays Powerful Role," *New York Times*, 10 August 1995.

35. This is not the case in Albania, where President Sali Berisha's Democratic party used police force to intimidate his rivals, blatantly rigged electoral votes, and achieved a dubious parliamentary majority in the May 1996 elections.

36. This strong conclusion does not apply to the Baltic states, the Czech Republic, Poland, and Hungary, where public opinion polls indicate deep civic commitment to pluralist values and a free market. On the other hand, the fact that in the June 1996 Russian presidential elections Communist party candidate Gennady Zyuganov received 40.31 percent, or 30.1 million votes, is indicative of a deep popular discontent with the post-Leninist order (often perceived as anarchy or disorder). For my comparative assessment of the post-communist countries, I gained a lot of information from the papers prepared for the workshop on democratization organized in 1995–1996 as a joint project by the University of Maryland and Johns Hopkins University-School of Advanced International Studies, directed by Karen Dawisha and Bruce Parrott.

37. Jean Rouvier, *Les grandes idées politiques de Jean-Jacques Rousseau à nos jours* (Paris: Plon, 1978), p. 159, quoted by André Reszler, p. 193.

38. Agnes Heller and Ferenc Fehér, *The Post-Modern Political Condition* (Cambridge: Polity Press, 1988); also by them, *The Grandeur and Twilight of Radical Universalism* (New Brunswick: Transaction Books, 1991). For the exploration of modernity and the exhaustion of ideological politics, see Leszek Kolakowski, *Modernity on Endless Trial* (Chicago: University of Chicago Press, 1990). These philosophers have long since noticed the dissolution of the "redemptive paradigms" and the rise of the alternative discourses, although they did not anticipate the ongoing rise of the narratives of hatred and revenge.

39. For instance, the Croat president Franjo Tudjman can easily dispense with his own party (at the moment critical voices are heard), use his influence on parliament (without having his own party) to approve any of his choices, and still appear as a "supporter of democracy." The same can be said of Romania's Ion Iliescu or Ukraine's Leonid Kuchma. For Latin American disillusionment with leftist radicalism, see Jorge Castañeda, *Utopia Unarmed: The Latin American Left after the Cold War* (New York: Knopf, 1993).

40. Daniel Chirot, *Modern Tyrants: The Power and Prevalence of Evil in Our Age* (New York: Free Press, 1994), p. 251.

41. See the chapter "Protoliberalism: Autonomy of the Individual and Civil Society," in Jerzy Szacki, *Liberalism after Communism* (Budapest and London: Central European University Press, 1995), pp. 73–117.

42. Adam Michnik, "An Embarrassing Anniversary," *New York Review of Books*, 10 June 1993, pp. 19–21.

43. See Bruce Ackerman, *The Future of the Liberal Revolution* (New Haven: Yale University Press, 1992).

44. About tribalism as the barbaric component lying at the core of modernity, see Hannah Arendt's masterpiece, *The Origins of Totalitarianism*, and the critique of Enlightenment by Frankfurt School theorists. Also see Stephen Eric Bronner and Douglas MacKay Kellner, *Critical Theory and Society: A Reader* (New York: Routledge, 1989). This critique was not a rejection de plano of modernity, but an invitation to an epistemology of doubt, opposed to the Voltairian exaltation of reason. See Wolf Lepenies, "The Future of Intellectuals," *Partisan Review*, no. 1 (Winter 1994), pp. 111–19. I insist on this because there is a growing trend to set up a barrier of sorts between the dark, unpredictable, Southeastern Europe, almost inherently irrational, tribal, and violent, and Central Europe, presumably more able to articulate and internalize the discourse of reason. See Adam Seligman, *The Idea of Civil Society* (New York: Free Press, 1992); Stjepan Mestrovic, M. Goreta, and S. Letica, *Habits of the Balkan Heart* (College Station: Texas A&M University Press, 1993).

45. Ken Jowitt, "The New World Disorder," *Journal of Democracy*, vol. 2, no. 1 (Winter 1991), pp. 16–17, and his *New World Disorder: The Leninist Extinction* (Berkeley and Los Angeles: University of California Press, 1992).

46. See John Rawls's discussion of criteria for assessing civic freedom and the idea of a well-ordered society in *Political Liberalism* (New York: Columbia University Press, 1993), pp. 30–40.

47. Llazar Semini, "Albania Warns Serbia on Kosovo," *Washington Post*, 16 August 1995.

48. For this use of Freud's terminology, see Michael Ignatieff, "The Balkan Tragedy," *New York Review of Books*, 13 May 1993, pp. 3–5. Again, these new (or not so new)

fantasies are part of a more widespread need to redefine identity and authority in a post-Leninist and post-utopian world. Were not the 1994 elections in Italy, or the massive vote for Jorg Haider's rightist Freedom party in Austria in 1996, just as disturbing as the fascist revival in the East? Until recently, one could make a strong argument that the absence of legitimizing signals from the West has diminished the chances for the Eastern neofundamentalists to enjoy a second life. But this seems to have been utterly revised by the events in Italy. See Olivier Mongin, *Face au scepticisme: Les mutations du paysage intellectuel ou l'invention de l'intellectuel démocratique* (Paris: Éditions La Découverte, 1994); and Anthony Lewis, "The Italy We Want?" *New York Times*, 26 June 1995.

49. Martin Palous, "Post-Totalitarian Politics and European Philosophy," *Public Affairs Quarterly*, vol. 7, no. 2 (April 1993), pp. 162–63.

50. Adam Michnik's remarks at the Conference "Eastern Europe: Today's Realities, Tomorrow's Prospects," University of Central Florida, January 1993. Many of Michnik's statements quoted in this book are based on intensive conversations I have had with him during the last five years in the U.S., Poland, Hungary, and Romania.

51. For the interpretation of mature Stalinism as Bolshevism of the extreme right, see Robert C. Tucker, *Stalin in Power: The Revolution from Above, 1928–1941* (New York: Norton, 1990), pp. 590–92.

52. Stoica was released from prison in July 1996, following Funar's victory in the Cluj mayoral elections. It was not the citizens of Cluj who lost when the scam was closed, but the gullible pilgrims from the most remote areas of the country, who had played during the last months of the game. Funar's electoral performance can be related both to the advantages many of the voters drew from Caritas as well as to the brazen anti-Hungarian rhetoric Funar used on an everyday basis. On various occasions he referred to Hungarians (who make up 23 percent of the city's population) as "barbaric descendants of the Huns who for one thousand years failed become civilized." Personal interviews in Cluj, May 1996. For the significance of the 1996 local elections in Cluj, see Laszlo Fey, "Nedumerire si explicatii" (Bewilderment and Explanations), 22 (Bucharest), no. 27, (3–9 July 1996), p. 6.

53. William McPherson, "Transylvania's S&L: The Pyramid Scheme That Is Eating Romania," *Washington Post*, 21 November 1993; Michael Shafir, "The Caritas Affair: A Transylvanian Eldorado," *RFE/RL Research Report*, vol. 2, no. 38 (24 September 1993), pp. 23–27; for a scholarly analysis of Caritas and the internecine struggle within Romania's old and new elites, see Verdery, "Faith, Hope, and Caritas in the Land of Pyramids," in *What Was Socialism*, pp. 168–203.

54. For information on the ongoing discussion on the legacy of the Polish People's Republic, I am grateful to my graduate student Beata Czajkowska, whose dissertation deals with the shifting role of the post-communist and post-romantic Polish intelligentsia. One can simply add that the discussion on the communist legacies is not uniquely Polish: it has been going on in all the post-communist societies, entailing similar outputs of symbols, emotions, and myths. Think of Yeltsin's use of the official TV station during the presidential elections in June 1996, when the audience was literally overwhelmed with documentary footage about the horrors of Stalinism. The point was not to revisit the past but to discredit the neo-Bolshevik candidate Zyuganov.

55. See Albert Hirshman's splendid analysis of the "perversity argument" in his *The*

Rhetoric of Reaction: Perversity, Futility, Jeopardy (Cambridge: Harvard University Press, 1991).

56. This is a point clearly made by Serb political philosopher Svetozar Stojanović, who describes Milošević as a "radical opportunist." Lecture by Stojanović, Institute for Philosophy and Public Policy, University of Maryland, December 2, 1996. See Svetozar Stojanović, "The Destruction of Yugoslavia," *Fordham International Law Journal*, vol. 19, no. 2 (December 1995), pp. 337–62.

57. Castañeda, *Utopia Unarmed*, p. 247.

58. For the former communists, see Andrew Nagorski's perceptive book, *The Birth of Freedom: Shaping Lives and Societies in the New Eastern Europe* (New York: Simon and Schuster, 1993), especially chapter 2, "The Communist Afterlife," pp. 55–91.

59. Populism is also convenient because it is neither left, nor right. As Argentine dictator Juan Domingo Perón once said: "I have two hands, a left and a right. I use each one whenever convenient." I heard this line frequently quoted by Latin American intellectuals during my stay in Venezuela between May and September 1982. For a myth-breaking analysis of Peronismo and other similar revolutionary-populist movements, see Carlos Rangel, *The Latin Americans: Their Love-Hate Relationship with the United States* (New York: Harcourt Brace Jovanovich, 1977) and *Third World Ideology and Western Reality* (New Brunswick, NJ: Transaction, 1986). For the threats to emerging democracies, including Perón-style populism, see Adam Michnik, "Market, Religion and Nationalism: Fundamentalisms in the New European Order," *International Journal of Politics, Culture, and Society*, vol. 8, no. 4 (1995), pp. 525–42.

60. Victor Eskenasy, "The Holocaust and Romanian Historiography: Communist and Neo-Communist Revisionism," in Randolph L. Braham, ed., *The Tragedy of Romanian Jewry* (New York: Columbia University Press, 1994), pp. 173–236; Mark Temple, "The Politicization of History: Marshal Antonescu and Romania," *East European Politics and Societies*, vol. 1, no. 3 (Fall 1996), pp. 457–503; Michael Shafir, "Marshal Ion Antonescu and Romanian Politics," *RFE/RL Research Report*, vol. 1, no. 29 (July 1992), pp. 22–28; Daniel Chirot, "Despre mareșalul Antonescu și viitorul României" (About Marshal Antonescu and the Future of Romania), *Meridian*, November-December 1991, pp. 15–16.

61. Successfully banking on mass disaffection with the government's ineptitude, Lukashenko declared: "The current privatization scheme will be stopped within days after I become President. We will just take everything back and get everybody working again." See Michael Specter, "Discontent of Belarus Voters Fueled Landslide for Outsider," *New York Times*, 7 December 1994.

62. For an analysis of the political mind of Russia's nationalist activists, see "The Rise of the New Right," *The Economist*, 28 January 1995, pp. 21–23. As in the case of Serbia and Romania, one notices the presence among these ethnic fundamentalists of former apparatchiks and secret police officers (the nomenklatura, or apparat nationalists). This phenomenon is linked to the use of nationalism by some late Leninist regimes to justify the need for cohesion and the rejection of political and economic reforms.

63. Maybe a postponement of historical discussions would be less deleterious for these societies than a continuation of these ruinous exercises in self-pity, anger and blatant rejection of factual verities. This point was made by Irena Grudzinska Gross at the international conference on "The Open Society and Its Rivals," organized by the Soros Foundation in Timișoara, Romania, 29–31 May 1996.

64. As Slavoj Žižek put it, "the dark side of the process current in Eastern Europe is
. . . the gradual retreat of the liberal-democratic tendency in the face of the growth of
corporate populism with all of its elements." See "Eastern Europe's Republics of Gilead,"
in *Dimensions of Radical Democracy: Pluralism, Citizenship, Community*, edited by Chantal
Mouffe (London: Verso, 1992), p. 199.

65. For the global impact in terms of norms definition, see James N. Rosenau, *Turbulence in World Politics: A Theory of Change and Continuity* (Princeton: Princeton University Press, 1990).

66. See Andrew Arato, "Revolution, Restoration and Legitimization: Ideological
Problems of the Transition from State Socialism," in *Envisioning Eastern Europe: Postcommunist Cultural Studies*, edited by Michael D. Kennedy (Ann Arbor: University of Michi-
gan Press, 1994), pp. 180–246.

67. These themes appear clearly in the discourse of the ethnocratic radicalism as
evinced by former student leader Marian Munteanu's "Movement for Romania," and
among supporters of Serbia's Slobodan Milošević or the xenophobic groups and movements generically described as the "Russian party."

68. The November 1996 elections in Romania, when the democratic forces managed to win both the parliamentary and presidential elections, suggest that this distinction should not be exaggerated. My point is that transitions in the northern tier have
moved much faster and with better results than in the south.

69. See "Poles Hold March over New Budget," *New York Times*, 10 February 1994.
This was one of the many voices protesting the austerity budget in February 1994 in
what turned out to be the largest anti-government demonstration since the collapse of
communism (about 30,000).

70. Peter Reddaway, "Russia on the Brink," *The New York Review of Books*, 28 January
1993, pp. 30–35. Reddaway notices a multilayered feeling of moral and spiritual injury
related to loss of empire and damaged identity: "Emotional wounds as deep as these tend
to breed anger, hatred, self-disgust and aggressiveness. Such emotions can only improve
the political prospects for the nationalists and neo-communists, at any rate for a time."
Needless to add, in the meantime, Reddaway has become even more pessimistic.

71. For the immense power of the new mafiosi that have become a challenge second
to none to the establishment of the rule of law in Russia, see K. S. Karol, "Moscou sous
la loi des gangs," *Le Nouvel observateur* (Paris), 17–23 March 1994, pp. 36–37; Claire
Sterling, "Redfellas: Inside the New Russian Mafia," in *New Republic*, vol. 210, no. 15
(11 April 1994), pp. 19–22; Steven Erlanger, "A Slaying Puts Russian Underworld on
Parade," *New York Times*, 14 April 1994, p. A3.

72. See for instance Pavel Coruţ, *Fiul Geto-Daciei* (Bucharest: Editura Gemenii,
1995).

73. Daniel Chirot, "Modernism without Liberalism: The Ideological Roots of Modern Tyranny," *Contentions*, vol. 5, no. 1 (Fall 1995), pp. 155–56.

74. Giovanni Sartori, "How Far Can Free Government Travel?" *Journal of Democracy*,
vol. 6, no. 6 (July 1995), p. 106; for a comparative analysis of post-communist elites
and their role in democratic development in East-Central Europe and Russia, see John
Higley, Judith Kullberg, and Jan Pakulski, "The Persistence of Postcommunist Elites,"
Journal of Democracy, vol. 7, no. 2 (April 1996), pp. 133–47.

75. Corruption is seen as a pandemic disease in East-Central Europe, which makes
these societies more like Latin America or Southern Europe than like any Anglo-Saxon

model of pluralism. Russian democrats, for instance, often complain about the "Colombianization" of their country, by which they understand a corrupt political structure and a weak judicial system unable to hold in check an all-powerful underworld.

76. This is the thesis maintained by Lev Timofeyev in his book *Russia's Secret Rulers* (New York: Knopf, 1993).

77. It took the presidential elections of June 1996 and the pressures exerted by different allies for Yeltsin to dismiss Korzhakov from his position of principal presidential advisor.

78. "From the Party of War to the Party of Power," *Economist*, 8 July 1995.

79. The Baltic states have moved in the direction of liberal constitutionalism, although there are serious problems regarding the definition of citizenship and the granting of equal rights to the Russian minorities on their territories. Most of the former Soviet republics have evolved in the direction of authoritarian populism, using democratic language to cover illiberal practices and attitudes. For a provocative examination of the post-communist dilemmas and the relationship between legality and legitimacy, see Jacques Rupnik, "The Post-Totalitarian Blues," *Journal of Democracy*, vol. 6, no. 2 (April 1995), pp. 61–73.

80. See Vesna Pusić, "Dictatorship with Democratic Legitimacy: Democracy versus Nation," *East European Politics and Societies*, vol. 8, no. 3 (Fall 1994), p. 393.

81. See James L. Gibson, "The Resilience of Mass Support for Democratic Institutions and Processes in the Nascent Russian and Ukrainian Democracies," in *Political Culture and Civil Society in Russia and the New States of Eurasia*, edited by Vladimir Tismaneanu (Armonk, NY: M.E. Sharpe, 1995), pp. 53–111.

82. Adam Michnik, "The Church and the Martyr's Stake in Poland," *New Perspectives Quarterly*, vol. 10, no. 3 (Summer 1993), p. 32.

83. Judith Shklar, "The Liberalism of Fear," in *Liberalism and the Moral Life*, edited by Nancy L. Rosenblum (Cambridge: Harvard University Press, 1989), pp. 23–38. For the need to redefine the liberal agenda after the Cold War, see Ira Katznelson, *Liberalism's Crooked Circle: Letters to Adam Michnik* (Princeton: Princeton University Press, 1996).

84. Jacques Rupnik insists that as long as ethnic and political borders do not correspond, and modernity is still belated as an institutionalized form of international cooperation between democratic actors, there is always potential for new conflicts, including violent ones. See his "Europe's New Frontiers: Remapping Europe," in *Daedalus*, vol. 123, no. 3 (Summer 1994), pp. 91–114 (special issue, "After Communism, What?").

85. For such a pessimistic approach, see Jan Urban, "Europe's Darkest Scenario," *Washington Post* (Outlook Section), 11 October 1992, pp. 1–2.

86. Gale Stokes, *When the Walls Came Tumbling Down: The Collapse of Communism in Eastern Europe* (New York: Oxford University Press, 1993), p. 218.

87. Zbigniew Brzezinski, *Out of Control: Global Turmoil at the End of the Twentieth Century* (New York: Charles Scribner and Son, 1993), p. 19.

88. See "The Rise of the New Right," *Economist*, 28 January 1995, pp. 21–23. More on these movements can be found in Walter Laqueur, *Black Hundred: The Rise of the Extreme Right in Russia* (New York: HarperCollins, 1993).

89. Quoted in "The Rise of the New Right." For Vasiliev's early views, see John B. Dunlop, "A Conversation with Dmitri Vasiliev: the Leader of Pamiat," *Report on USSR*, 15 December 1989, pp. 12–16. For authoritative analyses of Russian nationalist ideolo-

gies and movements, see Yitzhak Brudny, "Russian Nationalist Intellectuals and the Soviet State" Ph.D. dissertation, Princeton University, 1992, and John Dunlop, *The Rise of Russia and the Fall of the Soviet Empire* (Princeton: Princeton University Press, 1993). Alexander Yanov was prescient in highlighting the rise of radical right movements in Russia. See his *The Russian New Right* (Berkeley: Institute of International Studies, 1978).

90. See Samuel Huntington's, somewhat ramshackle hypotheses in "The Clash of Civilizations?" *Foreign Affairs*, vol. 72, no. 3 (Summer 1993), pp. 22–49.

91. A point raised by Ilya Prizel.

92. These trends are, after all, linked to many variables other than the purely political ones, as suggested by the high suicide rates in Sweden, Finland, and Hungary (and in Hungary this was true even before the fall of Kadarism). Surprisingly, Eberstadt tends to take the North Korean and Cuban statistical reports much too seriously when he compares information from these countries to the one provided by post-communist governments. I also wonder to what extent one can deduce qualitative conclusions form demographic indicators that are taken out of context of cultural, "identitarian" shifts. See Nicholas Eberstadt, "Marx and Mortality: A Mystery," *New York Times*, 6 April 1994. I do not see any reason to be astonished that a nondictatorial world allows for more risk than the police states, with their strict mechanisms of "discipline and punish." See Gail Kligman, "The Politics of Reproduction in Ceauşescu's Romania," *East European Politics and Societies*, vol. 6, no. 3 (Fall 1992), pp. 364–418.

93. Giuseppe DiPalma, "Legitimation from the Top to Civil Society: Politico-Cultural Change in Eastern Europe," *World Politics*, vol. 44, no. 1 (October 1991), pp. 49–80; my concept of "legitimation from the past" echoes Eric Hobsbawm's insightful analysis of the new discourses of hatred and self-aggrandizement in "The New Threat to History," *New York Review of Books*, 16 December 1993, pp. 62–64.

94. George Steiner, *Language and Silence: Essays on Language, Literature and the Inhuman* (New York: Atheneum, 1982), p. 152.

95. For an excellent discussion on nationalism, see Tzvetan Todorov, *On Human Diversity: Nationalism, Racism and Exoticism in French Thought* (Cambridge: Harvard University Press, 1993).

Three
Vindictive and Messianic Mythologies

1. In other words, how can one tame that violent propensity that a Georgian philosopher aptly called "the illiberal flesh of ethnicity"? See Ghia Nodia, "Rethinking Nationalism and Democracy in the Light of the Post-Communist Experience," in N. V. Chavchavadze, Ghia Nodia, and Paul Peachey, *National Identity as an Issue of Knowledge and Morality: Georgian Philosophical Studies* (Washington, DC: Paideia Press and Council for Research in Values and Philosophy, 1994), p. 54.

2. Andrzej Walicki, "The Three Traditions in Polish Patriotism," in *Polish Paradoxes*, edited by Stanislaw Gomulka and Antony Polonsky (London and New York: Routledge, 1990), pp. 30–31.

3. Fyodor Dostoevsky, *The Possessed*, quoted by Czeslaw Milosz in his essay "On Nationalism." See Czeslaw Milosz, *Beginning with My Streets* (New York: Farrar Straus Giroux, 1991), p. 85. Milosz's essay is one of the most perceptive interpretations of the recrudescence of nationalism at the end of the twentieth century.

4. Stephen Holmes, "Liberalism for a World of Ethnic Passions and Decaying States," *Social Research*, vol. 61, no. 3 (Fall 1994), p.601.

5. For the role of illiberal nationalism in constructing a sense of national cohesion and mobilization against presumed enemies (internal and external), see Tom Gallagher, *Romania after Ceauşescu: The Politics of Intolerance* (Edinburgh: Edinburgh University Press, 1995).

6. As Janusz Bugajski writes: "A nationalist-civic spectrum has intersected with the traditional left-right continuum, often making the ideological identity of specific parties confusing. Both the non-ethnic civic orientation and the collectivist ethnic-based option have been adopted by parties espousing either right-wing, centrist, or left-wing programs." Janusz Bugajski, "The Many Faces of Nationalism," *Uncaptive Minds*, vol. 8, no. 3–4 (Fall-Winter 1995–1996), p. 9.

7. See Romanian exiled writer Norman Manea's contribution in "Intellectuals and Social Change in Central and Eastern Europe," *Partisan Review* (Special Issue), no. 4 (Fall 1992), pp. 573–74.

8. Writer Judita Vaiciunaite, quoted in Anatol Lieven, *The Baltic Revolution: Estonia, Latvia, Lithuania and the Path to Independence* (New Haven: Yale University Press, 1993), p. 121.

9. For the politics of intolerance in Tudjman's Croatia, see Goran Vezić, "A Croatian Reichstag Trial: The Case of Dalmatian Action," *Uncaptive Minds*, vol. 7, no. 3 (Fall-Winter 1994), pp. 17–24.

10. Robert M. Hayden, "Constitutional Nationalism in the Former Yugoslav Republics," *Slavic Review*, vol. 51 (1992), pp. 654–73.

11. Andrei Cornea, "Mentalitatea locatarului principal," *22* (Bucharest), 2–8 August 1995, p. 4.

12. See S. Frederick Starr, ed., *The Legacy of History in Russia and the New States of Eurasia* (Armonk, NY: M.E. Sharpe, 1994); Roman Szporluk, ed., *National Identity and Ethnicity in Russia and the New States of Eurasia* (Armonk, NY: M.E. Sharpe, 1994).

13. For the essential distinction between the legitimate attachment to national cultural heritage and language and the desire to make one's nation more civilized, on the one hand, and the "rapacious and potentially totalitarian nationalism" which implies an "idolatrous belief in the absolute supremacy of national values when they clash with the rights of persons who make up this very nation," see Leszek Kolakowski, "Uncertainties of a Democratic Age," *Journal of Democracy*, vol. 1, no. 1 (Winter 1990), p. 49.

14. Israeli political philosopher Shlomo Avineri correctly remarked that this cosmopolitan slogan did in fact reflect the real cognitive situation of a certain class of people: "not the proletarians, but the multitude of modern educated, deracinated Jewish intellectuals, without whom a revolutionary movement would have been unthinkable in Central and Eastern Europe." For these secularized Jews, Zionism and Bolshevism became the two magnets in their attempt to solve the problem of identity and radical emancipation. See Shlomo Avineri, "Reflections on Eastern Europe," *Partisan Review*, no. 3 (Summer 1991), p. 447.

15. See for instance Walter C. Clemens, *Baltic Independence and the Russian Empire* (New York: St. Martin's Press, 1991).

16. For an illuminating analysis of "charismatic saviors," see André Reszler, *Mythes politiques modernes* (Paris: Presses Universitaires de France, 1981), pp. 188–205; Gerard Challiand, *Mythes révolutionnaires du tiers monde: Guerrillas et socialismes* (Paris: Éditions du Seuil, 1979).

17. For Tudjman's background, see Raymond Bonner, "A Would-Be Tito Helps to Dismantle His Legacy," *New York Times*, 20 August 1995. One should, however, emphasize that Croat state nationalism under Tudjman has not become a totally exclusionary ideology similar to the ethnic cleansing advocated by partisans of Great Serbia. The purges of the Serbs from significant state and media positions in the first years of independent Croatia were related to their previous prominent status. Much of the Serbian wave of refugees in the summer of 1995 was the result of panic and mass anguish feverishly entertained by Serbian nationalist politicians and intellectuals. One should insist on these points especially in relationship to current attempts to present all participants in the Yugoslav conflict as equally guilty and equally vicious. See the interview with Mirko Grmek, "L'ex-Yougoslavie: la guerre comme maladie sociale," *Le Messager Européen*, no. 9 (Paris: Gallimard, 1996), pp. 95–108.

18. See John Dunn, *Western Political Theory in the Face of the Future* (Cambridge: Cambridge University Press, 1993), p. 57, on the ambivalent role of nationalism in the twentieth century.

19. See Daniel Chirot, "Modernism without Liberalism: The Ideological Roots of Modern Tyranny," *Contentions*, vol. 5, no. 1 (Fall 1995), pp. 156–57.

20. Zbigniew Brzezinski, "Post-Communist Nationalism," *Foreign Affairs*, vol. 68, no. 5 (Winter 1989/1990), pp. 1–2.

21. Quoted in Stanislaw Gomulka and Antony Polonsky, "Introduction," to *Polish Paradoxes*, p. 7. Similar points could easily be made about the manufacturing of national mythologies in Serbia or Ukraine, Russia or Romania.

22. Yael Tamir, *Liberal Nationalism* (Princeton: Princeton University Press, 1993), p. 6. This view presupposes the existence of a liberal tradition, as well as the functioning of liberal institutions that would be the necessary counterpart to the nationalist vision and aspirations. The trouble is that in most of East and Central Europe, liberalism is still infant and under strong attack. Democratic individualism is widely regarded as a Western product, whereas the cult of ancestry and the focus on organic links appeal to intellectuals of different persuasions, from socialists to Christian Democrats. Furthermore, liberalism means protection from governmental intrusion, whereas these societies are still based on the widespread belief in the economic and social omnipotence of the state. For the difficulties of liberalism in post-communist East-Central Europe, see George Schöpflin, "Obstacles to Liberalism in Post-Communist Polities," *East European Politics and Societies*, vol. 5, no. 1 (Winter 1991), pp. 189–94.

23. Ernest Gellner, *Thought and Change* (London: Weidenfeld and Nicholson, 1971), p. 169

24. Benedict Anderson, *Imagined Communities* (London: Verso, 1991), pp. 6–7.

25. Isaiah Berlin, *The Crooked Timber of Humanity: Chapters in the History of Ideas* (New York: Knopf, 1991), p. 245.

26. Liah Greenfeld, *Nationalism: Five Roads to Modernity* (Cambridge: Harvard University Press, 1992), p. 487. Emphasis in original.

27 Elie Kedourie, "Introduction to the fourth edition," in *Nationalism* (Oxford: Basil Blackwell, 1993), p. xvii.

28. Bogdan Denitch, "Really Existing Nationalism," *New Politics*, Summer 1993, p. 121.

29. Michel Wieworka, *La démocratie à l'épreuve: Nationalisme, populisme, ethnicité* (Paris: La Découverte, 1993), pp. 92–93.

30. This theme has been developed by Gail Kligman in her forthcoming book on the politics of reproduction in Ceauşescu's Romania.

31. See Katherine Verdery's rejoinder to E. J. Hobsbawm, "Ethnicity and Nationalism in Europe Today," *Anthropology Today*, vol. 8, no. 1 (February 1992), p. 10. For a sophisticated analysis of post-communist nationalism, see Katherine Verdery, "Nationalism and National Sentiment in Post-Socialist Romania," *Slavic Review*, vol. 52, no. 2 (Summer 1993), pp. 179–203. Verdery's argument challenges the "ancient hatred" theory about the resurgence of nationalism after the demise of communism. In her view, state socialism never suppressed national consciousness but rather enhanced it, and "the supposed exit to democratic politics and market economies aggravate it further" (p. 180).

32. Charles Simic, "The Spider's Web," *New Republic*, 25 October 1993, p. 19.

33. Joseph Rothschild, *Ethnopolitics: A Conceptual Framework* (New York: Columbia University Press, 1981), p. 14.

34. Yael Tamir, "The Enigma of Nationalism," *World Politics* vol. 47 (April 1995), p. 430. Ethnocentrism is a form of nationalism that turns the real distinction between the in-group and the others into a fact of destiny that places one's nation into a position superior to all others. Under post-communist circumstances, this ethnocentric version of nationalism tends to get the upper hand.

35. For the distinction between civic and ethnic nationalism, see Greenfeld, *Nationalism*, p. 11.

36. It is close to the "new nationalism" described by Polish political philosopher Marcin Krol. See the summary of Krol's presentation on "The New Polish Nationalism," in the newsletter published by the Woodrow Wilson Center, *East European Studies*, May-June 1992, pp. 4–5. Also a personal interview with Krol, Warsaw, September 1993.

37. Respected Russian cultural historian Dimitrii Likhachev accurately contrasts *patriotism* with *nationalism* as a conscious love for one's own nation and its national qualities and, by extension, acceptance of others, since it is inseperable from an attitude of tolerance. The nationalism of the French Revolution or of the 1848 movements was romantic, generous, and in many senses universalistic. *Reflections on Russia* (Boulder: Westview Press, 1991), p. 59.

38. Ernest Renan, "What Is a Nation?" in *The Nationalism Reader*, edited by Omar Dahbour and Micheline R. Ishay (Atlantic Highlands, NJ: Humanities Press, 1995), p. 154.

39. Hans Kohn, *The Idea of Nationalism*, second ed. (New York: Macmillan, 1961), p. 330. For Eastern Europe's nationalist traditions, see Peter Sugar and Ivo John Lederer, eds., *Nationalism in Eastern Europe* (Seattle: University of Washington Press, 1994).

40. For a most informative analysis of the Yugoslav crisis and the role of political elites in feeding ethnic conflict, see Laura Silber and Allen Little, *Yugoslavia: The Death of a Nation* (New York: TV Books/Penguin, 1996); for an outstanding scholarly exploration of the Yugoslav debacle, see Susan Woodward, *Balkan Tragedy: Chaos and Dissolution after the Cold War* (Washington, DC: Brookings Institution, 1995).

41. Quoted by Nebojsa Popov, "Serbian Populism and the Fall of Yugoslavia," *Uncaptive Minds*, vol. 8, no. 3–4 (Fall-Winter 1996–1996). Popov's analysis of Serbian populism is among the most lucid autopsies of the Milošević authoritarian-socialist

regime and its uses of revolutionary and chauvinistic rhetoric to forge a national, panic-ridden consensus.

42. Celestine Bohlen, "Cradle of Russian Revolution a Hotbed of Disgust," *New York Times*, 22 June 1993.

43. The "National Salvation Front" name was first used in Romania by the group that took over power in December 1989.

44. "Serbian Populism: Epilogue," an interview with Nebojsa Popov, *Uncaptive Minds*, vol. 8, no. 3–4 (Fall-Winter 1995–1996), pp. 114, 118.

45. On the history of the term "populism" as part of the Russian radical tradition, see Richard Pipes, "Narodnichestvo: A Semantic Inquiry," in his book *Russia Observed: Collected Essays on Russian and Soviet History* (Boulder: Westview Press, 1989), pp. 103–21.

46. Quoted in Popov, "Serbian Populism and the Fall of Yugoslavia," p. 89.

47. Ibid., p. 91. It should be noted that important figures of the Orthodox Church openly call for the establishment of a "theodemocracy." Slavophilism has resurfaced and slogans are circulated that call for the formation of a great Orthodox empire stretching "from the Adriatic Sea to Japan."

48. See Laura Silber, "Serbia Has No Václav Havel," *New York Times*, 12 December 1996.

49. Funar was reelected in June 1996 on a platform imbued with anti-Hungarian, ultra-nationalist slogans. The most striking example of Funar's uses of xenophobic propaganda is his order to open archeological excavations in front of the statue of King Mátyas (Matei) Corvin, in the very heart of Cluj. The ostensible argument for this urban devastation is the search for Roman relics. The direct continuity between the occupying Romans and the contemporary Romanians is a major point of Romanian historiography. In 1996, Funar staunchly opposed the signing of a friendship treaty between Romania and Hungary, and called for the expulsion of ethnic Hungarians to "their country."

50. For a thorough examination of the nationalist movements in post-communist societies, see Janusz Bugajski, *Nations in Turmoil: Conflict and Cooperation in Eastern Europe* (Boulder: Westview Press, 1993). See also Bugajski's useful taxonomy of the post-communist nationalist trends in his article "The Many Faces of Nationalism."

51. Furthermore, Ceontea described his perennial fears that Hungarians would want to rape and murder his wife and daughter. Ceontea's statement in *FBIS-EEU*, 5 February 1991, p. 42, as quoted by J. F. Brown, *Hopes and Shadows: Eastern Europe after Communism* (Durham: Duke University Press, 1994), p. 196.

52. Cosić quoted in Popov, "Serbian Populism and the Fall of Yugoslavia," pp. 88–89. For the abysmal consequences of the mythological vision of history and the longing for ethnically pure community, see Chantal de Rudder, "Le rêve en ruines de la Grande Serbie," *Le Nouvel Observateur*, 24–30 August 1995, pp. 30–31.

53. John Kifner, "Through the Serbian Mind's Eye," *New York Times*, 10 April 1994.

54. It is symptomatic that Bokan's glossy magazine, titled "Our Ideas," carried articles on Mussolini, Ezra Pound, and the Romanian Iron Guard.

55. Marian Munteanu's espousal of Guardist anti-liberal views and the danger that the Romanian student movement would repeat the ill-fated rightist adventures of the interwar period were noted by Istvan Deak in his article "Survivors," *New York Review of Books*, 5 March 1992, pp. 43–51.

56. See Michael Shafir, "The Movement for Romania: A Party of 'Radical Return,'" *RFE/RL Research*, vol. 1, no. 29 (17 July 1992).

57. Piotr Ogrodzinski and Henryk Szlajfer, "Is the Catholic Church a Threat to Democracy in Poland?" *East European Reporter*, vol. 5, no. 3 (May–June 1992), pp. 17–20.

58. G. M. Tamás, "The Legacy of Dissent: How Civil Society has Been Seduced by the Cult of Privacy," *Times Literary Supplement*, 14 May 1993, p. 14.

59. Slavenka Drakulić *The Balkan Express: Fragments from the Other Side of War* (New York: Norton, 1993), p. 3.

60. Henry Tudor, *Political Myth* (London: PallMall, 1972), p. 124.

61. For a refutation of the "reactionary" rejection of change, see Albert O. Hirschman, *The Rhetoric of Reaction: Perversity, Futility, Jeopardy* (Cambridge: Harvard University Press, 1991).

62. Mihai Botez, "A View from Bucharest," in *Debates on the Future of Communism*, edited by Vladimir Tismaneanu and Judith Shapiro (New York: St. Martin's Press, 1991), pp. 170–81.

63. This is not to say that Kravchuk adopted an exclusive version of nationalism. The point I want to make is the malleability of political beliefs in these transitional times. For a concise and informative examination of post-Soviet Ukraine, see Alexander Motyl, *Dilemmas of Independence: Ukraine after Totalitarianism* (New York: Council on Foreign Relations Press, 1993).

64. For a penetrating interpretation of the Csurka phenomenon, see Zoltan Barany, "Mass-Elite Relations and the Resurgence of Nationalism in Eastern Europe," paper presented at the convention of the American Association for the Advancement of Slavic Studies, Phoenix, 19–22 October 1992.

65. Radio Free Europe/Radio Liberty *Daily Report*, no. 125, 5 July 1993.

66. For the contemporary meaning of the traditional conflict between populists and Westernizers in Hungary, see Gabor Vermes, "Hungary's Unprecedented Opportunity: A Historical Interpretation," *Comparative Social Research*, vol. 14 (1994), pp. 19–47. Hungarian economist János Mátyás Kovács proposed a sobering reassessment of the conventional ideological dichotomies in East-Central Europe in his paper "The Uncertain Ghosts: 'Populists' and 'Westernizers' in Post-Communist Eastern Europe," presented at the conference "Europe: The One and the Many," University of Notre Dame, 20–22 April 1996.

67. Carnogursky quoted in Arista Maria Cirtautas, "Nationalism in East European Latecomers to Democracy," in *Can Europe Work? Germany and the Reconstruction of Postcommunist Societies*, edited by Stephen E. Hanson and Willfried Spohn (Seattle: University of Washington Press, 1995), pp. 41–42.

68. Arthur Koestler, "The Urge to Self-Destruction," in *The Heel of Achilles: Essays 1968–1973* (New York: Random House, 1974), p. 14.

69. For the intellectual foundations of extreme Russian nationalism, see the chapters on Igor Shafarevich and Lev Gumilev in Alexander Yanov, *Weimar Russia* (New York: Slovo/Word Publishing House, 1995), pp. 230–67.

70. For Belov's and other similar anti-liberal views, see Lee Hockstader, "New Russian Communists Put on Moderate Face," *Washington Post*, 20 May 1996.

71. For the Polish extreme right and the views expressed by Boleslaw Tejkowski, chairman of the "Polish National Community-Polish National Party," see John Micgiel, "Poland: A Case-Study," *Political Science Quarterly*, vol. 108, no. 3 (Fall 1993), p. 7.

72. For the threat of fascism in post-communist societies, see Ralf Dahrendorf, *Reflections on the Revolution in Europe* (New York: Random House, 1990), p. 115.

73. Isabel Fonseca, *Bury Me Standing: The Gypsies and Their Journey* (New York: Knopf, 1995).

74. Vladimir Tismaneanu, *Reinventing Politics: Eastern Europe from Stalin to Havel*, updated edition (New York: Free Press, 1993), especially the Afterword ("Nationalism, Populism, Fascism, and Other Threats to Pluralism in Eastern Europe").

75. Stephen Sestanovich, "The Hour of the Demagogue," *National Interest*, Fall 1991, p. 15.

Four
Scapegoating Fantasies

1. Walter L. Adamson, "Avant-Garde Political Rhetorics: Prewar Culture in Florence as a Source of Postwar Fascism," *History of European Ideas*, vol. 16, nos. 4–6 (1993), p. 754.

2. It is not my purpose in this chapter (or, for that matter, in this book) to present fascism as looming large in post-communist societies. After all, public opinion polls in these countries indicate mass approval for democratic values and institutions. What I want to highlight is the connection between the current social and cultural turbulent circumstances, on the one hand, and the configuration of constellations of resentful symbols and attitudes. At the same time, the impact of political myths cannot be underestimated, as the 1996 Russian presidential elections have so clearly shown: it was precisely the use of narratives of betrayal and victimization that allowed Zyuganov and his reconstructed Communist party get out their initial political ghetto and become a national force.

3. See Sigmund Neumann, *Permanent Revolution: Totalitarianism in the Age of International Civil War* (New York: Praeger, 1965), pp. 31–32. The preface to this second edition of Neumann's book was written by Hans Kohn, one of the most perceptive students of nationalism.

4. Fritz Stern, *Dreams and Delusions: The Drama of German History* (New York: Knopf, 1987), p. 149.

5. Warren Zimmermann, "Origins of a Catastrophe," *Foreign Affairs*, vol. 74, no. 2 (March-April 1995), p. 12.

6. Franjo Tudjman, *Nationalism in Contemporary Europe* (New York: Columbia University Press, 1981), p. 272.

7. Slavenka Drakulic, *The Balkan Express: Fragments from the Other Side of the War* (New York: Norton, 1993), p. 51.

8. Samuel Huntington, "The Clash of Civilizations?" *Foreign Affairs*, vol. 72, no. 3 (Summer 1993), p. 31. Can one seriously see the conflict between Milošević and Tudjman as an East-West clash?

9. For an excellent examination of the role of cultural elites in both the assumption and the denial of the past (fascist and communist) in Romania, see Dan Pavel, *Etica lui Adam, sau de ce rescriem istoria* (The Ethics of Adam, or Why We Rewrite History) (Bucharest: Editura Du Style, 1995).

10. René Girard, *The Scapegoat* (Baltimore: Johns Hopkins University Press, 1986), p. 39.

11. Ibid., pp. 40–41.

12. The origins of this exclusionary urge can be traced back to the times of the French Revolution. On 25 December 1793, Maximilien Robespierre, in his *Report on the Principles of Revolutionary Government*, attacked foreigners as the cause of all crises. In April 1794, the Committee on Public Safety drew up a law on foreigners, excluding them from public service and public rights. Using the Jacobin logic of "amalgamation," the law applied to former members of the nobility, as well. See Julia Kristeva, "The Strangers," *Partisan Review*, Winter 1991, pp. 88–100.

13. Zimmermann, "Origins of a Catastrophe," p. 20.

14. See Graham Frazer and George Lancelle, *Absolute Zhirinovsky: A Transparent View of the Distinguished Russian Statesman* (New York: Penguin Books, 1994), p. 139.

15. Georges Sorel, *Reflections on Violence* (London and New York: Collier Books, 1961), p. 50. For a thoughtful discussion of Sorel's political philosophy, see Zeev Sternhell with Mario Sznajder and Maia Asheri, *The Birth of Fascist Ideology: From Cultural Rebellion to Political Revolution* (Princeton: Princeton University Press, 1994).

16. Slavoj Žižek, *The Sublime Object of Ideology* (London: Verso, 1989), p. 127.

17. Johann Gottlob Fichte, *Addresses to the German Nation* (1808), excerpted in *Communism, Fascism, and Democracy*, edited by Carl Cohen (New York: Random House, 1972), p. 286.

18. In September 1994, for instance, Mitterrand declared: "I will not apologize in the name of France. The Republic has nothing to do with this. I do not believe France is responsible." Ironically, it was only in 1995 that the newly elected Gaullist president Jacques Chirac put an end to this refusal to accept responsibility by openly declaring. "These dark hours forever sully our history and are an insult to our past and traditions. Yes, the criminal folly of the occupiers was seconded by the French, by the French state." See Marlise Simons, "Chirac Affirms France's Guilt in Fate of Jews," *New York Times*, 17 July 1995. For a major contribution to this topic, see Susan Zucotti, *The Holocaust, the French and the Jews* (New York: Basic Books, 1993). For young Mitterrand's association with the interwar radical right see especially Tony Judt, "Truth and Consequences," *New York Review of Books*, 3 November 1994, pp. 8–12.

19. See Sternhell et al. *The Birth of Fascist Ideology*; see also Sir Isaiah Berlin's masterful study "Joseph de Maistre and the Origins of Fascism," in his book *The Crooked Timber of Humanity: Chapters in the History of Ideas* (New York: Knopf, 1991), pp. 91–174. Like Sorel, de Maistre exterted a significant influence in the formation of the political doctrines of Romania's mystical revolutionaries, primarily on young Mircea Eliade and E. M. Cioran. Later, after he emigrated to France and completely broke with his fascist past, Cioran wrote one of the most thoughtful interpretations of Joseph de Maistre's attack on modernity; Isaiah Berlin highly praised Cioran's insights. See E. M. Cioran's essay "Joseph de Maistre: An Essay on Reactionary Thought," in his book *Anathemas and Admirations* (New York: Arcade Publishing/Little Brown, 1991).

20. See Alan Cowell, "Leader of Italian Neo-Facists Praises Mussolini," *New York Times*, 2 April 1994. For Italian fascism, the best source remains Renzo de Felice, *Le fascisme: Un totalitarisme à l'italienne* (Paris: Presses de la Fondation Nationale de Sciences Politiques, 1988). The original Italian edition appeared in 1981.

21. The denial of the past and the resurgence of "generic fascism" are masterfully explored by Umberto Eco in "Ur-Fascism," *The New York Review of Books*, 22 June 1995, pp. 12–15.

22. See Alan Cowell, "Italy's Neo-Fascists: Have They Shed Their Past?" *New York Times*, 31 March 1994.

23. See Craig Whitney, "In Europe, the Right Also Rises," *New York Times*, 14 November 1994.

24. See William Drozdiak, "Italian Neo-Fascists Move toward Center, but Europe Still Frets," *Washington Post*, 20 May 1994.

25. For a comprehensive and lucid analysis of the historical debate in Germany, see Charles Maier, *The Unmasterable Past: History, Holocaust, and the German National Identity* (Cambridge: Harvard University Press, 1988).

26. For a penetrating analysis of the post-1989 German human and political dramas, see Mark Fisher, *After the Wall: Germany, the Germans and the Burdens of History* (New York: Simon and Schuster, 1995).

27. Etienne Balibar, *Masses, Classes, Ideas: Studies on Politics and Philosophy before and after Marx* (New York and London: Routledge, 1994), p. 199. According to Balibar, for whom class conflict remains the main interpretive paradigm of the political process, any form of nationalism is conducive to excesses: "I have never found any means to draw the line of demarcation between 'patriotism' and 'nationalism,' or if you prefer between clean, moderate, defensive nationalism which only aims at preserving an identity, and dirty, excessive and aggressive nationalism which leads to imperialist policies or to internal oppression of ethnic minorities" (p. 202). Whatever one may think of his theory, Balibar points to a very serious issue: how to draw the distinction between exclusive and inclusive nationalism.

28. John Lukacs, "Back from the Dead: Benito Mussolini," *New York Times Magazine*, 24 July 1994, p. 17.

29. Isaiah Berlin, *Against the Current: Essays in the History of Ideas* (Harmondsworth and New York: Penguin Books, 1982), p. 343.

30. See Eugen Weber, *Varieties of Fascism: Doctrines of Revolution in the Twentieth Century* (Malabar, FL: Krieger, 1982), pp. 17–18.

31. Gennady Zyuganov, *Derzhava* (Moscow: Informpechat', 1995), p. 33, quoted by Veljko Vujacic in his paper "Between Left and Right: Russian Nationalism and the Third Way," presented at the conference on "Neo-Communism and Democratic Change," Freedom House and Johns Hopkins University Foreign Policy Institute, Washington, DC, 9–10 November 1995, p. 18.

32. István Bibo, *Misère des petits états d'Europe de l'Est* (Paris: L'Harmattan, 1986), p. 299 (italics in the original).

33. A. J. Langbehn, *Rembrandt als Erzieher* (Leipzig, 1891), p. 292, quoted in Peter Pulzer, *The Rise of Political Anti-Semitism in Germany and Austria* (Cambridge: Harvard University Press, 1988), p. 236.

34. See Norman Cohn, *Warrant for Genocide: The Myth of the Jewish World-Conspiracy and the "Protocols of the Elders of Zion"* (New York: Harper Torchbooks, 1969), esp. pp. 264–65.

35. James H. Billington, "Let Russia Be Russian," *New York Times*, 16 June 1996.

36. For a penetrating analysis of the Legionary doctrine, the myth of the Fourth Rome, and Codreanu's "puritanic revolution" in Romania, see Ioan Petru Culianu, *Mircea Eliade* (Bucharest: Editura Nemira, 1995), pp. 175–86. See also Zigu Ornea, *Anii treizeci: Extrema dreaptă românească* (The 1930s: The Romanian Extreme Right) (Bucharest: Editura Fundatiei Culturale Române, 1995).

37. Hannah Arendt, *The Origins of Totalitarianism* (San Diego and New York: Harcourt Brace Jovanovich, 1973), pp. 242–43.

38. This point was brought to my attention by Ilya Prizel.

39. Mark Thompson, "Greater Croatia," *London Review of Books*, 13 May 1993, pp. 10–11.

40. See Drago Roksandić, "The Myth of 'Historical Conflict,'" *Labour Focus on Eastern Europe*, issue 41, no. 1 (1992), pp. 18–20.

41. E. M. Cioran, "Mon pays," cited in Alain Finkielkraut, "Cioran mort et son juge," *Le Messager Européen*, no. 9 (Paris: Gallimard, 1996), pp. 66–67.

42. Czeslaw Milosz, *The Captive Mind* (New York: Vintage Books, 1981), pp. 112–13.

43. For an interpretation of the ongoing debate on the legacies of Cioran's youthful fascination with fascism, see my essay "Romania's Mystical Revolutionaries," *Partisan Review*, Fall 1994, pp. 600–9. For the Guardist echoes in contemporary Romania and the search for an anti-parliamentary and anti-political "revolution," see Mircea Mihăieş, "Che Guevara sau Căpitanul?" *Lumea liberă* (New York), no. 406 (13 July 1996), p. 11.

44. See the summary of a report on the "Skinhead International" released by the Anti-Defamation League, "Some Music, It Turns out, Inflames the Savage Breast," *New York Times*, 2 July 1995.

45. For a succinct and accurate analysis of the relationship between nationalism and philosophical romanticism (especially Fichte), see Elie Kedourie's *Nationalism*, fourth, expanded edition (Oxford: Basil Blackwell, 1993), pp. 1–43.

46. See Eugen Weber, "Romania," in *The European Right: A Profile*, edited by Hans Rogger and Eugen Weber (Berkeley and Los Angeles: University of California Press, 1965), pp. 501–74; Andrew Janos, *The Politics of Backwardness in Hungary* (Princeton: Princeton University Press, 1982); Stanley Payne, *A History of Fascism, 1914–1945* (Madison: University of Wisconsin Press, 1995), pp. 267–89.

47. Matei Calinescu, "Romania's 1930's Revisited," *Salmagundi*, no. 97 (Winter 1993), pp. 133–51; Vladimir Tismaneanu and Dan Pavel, "The Generation of Angst and Adventure Revisited," *East European Politics and Societies*, vol. 8, no. 3 (Fall 1994), pp. 402–38; Irina Livezeanu, "Fascists and Conservatives in Romania: Two Generations of Nationalists," in *Fascists and Conservatives: The Radical Right and the Establishment in Twentieth-Century Europe*, edited by Martin Blinkhorn (London: Unwyn Hyman, 1990), pp. 218–39.

48. On the other hand, many Catholics participated during World War II in rescuing Jews. These gestures were all the more significant since Poland's occupation regime was particularly brutal, and assistance to the Jews was punished with the death penalty. See the special section on Polish-Jewish relations in *Le Messager Européen*, no. 9 (Paris: Gallimard, 1996), pp. 155–278 and also Adam Michnik's article "The Madness of Fanaticism," *Gazeta Wyborcza*, 8 August 1996 (English translation in *FBIS-Eastern Europe*, 8 August 1996, pp. 46–47), in which he opposes attempts "to build up the image of Poland as a country of anti-Semites and criminals."

49. Jane Perlez, "50 years after Pogrom, City Shrinks at Memory," *New York Times*, 6 July 1996.

50. The Jewish communists included Mátyas Rákosi, Erno Gerö, Ana Pauker, Iosif Chişinevschi, Jakub Berman, Roman Zambrowski, Bedřich Geminder, Rudolf Slansky, to mention just the most visible ones.

51. For important data regarding the persecution of the Romanian Zionist leaders in the early 1950s, see A. I. Zissu, *Sionisti sub anchetă: Declaratii, confruntări, interogatorii, 10 mai 1951–1 martie 1952* (Zionists under Investigtion: Declarations, Confrontations, Interrogations, 10 May 1951–1 March 1952) (Bucharest: Edart/FFP, 1993).

52. Katherine Verdery, *National Ideology under State Socialism* (Berkeley and Los Angeles: University of California Press, 1991).

53. Ernest Gellner, *Encounters with Nationalism* (Oxford: Basil Blackwell, 1994), pp. x–xi; Michael Walzer, "The New Tribalism: Notes on a Difficult Problem," *Dissent*, Spring 1992, pp. 164–71.

54. For the uses of anti-Semitism in contemporary Romanian politics, see Michael Shafir, "Antisemitic Candidates in Romania's 1996 Elections," *East European Jewish Affairs*, vol. 26, no. 1 (1996), pp. 89–105.

55. See Ken Jowitt, "Our Republic of Fear: Chomsky's Denunciation of America's Foreign and Economic Policies," *Times Literary Supplement*, 10 February 1995, pp. 3–4.

56. See Léon Poliakov, *Histoire de l'antisémitisme* (Paris: Calmann Lévy/Pluriel, 1981), vol. 2, p. 291.

57. For Jews and Polish communism, see Jaff Schatz, *Generation: The Rise and Fall of the Jewish Communists of Poland* (Berkeley and Los Angeles: University of California Press, 1991).

58. K. S. Karol, "Les silences de Walesa," *Le Nouvel Observateur*, 29 June–5 July 1995, p. 39.

59. Christine Spolar, "Sermon by Walesa's Priest Puts Spotlight on Polish Antisemitism," *Washington Post*, 8 July 1995.

60. Jane Perlez, "Polish Jews Ask Walesa to Disavow Priest's Remarks," *New York Times*, 17 June 1995. Eventually, under pressure from the Polish episcopate, Jankowski did express regrets, but in a very brief and ambiguous statement.

61. About Nae Ionescu's destructive role in Romania's political and spiritual life, see the letters addressed in 1945 by Eugène Ionesco from Paris to literary critic and cultural philosopher Tudor Vianu: *Scrisori către Tudor Vianu* (Bucharest: Editura Minerva, 1994), esp. pp. 274–75.

62. For a critique of this trend, see Ioan Buduca, "Nationalismul extremist în lumea post-comunistă," *Cuvîntul* (new series), Bucharest, February 1995.

63. Radu Ioanid, "Antisemitism and the Treatment of the Holocaust in Postcommunist Romania," in *Antisemitism and the Treatment of the Holocaust in Postcommunist Eastern Europe*, edited by Randolph Braham, The Rosenthal Institute for Holocaust Studies Graduate Center/CUNY and Socials Science Monographs, distributed by Columbia University Press (New York, 1994), p. 170. For analyses of the Antonescu myth and efforts to examine the role of the former dictator, see the special issue on "The Ion Antonescu Case," *Dilema* (Bucharest), no. 165 (8–14 March 1996). The Antonescu myth has been used by pro-Iliescu groups for definite political reasons, as an archetype opposed to the attempts to restore Romania's constitutional continuity. The opposition, in turn, used monarchist symbols and the figure of exiled King Michael as component of a countermyth meant to delegitimize the power holders. For the role of myth in post-1989 Romanian politics, see Leonard Drula, "Ion Antonescu si Mihai I. Între istorie si politică," in *Mituri istorice românesti*, edited by Lucian Boia (Bucharest: Editura Universitatii Bucuresti, 1995), pp. 220–54.

64. Tony Judt, *Past Imperfect: French Intellectuals, 1944–1956* (Berkeley and Los Angeles: University of California Press, 1992).

65. It was only in April 1995 that the Czech authorities finally admitted the significance of Terezin (Theresienstadt) as part of the Holocaust.

66. This problem is analyzed by Dominique Arel, "Ukraine: The Temptation of the Nationalizing State," in *Civil Society and Political Culture in the Countries of the Former Soviet Union*, edited by Vladimir Tismaneanu (Armonk, NY: M.E. Sharpe, 1995), pp. 157–88.

67. To remember the absolute evil is not to deny the existence of the other radical form of inhumanity, the Gulag and its ramifications in the Sovietized countries of Eastern Europe. In reality, the quality of memory is often related to the one of psychological empathy, and those who try to understand Auschwitz can better capture the meaning of Kolyma. See Daniel Chirot, *Modern Tyrants* (New York: Free Press, 1994). For a poignant approach to the similarities between Nazi and Stalinist camps, between Dachau and Kolyma, see Adam Hochschild, *The Unquiet Ghost: Russians Remember Stalin* (New York: Penguin Books, 1994).

68. For the complex relationship between Jews, communism, and anti-Semitism in Eastern Europe, see Annie Kriegel, "L'antisémitisme en Europe orientale: Notes pour une problématique," *Commentaire*, no. 60 (Winter 1992–1993), pp. 835–37; for the Romanian communist intellectual Valter Roman's political career, and also for a fascinating exploration of the Stalinist experience in Eastern Europe, see Christian Duplan and Vincent Giret, *La vie en rouge: Les Pionniers. Varsovie, Prague, Budapest, Bucarest, 1944–1968* (Paris: Éditions du Seuil, 1994).

69. Jeffrey Herf, "East German Communists and the Jewish Question: The Case of Paul Merker," *Journal of Contemporary History*, vol. 29, no. 4 (October 1994), pp. 627–61.

70. Jaff Schatz, "The Last True Communists," *Nationalities Papers*, vol. 23, supplement no. 1 (1994), pp. 129–63 (special issue on "Ethnopolitics in Poland"). Lech Walesa resorted to anti-Semitic innuendo during the presidential electoral campaign of 1990: he hinted at Tadeusz Mazowiecki's alleged Jewish background and complained of the Jewish tendency to use pseudonyms rather than real names (this being of course a slander directly imported from the propaganda arsenal of the communist secret police). Not surprisingly, Walesa later expressed just the opposite views during his trip to Israel: using anti-Semitic slurs and slogans is thus a matter of convenience rather than of firm belief. See Konstanty Gebert, "Antisemitism in the 1990 Polish Presidential Elections," *Social Research*, vol. 58, no. 4 (Winter 1991), pp. 723–55.

71. "Cominternist" has become the code word most frequently used to denounce Jews for their role in the the establishment of Stalinism in that country. Csurka in Hungary used the same language, attacking both liberal leaders (children of the former Comintern nomenklatura) as well as their protectors, and primarily the Soros foundation. That George Soros himself does not have much patience for his own Jewishness (let alone for pro-Israel activities), that he sees too many Jewish members on the boards of his foundations in Eastern Europe as a danger to their popularity and credibility, is insignificant in this self-enclosed theory. See Connie Bruck, "The World According to Soros," *New Yorker*, 23 January 1995, pp. 54–78.

72. For the post-communist narratives of rancor and ressentiment, see Paul Hockenos, *Free to Hate: The Rise of the Right in Post-Communist Eastern Europe* (New York:

Routledge, 1994). For an insightful comparative analysis of the rightist trends in Eastern Europe, see Sabrina Petra Ramet, "Back to the Future in Eastern Europe: A Comparison of the Post-1989 with Post-1918 Tendencies," *Acta Slavica Iaponica* (Saporro, Japan), Vol. 13 (1995), pp. 61–82.

73. For the uncivil, authoritarian-chauvinistic movements in post-communist Eastern Europe, see Sabrina Petra Ramet, *Social Currents in Eastern Europe: The Sources and Consequences of the Great Transformation* (Durham, NC: Duke University Press, 1995), pp. 431–54.

74. Sorin Antohi's splendid discussion in *Civitas Imaginalis: Istorie si utopie în cultura română* (Civitas Imaginalis: History and Utopia in Romanian Culture) (Bucharest: Editura Litera, 1994); he uses the Jewish *selbsthass* (self-hatred) concept to explain much of the ongoing and excruciating discussions around the topic proposed once by E. M. Cioran: how can one be a Romanian? As for the novel phenomenon of the superfluous "Third World" populations, Hans Magnus Enzensberger's analysis is disturbingly accurate: "conspiracy theory only obscures the truth: in New York as well as in Zaire, in the industrial cities as well as in the poorest countries, more and more people are being permanently excluded from the economic system because it no longer pays to exploit them." See *Civil Wars from L.A. to Bosnia* (New York: New Press, 1994), p. 36.

75. This rejection of alterity has a long tradition in European culture, where marginality was often used as an argument for exclusion. See Hans Mayer, *Les Marginaux. Femmes, juifs et homosexuels dans la littérature européenne* (Paris: Albin Michel, 1994).

76. Simon Epstein, "Extreme Right Electoral Upsurges in Western Europe: The 1984–1995 Wave as Compared with the Previous Ones," *Analysis of Current Trends in Antisemitism*, no. 8 (1996), Hebrew University of Jerusalem, Vidal Sasoon International Center for the Study of Antisemitism.

77. Robert Wistrich, "Nationalism Reborn," *Partisan Review*, no. 1 (Winter 1995), p. 15; see also Adam Michnik's "Presence of Liberal Values," *East European Reporter*, vol. 4, no. 4 (Spring-Summer 1971), p.76

78. See Celestine Bohlen, "Where the Fires of Hatred Are Easily Stoked," *New York Times*, 4 August 1991.

Five
Is the Revolution Over?

1. For Berisha's populist authoritarian methods and the demagogic use of the decommunization rhetoric during the 1996 parliamentary elections, see Jane Perlez, "Albania's Reformer Turns Autocrat," *New York Times*, 1 June 1996. I owe much of my analysis of Albania's political life to Gramoz Pashko, cofounder with Berisha of the Democratic party and former deputy prime minister, who broke with the president and became a main voice of the liberal opposition in that country. For the implications of the Albanian electoral fraud as a precedent to be emulated in other post-communist countries, see Thomas Carothers, "In Albania, One for the Thugs," *Washington Post*, 6 June 1996.

2. See George Konrád, *The Melancholy of Rebirth: Essays from Post-Communist Central Europe, 1989–1994* (San Diego, New York, and London: Harcourt Brace, 1995), pp. 2–3

3. Statements made by Adrian Năstase in Washington, DC, at the International Foundation for Electoral Systems, 20 January 1995 (personal notes).

4. Gregor Gysi, "Five Years of the PDS," *New Politics*, vol. 5, no. 3 (new series) (Summer 1995), p. 139.

5. See Serge Schmemann, "End of Line: Leaders at Communism's Finish," *New York Times*, 16 November 1990.

6. See Ken Jowitt's discussion of inclusion and neotraditionalism in his book *New World Disorder: The Leninist Extinction* (Berkeley and Los Angeles: University of California Press, 1992), pp. 88–158.

7. Andrew Nagorski, *The Birth of Freedom: Shaping Lives and Societies in the New Eastern Europe* (New York: Simon and Schuster, 1994), p. 59.

8. Polish historian, Solidarity advisor, and prominent dissident Bronislaw Geremek was a party member between 1950 and 1968. He gave up party membership to protest the invasion of Czechoslovakia and the increasingly xenophobic turn of the Polish Communist party: "I considered that I had a special obligation to oppose totalitarianism, communism, and the Party precisely because I had previously been a member. I felt I was duty bound to reimburse the debt I contracted for having carried the party card for twenty years." See Bronislaw Geremek, *La Rupture: La Pologne du communisme à la démocratie. Entretiens avec Jacek Zakowski* (Paris: Éditions du Seuil, 1991).

9. Jeffrey Isaac, "Adam Michnik: Politics and the Church," *Salmagundi*, no. 103 (Summer 1994), pp. 199–212. Isaac discusses Michnik's failure to address in an uninhibited way the presence of anti-Semitism in the Polish political culture as well his toying with the idea of Europe as a "Christian civilization." See, on the same issue, Robert Kaplan's discussion of the refusal to address the past in Romania and Croatia, *Balkan Ghosts: A Journey through History* (New York· St. Martin's Press, 1993).

10. For instance, political scientists Guillermo O'Donnell and Philippe C. Schmitter write: "It is difficult to imagine how a society can return to some degree of functioning which would provide social and ideological support for political democracy without somehow coming to terms with the most painful elements of its own past." See *Transitions from Authoritarian Rule: Tentative Conclusions about Uncertain Democracies* (Baltimore and London: Johns Hopkins University Press, 1991), p. 30.

11. Nanci Adler, *Victims of the Soviet Terror: The Story of the Memorial Movement* (Westport, CT and London: Praeger, 1993).

12. John Tagliabue, "New Pariahs Have East Europe Astir," *New York Times*, 18 March 1992.

13. Of all the categories targeted by the lustration law, the members of the People's Militia had been lately the least politically involved in the communist repression. Actually, as the late Rita Klimova, the first Czech ambassador to Washington after the Velvet Revolution, told me, the militia consisted by the end of the communist regime of nothing more than old-buddy hunting and drinking clubs. Personal interview with Rita Klimova, Washington, DC, November 1992. In spite of her impressive dissident credentials and qualified support for lustration, Klimova herself was attacked by the radicals because of her participation in her youth in the purges of the "bourgeois" intelligentsia.

14. Jennifer Yoder, "Corrective Justice in the Former GDR," unpublished manuscript.

15. Timothy Garton Ash, "Central Europe: The Present Past," *New York Review of Books*, 13 July 1995, p. 13.

16. "Czech Parliament Passes Law on Illegitimacy of Communist Regime," *Radio*

Free Europe/Radio Liberty Daily Report, 10 July 1993; for extensive excerpts of this law and an excellent discussion of the avatars of decommunization in the Czech republic, see Erazim Kohak, "Political Correctness in Prague," *Dissent*, Winter 1994, pp. 35–38. Kohak, a distinguished Czech political philosopher, objects to the 1991 lustration law as well as to the 1993 document on the basis of their moral absolutism combined with lack of interest in such fundamental principles as individual guilt and presumption of innocence. With regard to the latter he writes, "The problem is not simply that some innocent people will be hurt by it. That, again, is a problem one could counter with the principle of the greatest food for the greatest number. Far more serious is that the law enshrines in our legal practice the principle of collective guilt" (p. 38).

17. Quoted by Ethan Klingsberg, "File Fever," *New York Times*, 22 November 1993.

18. Petr Pithart, "Intellectuals in Politics: Double Dissent in the Past, Double Disappointment Today," *Social Research*, vol. 60, no. 4 (Winter 1993), p. 761.

19. For decommunization in Bulgaria, see Kjell Engelbrekt, "Bulgaria's Communist Legacy: Settling Old Scores," *Radio Free Europe/Radio Liberty Research Report*, vol. 1, no. 28 (10 July 1992), pp. 6–10. Henry Kamm in "An Old Red Fumes in His Villa Prison," *New York Times*, 9 July 1993, depicts an unrepentant Zhivkov serving a seven-year sentence on the charge of misuse of public funds, the only offense the government could find legal provisions for indicting the former leader with. Instead of admitting any personal guilt, Zhivkov stated: "If every head of state were tried for what I did, there wouldn't be a single head of state out of prison." Several years earlier, Zhivkov rejected responsibility for any crime: "I am not legally responsible," he declared about his times in power. "I made political errors, but I have not committed a crime against my people or the world." He admitted, however, that the foundation of Soviet-style socialism was wrong, and that "at its very inception the idea of socialism was stillborn." See Chuck Sudetic, "Bulgarian Communist Stalwart Says He'd Do It All Differently," *New York Times*, 28 November 1990.

20. Jane Perlez, "Job Shake-Out Pushes Poles to Ex-Communists," *New York Times*, 18 September 1993.

21. "The Party Isn't Over," *Economist*, 26 June 1993, p. 57.

22. William Safire, "Communostalgia," *New York Times*, 11 March 1993. Safire defines communostalgia as "the habit of forgetting the painful tyranny of the past in the uncomfortable freedom of the present."

23. György Bence, "Political Justice in Post-Communist Societies; The Case of Hungary," Occasional Paper no. 27, Wilson Center (Washington, DC), East European Program, April 1991, p. 6.

24. Alessandra Stanley, "Russia's New Rulers Govern, and Live, in Neo-Soviet Style," *New York Times*, 23 May 1995.

25. Alina Mungiu, *România: Mod de folosire* (Bucharest: Editura Staff, 1994), pp. 22–23; Jane Perlez, "With Old Tricks, Romania's Old Reds Curb Press," *New York Times*, 8 June 1995.

26. Jane Perlez, "Romania's Anti-Communist Revolutionary," *New York Times*, 19 November 1996.

27. Adam Michnik and Václav Havel, "Justice or Revenge?" *Journal of Democracy*, vol. 4, no. 1 (January 1993), pp. 21–22.

28. Vojtech Čepl, "Ritual Sacrifices," *East European Constitutional Review*, Spring 1992, pp. 25–26.

29. Eva Hoffman, *Exit into History: A Journey through the New Eastern Europe* (New York: Viking, 1993), pp. 175–80; Nagorski, *The Birth of Freedom*, pp. 87–90.

30. Jan Kavan's letter to the author (1993). As Tina Rosenberg reports, among the first hundred cases of individuals who appealed to the court and sued the Ministry of the Interior, only ten lost, all of them on technicalities. See *Haunted Land: Facing Europe's Ghosts after Communism* (New York: Random House, 1995), pp. 100–1.

31. Nagorski, *The Birth of Freedom*, p. 82.

32. Ibid., pp. 90–91.

33. Anne Applebaum, "Learning to Love Lustration," *Wall Street Journal*, 26–27 May 1995.

34. For the situation in Romania prior to the watershed November 1996 elections, see Vladimir Tismaneanu, "Democracy, Romanian-Style," *Dissent*, Summer 1995, pp. 220–22.

35. See Anne Applebaum, "The Fall and Rise of the Communists: Guess Who's Running Central Europe," *Foreign Affairs*, November-December 1994, pp. 7–13.

36. Richard Pipes, "The Past on Trial: Russia, One Year Later," *Washington Post* (Outlook), 16 August 1992.

37. Leonard Shapiro, *The Communist Party of the Soviet Union* (New York: Vintage, 1971), pp. 619–29.

38. Jacques Rupnik, "Post-Totalitarian Blues," *Journal of Democracy*, vol. 6, no. 2 (1995), pp. 61–73.

39. This topic is wonderfully and disquietingly analyzed by Julian Barnes in *The Porcupine* (New York: Knopf, 1992), a novel whose main character is modeled after the former Bulgarian dictator Todor Zhivkov.

40. Rosenberg, *Haunted Land*, p. xix.

41. "The Clean-up Bureau," an interview with Pastor Joachim Gauck originally published in the Polish newsweekly *Wprost* (Wroclaw), reprinted in *Uncaptive Minds*, vol. 5, no. 2(20) (Summer 1992), p. 128.

42. In Romania, despite much rhetoric and the intensity of the first anti-communist wave that followed the execution of Nicolae and Elena Ceauşescu, the new ruling team has institutionalized a policy of deliberate amnesia. Although, starting in 1994, important documents have been released by the Romanian Service of Information (SRI) regarding the crimes of the 1950s, including the atrocious experiments in "reeducation" in Gherla and Piteşti, there is still too little information about what happened six or seven years ago, when the same secret police played such a pivotal role in the quasi revolution, the miners' devastation of Bucharest in June 1990, and so many other still obscure events.

43. Françoise Thom, "The Second Echelon," *Uncaptive Minds*, vol. 4, no. 4 (18) (Winter 1991–1992), p. 8.

44. Quoted by Rosenberg, *Haunted Land*, p. 240.

45. See Adam Michnik's essays, "The Two Faces of Europe," *New York Review of Books*, 19 July 1990, p. 7, and "An Embarrassing Anniversary," *New York Review of Books*, 10 June 1993, pp. 19–21.

46. "Hatred and Democracy," interview with President Zhelyu Zhelev by Adam Michnik, *Gazeta Wyborcza*, 3–4 July 1993, pp. 14–15; English translation in *FBIS-Eastern Europe*, 8 July 1993, pp. 7–9. In the fall of 1996 a Polish parliamentary commission decided that all state officials from deputy governor to the president, including

parliamentary deputies, judges, prosecutors, and candidates for those posts would be screened to determine if they had cooperated with the communist-era secret services. Ironically, this law was adopted by a parliament in which the post-communists enjoy a plurality of seats. See *OMRI Daily Digest*, 2 December 1996.

47. Rosenberg, *The Haunted Land*, p. 250. For Olszewski, see Jan Josef Lipski, *KOR: A History of the Workers' Defense Committee in Poland, 1976–1981* (Berkeley and Los Angeles: University of California Press, 1985), as well as Jacek Kuron's memoirs, *La foi et la faute* (Paris: Fayard, 1991).

48. Quoted in Jacques Rupnik, "Post-Totalitarian Blues," *Journal of Democracy*, vol. 6, no. 2 (April 1995), p. 63.

49. Adam Michnik quoted in Rosenberg, *The Haunted Land*, pp. 247–48.

50. Havel and Michnik, "Justice or Revenge?" pp. 25–26.

51. Stephen Holmes, "The End of Decommunization?" *East European Constitutional Review* (double issue), vol. 3, nos. 3–4 (Summer–Fall 1994), pp. 33–36.

52. Bruce Ackerman, *The Future of the Liberal Revolution* (New Haven: Yale University Press, 1992), pp. 80–82.

53. Arpad Göncz, "Breaking the Vicious Circle," *Common Knowledge*, vol. 2, no. 1 (Spring 1993), p. 5.

54. Petruska Sustrova, "The Lustration Controversy," *Uncaptive Minds*, vol. 5, no. 2 (20) (Summer 1992), pp. 129, 134.

55. Josef Darski, "Decommunization in Eastern Europe," *Uncaptive Minds*, vol. 6, no. 1 (22) (Winter-Spring 1993), p. 78.

56. Ibid., p. 81.

57. Horaţiu Pepine, "Metafora KGB," *22* (Bucharest), no. 21 (24–30 May 1995), p. 1.

58. Discussion with Bronislaw Geremek at the Group for Social Dialogue, *22* (Bucharest), no. 21 (24–30 May 1995), pp. 8–9.

59. General Wojciech Jaruzelski is rather the exception in this respect, but even he tries to vindicate his decision to impose martial law and ban Solidarity in December 1981: "I still believe I couldn't have acted any other way. But I deeply regret it. It was a nightmare. It is a great burden for me, and it will be until the end of my days." See John Darnton, "Jaruzelski Is Now Sorry He Ordered Martial Law," *New York Times*, 4 March 4, 1993. For an in-depth analysis of Jaruzelski's mindset and inner psychological torments, see Rosenberg, *Haunted Land*, pp. 125–222. For Jaruzelski's attempts to engage in dialogue with prominent democratic activists like Adam Michnik and Bronislaw Geremek, see Christine Spolar, "Twilight of the General," *Washington Post*, 22 September 1995.

60. Stephen Kinzer, "A Relic Who's Red and Unrepentant," *New York Times*, 20 July 1996. Kessler's unreconstructed Leninist beliefs prevented him from acquiring membership in the Party of Democratic Socialism, the successor to the East German Communist party, which has tried to convey a modern, moderate, and democratic image.

61. Money for *Nie* came primarily from the mass sales of Urban's outrageous memoir entitled "Urban's Alphabet" in which he attacked virtually all famous Polish elite figures, focusing on their private lives and indulging in what an American journalist called "gutter con brio." The book was a tremendous hit: 750,000 copies were in circulation after a month (in a country of about 40 million people). For a masterful investigation of Urban's career, see Lawrence Weschsler, "Urban Blight," *New Yorker*, 11 December 1995, pp. 54–69.

62. See "I Don't Believe the Files Were Falsified," interview with Bogdan Borusewicz, *Uncaptive Minds*, vol. 5, no. 2 (20) (Summer 1992), p. 117.

63. See George Konrád's scheme for a realistic approach in "Authority and Tolerance," *East European Reporter*, May-June 1992, pp. 45–47.

64. Following the victory of the democratic forces in the November 1996 elections, Adrian Severin became Romania's foreign minister.

65. *Mediafax* (Bucharest), 1 July 1996. It is noteworthy that the Severin report includes major points suggested in the Timişoara Proclamation (March 1990), one of the first East European calls for legal decommunization. At the time the proclamation was issued, the Roman government denounced it as a call for civil war.

66. For anti-communist protest and human rights activism in Czechoslovakia, see Bernard Wheaton and Zdenek Kavan, *The Velvet Revolution: Czechoslovakia, 1988–1991* (Boulder: Westview Press, 1992).

67. For Wolf, see Alan Cowell, "East Germany's Old Spymaster Talks: So Many Regrets, but Uncontrite," *New York Times*, 6 June 1995.

68. Tina Rosenberg, "Where's the Crime?" *New York Times*, 2 June 1995.

69. Ibid.

70. See Andrei Ursu, "Scrisoare deschisă către preşedintele României, d-l Ion Iliescu" (An Open Letter to the President of Romania, Mr. Ion Iliescu), 22 (Bucharest), no. 28 (10–16 July 1996), pp. 15–16. It remains to be seen whether the anti-communist Romanian government that came to power in November 1996 will open legal procedures against those Securitate officers who directly organized Ursu's assassination. See the interview with Andrei Ursu, 22, no. 51 (17–23 December 1996).

71. For Olszewski's right-wing anti-establishment rhetoric, see "Grab the Chance," *Economist*, 13 July 1996, pp. 47–48.

72. Personal interview with Miklós Haraszti, Orlando, FL, 4 January 1995.

73. See Wiktor Osyatinski, "Agent Walesa?" *East European Constitutional Review*, Summer 1992, pp. 28–30.

74. See Bronislaw Geremek, *La rupture: La Pologne du communisme à la démocratie* (Paris: Éditions du Seuil, 1991).

75. See Nial Ferguson, "The Trial," *New Republic*, 18 May 1992, pp. 20–21.

Six
A Velvet Counterrevolution?

1. See H. Stuart Hughes, *Sophisticated Rebels: The Political Culture of European Dissent, 1968–1987* (Cambridge: Harvard University Press, 1988).

2. This point was emphasized by Havel in his pathbreaking essay "The Power of the Powerless" in Václav Havel et al., *The Power of the Powerless: Citizens against the State* (Armonk, NY: M.E. Sharpe, 1985), pp. 23–96.

3. See Robert D. Putnam, "Bowling Alone: America's Declining Social Capital," *Journal of Democracy*, vol. 6, no. 1 (January 1995), pp. 65–78.

4. Tony Judt, "Nineteen Eighty-Nine: The End of Which European Era?" *Daedalus*, vol. 123, no. 3 (Summer 1994), p. 6.

5. G. M. Tamás, "The Legacy of Dissent," *Times Literary Supplement*, 14 May 1993, p. 14.

6. For an opposite view, insisting on the enduring significance of the dissident

search for a new political paradigm, reconciling social justice and individual rights, equality and pluralism, see Ira Katznelson, *Liberalism's Crooked Circle: Letters to Adam Michnik* (Princeton: Princeton University Press, 1996).

7. John Lukacs, *The End of the Twentieth Century and the End of Modern Age* (New York: Ticknor and Fields, 1993).

8. Havel himself confessed, not without a sense of melancholy, that he would like to write a little book on this current aversion expressed by large strata of the population toward the once admired dissidents. See the discussion between Havel and Jacques Rupnik in 22 (Bucharest), no. 18 (13–19 May 1993); the French original is in *Politique Internationale*, no. 58 (1993).

9. Irena Grudzinska Gross, "Post-Communist Resentment, or the Rewriting of Polish History," *East European Politics and Societies*, vol. 6, no. 2 (Spring 1992), pp. 141–51, and *Partisan Review*, "Intellectuals and Social Change in Central and Eastern Europe," special issue, no. 4 (Fall 1992).

10. Klaus is certainly not a proponent of any communal definition of identity, and his rejection of "ethical universalism" is essentially different from the populist discourse. At the same time, he has little patience for Havel's vision of civil society as a vehicle for strengthening group solidarities and collective initiatives from below. The difference between the two Václavs is more one of interpretation of liberalism and of the role of critical intellectuals in post-communist polities, rather than a conflict between two incompatible political philosophies. See "Rival Visions: Václav Havel and Václav Klaus with commentary by Petr Pithart," *Journal of Democracy*, vol. 7, no. 1 (January 1996), pp. 12–23.

11. For the dismissive attitude toward former dissidents as "naive humanists," see Vladimir Pasti, *România în tranziție: căderea în viitor* (Bucharest: Editura Nemira, 1995).

12. An exceptionally important document regarding the complexities of political justice in post-communist societies was the dialogue between Adam Michnik and Václav Havel, "Justice or Revenge?" *Journal of Democracy*, vol. 4, no. 1 (January 1993), pp. 20–27.

13. Attacks on political opponents and democratic activists developed in Belarus under Lukashenko's authoritarian leadership. Zenon Pozniak, chairman of the Popular Front and prominent democratic activist, applied in July 1996 for political asylum in the United States. Similar forms of harassment have occurred in Albania; Gramoz Pashko, a professor of economics at the University of Tirana and cofounder with Berisha of the Democratic party, was deprived of his parliamentary seat during the 1996 elections, and left the country for an indefinite period.

14. This was the case not only in the Czech Republic and Poland, but even more in the former GDR, where many exdissidents became firebrand advocates of legal actions against the former elite. For an informative analysis of the Polish debates on lustration and their impact on the new political system, see Frances Millard, "The Shaping of the Polish Party System, 1989–93," *East European Politics and Societies*, vol. 8, no. 3 (Fall 1994), pp. 467–94. For the role of exdissidents in the post-1989 German efforts to confront the past, see Tina Rosenberg, *Haunted Land: Facing Europe's Ghosts after Communism* (New York: Random House, 1995), pp. 261–394.

15. Adam Michnik, "An Embarrassing Anniversary," *New York Review of Books*, 10 June 1993, p. 19.

16. Personal interviews with Adam Michnik, Warsaw, 29–30 August 1993; Orlando, FL, 5 January 1994; Budapest, 22 March 1996.

17. Theodore Draper, "A New History of the Velvet Revolution," *New York Review of Books*, 14 January 1993. In a subsequent article, 28 January 1993, called "The End of Czechoslovakia," Draper further charged Havel with offering "little more than dreams."

18. Yegor Ligachev, *Inside Gorbachev's Kremlin* (New York: Pantheon, 1993).

19. This point is central for explaining the rise of nationalism rather than civic liberalism as a dominant successor ideology in the Balkans and the former USSR. See Slavenka Drakulić, *The Balkan Express: Scenes from the Other Side of the War* (New York: Norton, 1993).

20. "Adam Michnik: Patria intelectualului este adevărul," (Adam Michnik: Truth is the Intellectual's Motherland), an interview by Vladimir Tismaneanu and Mircea Mihăieş, *AGORA* (Philadelphia), vol. 5, no. 4 (October-December 1992), pp. 63–64.

21. Timothy Garton Ash, "Eastern Europe: The Year of Truth," *New York Review of Books*, 15 February 1990, p. 18.

22. On this point see Ernest Gellner, *Conditions of Liberty: Civil Society and Its Rivals* (New York: Allen Lane/Penguin Press, 1994), p. 53.

23. See Jan T. Gross, "Poland: From Civil Society to Political Nation," in *Eastern Europe in Revolution*, edited by Ivo Banac (Ithaca: Cornell University Press, 1992), pp. 56–71.

24. Garton Ash, "Eastern Europe: The Year of Truth," p. 20.

25. Daniel Chirot, "What Happened in Eastern Europe in 1989?" in *The Crisis of Leninism and the Decline of the Left*, edited by Daniel Chirot (Seattle: University of Washington Press, 1991), p. 22.

26. See Václav Havel, "New Year Address," *East European Reporter*, vol. 4, no. 1 (Winter 1989/1990), pp. 56–58.

27. See Aristide Zolberg, "Moments of Madness," *Politics and Society*, no. 2 (Winter 1972), p. 183, quoted by Katznelson, *Liberalism's Crooked Circle*, p. 183.

28. See Tony Judt, "Misjudgement of Paris: French Illusions and the Eastern Europe that Never Was," *Times Literary Supplement*, 15 May 1992, p. 3.

29. Ira Katznelson rightly insists that there is a close link between the health of a democracy and quality of the discourse public moralists generate. See *Liberalism's Crooked Circle*, pp. 34–35. The term "public moralists" comes from Stefan Collini, *Public Moralists: Political Thought and Intellectual Life in Britain, 1850–1930* (Oxford: Clarendon Press, 1991).

30. See Michael Ignatieff, "After the Revolutions," New Republic, 19 and 26 August 1996, pp. 42–45.

31. On the contrast between the thriving media in Central Europe and the authoritarian attempts to stifle the free press in the Balkans (Bulgaria, Serbia, Croatia), see the editorial "Eastern Europe's Ailing Press," *New York Times*, 6 August 1996.

32. See Gale Stokes, *The Walls Came Tumbling Down: The Collapse of Communism in Eastern Europe* (New York: Oxford University Press, 1993), p. 157.

33. See Michnik's preface to the American edition of his book *The Church and the Left* (Chicago: University of Chicago Press, 1993), p. xiii.

34. Tony Judt, "The Unmastered Future: What Prospects for Eastern Europe?" *Tikkun*, vol. 5, no. 2 (1990), p. 14.

35. See "Rival Visions: Václav Havel and Václav Klaus with commentary by Petr Pithart," *Journal of Democracy*, vol. 7, no. 1 (January 1996), p. 17.

36. Deploring the disappearance of high moral standards among Poland's former oppositionists, political essayist Jacek Zakowski insisted on the need to revive the ethos of civil society, especially in the efforts to prevent corruption and assert the primacy of the public good over personal interests. See his highly controversial essay, "Something Has Shattered in Poland, Something Has Come to an End," *Gazeta Wyborcza*, 16–17 April 1994, quoted in Michal Cichy, "Requiem for the Moderate Revolutionist," p. 148.

37. See Ernest Gellner, "The Last Marxists: Pretensions, Illusions and Achievements of the Frankfurt School," *Times Literary Supplement*, 23 September 1994, pp. 3–5.

38. See Gellner's *Conditions of Liberty*, as well as Michael Ignatieff's review essay, "On Civil Society: Why Eastern Europe's Revolutions Could Succeed," *Foreign Affairs*, vol. 74, no. 2 (March-April 1995), pp. 128–37.

39. Havel's search for authenticity is close to Hannah Arendt's vision of the possibility of a just order rooted in spontaneity of social interaction and the existence of non-institutionalized forms of political expression. See Jeffrey C. Isaac, "The Meanings of 1989," *Social Research*, vol. 63, no. 2 (Summer 1996), pp. 328–29; Melvyn A. Hill, ed., *Hannah Arendt: The Recovery of the Public World* (New York: St. Martin's Press, 1979).

Conclusion
The Mythological Construction of Reality

1. See Fred Hiatt, "Russians Seek Rosier Past, Even Revising Stalin Image," *Washington Post*, 30 October 1994.

2. Indeed, some of those who now lionize Ranković as a champion of Serbian nationalism may have lost members of their families in the atrocious Goli Otok concentration camp during the 1950s. I owe information about the reverence shown to Ranković to Nicholas J. Miller.

3. Some Romanian nationalists have gone so far as to describe the Zhdanovist cultural policies of the 1950s as the "Holocaust of the Romanian culture." A series of articles under this title was published by Mihai Ungheanu in the ultra-chauvinist weekly *România Mare* in 1991–1992. Between 1993 and 1996, Ungheanu served as secretary of state in the Ministry of Culture.

4. Ferenc Kulin quoted by Gábor Gyany, "Political Uses of Tradition in Postcommunist East Central Europe," *Social Research*, vol. 60, no. 4 (Winter 1993), p. 897.

5. For the development of the nationalist ideology in Central and Eastern Europe, see Peter F. Sugar and John Lederer, eds., *Nationalism in Eastern Europe* (Seattle and London: University of Washington Press, 1994).

6. See Hans Magnus Enzensberger's intervention at the conference on "Intellectuals and Social Change in Central and Eastern Europe," *Partisan Review*, Fall 1992, p. 686. Along the same lines, see the contributions by Slavenka Drakulić, Adam Michnik, Norman Manea, and Dubrovka Ugresić.

7. See Mircea Eliade, *Myths, Dreams and Mysteries: The Encounter between Contemporary Faiths and Archaic Realities* (New York: Harper Torchbooks, 1967), pp. 25–26.

8. Adam Michnik, quoted by John Lloyd, "The Comrades' Last Fight," *Financial Times*, 3 September 1989. Paradoxically, Lloyd did not notice that Michnik's statement

could apply very well to a possible transmogrification of the former communists. Indeed, what is post-communist nationalism if not "the greed for power clothed in the gown of justice"? How else can one make sense of Slobodan Milošević's metamorphosis from Marxist ideological hack into apostle of Serbian nationalism?

9. For a persuasive critique of "third way" illusions in contemporary Romania, see Adrian Marino, *Politică și cultură* (Iasi: Editura Polirom, 1996), pp. 92–93. For the persistence of subliminal anti-capitalist sentiments among Hungary's post-1989 political formations, see G. M. Tamás, "Farewell to the Left," *East European Politics and Societies*, vol. 5, no. 1 (Winter 1991), pp. 92–112.

10. This possible scenario was mentioned by Ivan Szelenyi as early as 1990. See his article "Social and Political Landscape, Central Europe, Fall 1990," in *Eastern Europe in Revolution*, edited by Ivo Banac (Ithaca: Cornell University Press, 1992), p. 228. Szelenyi spelled out strong misgivings about the prospects for European integration for Eastern Europe and expressed worries about the region's transformation into Germany's semicolony.

11. See Furio Cerutti, "Can There Be a Supranational Identity?" *Philosophy and Social Criticism*, vol. 18, no. 2 (1992), pp. 147–62.

12. Wolf Lepenies, "The Future of Intellectuals," *Partisan Review*, no. 1 (Winter 1994), pp. 118–19.

13. See Anthony D. Smith, *National Identity* (London: Penguin, 1991), p. 175.

14. Adam Michnik, "After the Revolution," *New Republic*, 2 July 1990, p. 28.

15. I analyzed the fate of this doctrine under state socialism in *The Crisis of Marxist Ideology in Eastern Europe: The Poverty of Utopia* (New York and London: Routledge, 1988). For the post-1989 crisis of the Left, see Daniel Chirot, ed., *The Crisis of Leninism and the Decline of Left: The Revolutions of 1989* (Seattle: University of Washington Press, 1991).

16. See Vladimir Tismaneanu, "Tenuous Pluralism in Post-Ceaușescu Romania," *Transition*, no. 26 (1996), pp. 6–11.

17. See the special issue of *World Politics* edited by Nancy Bermeo, vol. 44, no. 1 (October 1991), "Liberalization and Democratization in Eastern Europe and the Soviet Union."

18. See primarily Timothy Garton Ash, *The Uses of Adversity: Essays on the Fate of Central Europe* (New York: Random House, 1989), pp. 300–24.

19. The confusion within the top echelons of the Leninist parties is convincingly documented in a number of memoirs written by people once very close to Mikhail Gorbachev. See for instance Aleksandr Yakovlev, *The Fate of Marxism in Russia* (New Haven: Yale University Press, 1994); Valery Boldin, *Ten Years That Shook the World: The Gorbachev Era as Witnessed by His Chief of Staff* (New York: Basic Books, 1994). See also Vladimir Tismaneanu, "The Legacy of Perestroika," *ORBIS* (Philadelphia), Summer 1994, pp. 505–9.

20. Leszek Kolakowski, "Amidst Moving Ruins," *Daedalus*, vol. 121, no. 2 (Spring 1992), p. 49. This is indeed fundamental for the endurance and impact of political myth: In addition to its positivistic, facts-oriented component, Marxian Communism was the consummate secular eschatology. Among the most penetrating analyses of the meaning of the Marxian mythology are Robert C. Tucker, *Philosophy and Myth in Karl Marx* (Cambridge: Cambridge University Press, 1972), and Ferenc Fehér, "Marxism as Politics: An Obituary," *Problems of Communism*, January-April 1992, pp. 11–18. For my

response to this line of argument, see Vladimir Tismaneanu, "Secular Prophecy and Radical Dreams: Reflections on the Fate of Marxism," ibid., pp. 24–28.

21. For twentieth-century political mythologies, see François Furet, "La passion révolutionnaire au XXe siècle," in *Écrire l'histoire du XXe siècle: la politique et la raison*, edited by Marcel Gauchet, Pierre Manent, and Pierre Rosenvallon (Paris: Gallimard/ Seuil, 1994), pp. 11–43; Raoul Girardet, *Mythes et mythologies politiques* (Paris: Seuil, 1986). For the competition between national and social political radicalisms, see Jacob L. Talmon, *Myth of the Nation and Vision of the Revolution* (New Brunswick, NJ: Transaction, 1991).

22. See Tariq Ali's reference to the similarity between the current European moral landscape and the world portrayed by Balzac in *Les illusions perdues* in "Literature and Market Realism," *New Left Review*, no. 199 (May-June 1993), pp. 140–45.

23. See Andrzej W. Tymowski, "Left Turn in Polish Elections?" *New Politics*, no. 16 (Winter 1994), pp. 99–105.

24. Nancy Bermeo, "Democracy in Europe," *Daedalus*, vol. 123, no. 2 (Spring 1994), pp. 164, 166.

25. See Víctor M. Pérez-Díaz, *The Return of Civil Society: The Emergence of Democratic Spain* (Cambridge: Harvard University Press, 1993).

26. Timothy Garton Ash, "The Year of Truth," *New York Review of Books*, 15 February 1990, pp. 18–20.

27. This revolutionary role for the intelligentsia as a "new political class" was first noticed, although in a different sense and context, by György Konrád and Ivan Szelenyi, *The Intellectuals on the Road to Class Power* (New York: Harcourt Brace Jovanovich 1979).

28. Among the first was Adam Michnik, who noticed the revival of the clericalist, ethnocentric trends in Polish politics. See especially Michnik's preface to the English-language translation and the chapter "Troubles" in *The Church and the Left* (Chicago and London: University of Chicago Press, 1993).

29. See Bruce Ackerman, *The Future of Liberal Revolution* (New Haven and London: Yale University Press, 1992), pp. 72–73.

30. Economically it is obvious that the former nomenklatura had an advantage from the start: large amounts of foreign currency, know-how, connections—all these elements concurred to make them the new economic rulers. See especially Lev Timfoyev, *Russia's Secret Rulers* (New York: Knopf, 1993) and K. S. Karol's devastating report on the relations between the power elite and the organized mob in contemporary Russia, "La maison Eltsine à la dérive," *Le Nouvel Observateur*, 10–16 November 1994, pp. 38–40.

31. Valerie Bunce and Maria Csanadi, "Uncertainty in the Transition: Post-Communism in Hungary," *East European Politics and Societies*, vol. 7, no. 2 (Spring 1993), pp. 240–75.

32. See Rick Atkinson, "The Wall Is Gone, but Berlin Remains a City That Is Badly Divided," *Washington Post*, 9 November 1994.

33. Eric Hobsbawm, "The New Threat to History," *New York Review of Books*, 16 December 1993, pp. 62–63.

34. For the role of corruption in the self-destruction of communist regimes, see Leslie Holmes, *The End of Communist Power: Anti-Corruption Campaigns and Legitimation Crisis* (New York: Oxford University Press, 1993).

35. See Vladimir Tismaneanu, ed., *Political Culture and Civil Society in the Countries of the Former Soviet Union* (Armonk, NY: M.E. Sharpe, 1995). For an excellent interpretation of post-Leninist Russian politics, see M. Steven Fish, *Democracy from Scratch: Opposition and Regime in the New Russian Revolution* (Princeton: Princeton University Press, 1995), and also by him, "The Travails of Liberalism," *Journal of Democracy*, vol. 7, no. 2 (April 1996), pp. 104–17.

36. Jürgen Kocka, "Crisis of Unification: How Germany Changes," *Daedalus*, vol. 123, no. 1 (Winter 1994), p. 174. I would argue with Kocka that the revolutions of 1989 did offer more than a revisiting of the Western liberal tradition of civil society. The dissident philosophy of freedom, the concept of anti-politics, and the dream of Central Europe may have been quixotic, but they were also signals that not all political formulas had been exhausted by the Western practices.

37. See Mircea Eliade, *Myth and Reality* (New York: Harper & Row, 1963), p. 141.

38. See Heller and Fehér, *The Postmodern Political Condition*, p. 9. As the Hungarian authors emphasized, post-modernity includes a minimally defined, nonuniversalistic ethical agenda. With its normative thrust, however, the dissident concept of freedom belongs to the legacy of modernity rather than to its post-modern critique.

39. Quoted in John Pomfret, "Reform Wins; Dissidents Lose," *Washington Post*, 24 October 1994.

40. Ken Jowitt, *New World Disorder: The Leninist Extinction* (Berkeley and Los Angeles: University of California Press, 1992).

41. See Vladimir Tismaneanu, ed., *In Search of Civil Society* (New York and London: Routledge, 1990); Garton Ash, *The Uses of Adversity*.

42. See Furet, "La passion révolutionnaire au XXe siècle," pp. 11–43.

43. See Anna Husarska, "Altared State: Permissive Poland Rebels against the Church," *Washington Post*, 26 November 1995.

44. See Timothy Garton Ash, "'Neo-Pagan' Poland," *New York Review of Books*, 11 January 1996, p. 14. Cardinal Glemp used the term "neo-paganism" against those who reject the Church's privileged role in what they want to be a secular Poland.

45. For a detailed analysis of the communists' afterlife in Central Europe, see Andrew Nagorski, *The Birth of Freedom: Shaping Life and Societies after Communism* (New York: Simon and Schuster, 1993), pp. 55–91.

46. See "UDF Memorandum on the Situation in Bulgaria," *Uncaptive Minds*, vol. 8, no. 2 (Summer 1995), pp. 93–95.

47. Again, each case is different: in Russia's 1996 presidential elections, Yeltsin successfully played the anti-communist card against Zyuganov's uneasy coalition of Bolsheviks and ethno-religious imperial fundamentalists. A highly personalized campaign that literally ruined Yeltsin's health was accompanied by the use of government-controlled TV to remind voters methodically of the abysmal economic and political conditions of Stalin's times.

48. For the political and intellectual metamorphoses of the post-communists and their relationship to at least a major faction of the post-dissident communities, see Bernard Guetta, "Les habits neufs des ex-communistes," *Le Nouvel Observateur*, 10–16 November 1994, pp. 12–15.

49. See Hannah Arendt, "Some Questions of Moral Philosophy," lecture delivered at the New School for Social Research, 10 February 1965, *Social Research*, vol. 61, no. 4 (Winter 1994), p. 740. Arendt deals in this lecture with the unmasterable past, the past

that doesn't pass away because it had not been either comprehended or exorcized. As in the case of the Nazi past, there is enough unspeakably reprehensible in the Communist experience in the former Soviet Union and East-Central Europe that would justify an approach similar to Arendt's. Indeed the world of the Gulag exploded the validity of the moral imperative: good and evil as understood by the founders of the bourgeois order, or by Christianity, or even by Karl Marx, were simply discarded as vital issues. And thus we return to the issue of the possibility of decommunization (or de-Nazification): is it in the powers of humans to judge crimes so horrible, so much beyond the nature of human conduct? But then, how can one renounce this most human affair, which is retribution for trespassing the laws and customs of the civilized world and turning mass crime into state politics: "this is something which should never have happened, for men will be unable to punish it or to forgive it. . . . It is a past which has grown worse as the years have gone by, and this is partly because the Germans for such a long time refused to prosecute even the murderers among themselves, but partly also because this past could not be 'mastered' by anybody. Even the famous healing power of time has somewhat failed us." Ibid., p. 745.

Index _____

About the Author

Vladimir Tismaneanu is Profesor of Government and Politics, University of Maryland at College Park. He is the author of *Reinventing Politics: Eastern Europe from Stalin to Havel*.